Conventional Lies of our Civilization

MAX NORDAU

Chicago 1883

TABLE OF CONTENTS

PREFACE OF THE FIRST EDITION

This book claims to be a faithful presentation of the views of the majority of educated, cultivated people of the present day. There is no doubt but what millions living in the midst of our civilization have learned by their own reflection and experience to regard and criticise the existing conditions of State and society as they are criticised in the following pages, and will coincide in the opinion expressed in them, that the present social, political and economic institutions are utterly at variance with the views and conceptions of the universe based upon natural science, and therefore untenable and doomed to destruction. Notwithstanding this fact, the author knows that many people will hold up their hands in holy horror when they read it, and not the least ostentatiously those who find their own most secret sentiments expressed in it. This is the very reason why the author believed that it was necessary, that it was imperative upon him, to write this book. The greatest evil of our times is the prevailing cowardice. We do not dare to assert our opinions, to bring our outward lives into harmony with our inward convictions; we believe it to be worldly policy to cling outwardly to relics of former ages when at heart we are completely severed from them. We do not wish to shock anyone, nor offend anyone's prejudices, and we call this "respecting the convictions of others"—those others who in return do not respect our convictions, who ridicule them, who persecute them, and who would like best to exterminate them and us at the same time. This lack of sincerity and manly courage prolongs the period of falseness, and postpones indefinitely the triumph of truth. The author at least wished to fulfill his duty to himself, to truth, and to his comrades in sentiment. He has expressed his convictions openly and without the slightest hesitation. If all those who are dissembling—acting contrary to their convictions, diplomatizing and feigning were to do the same as the author, they would find perhaps to their amazement that they formed the majority in many places, and that it would soon be to their advantage to lead sincere and consistent lives, instead of their present careers of hypocrisy and double dealing.

In the summer of 1883,

The Author.

PREFACE TO THE SIXTH EDITION

The Imperial Council of Vienna has prohibited the further sale of this book in Austria and confiscated all copies of it to be found. The official decree condemns the book on account of the "Crime of insulting the members of the imperial family," the "Crime of disturbing the public peace by attempting to arouse contempt or hatred for the person of the Emperor, etc.," the "Crime of denouncing religion," the "Crime of inciting hostility against religious communities, etc.," and in conclusion,, the "Crime of insulting a church and sect recognized by the State." Every word of these indictments is a calumny from first to last. It is not true that I have "insulted any member of the imperial family;" it is not true that I have attempted to "arouse contempt or hatred for the person of the Emperor." I do not attack persons, neither high nor low, but ideas. Further it is not true that I have disturbed any one in the exercise of his religion (how could a book do this?) nor incited hostility against religious communities at the most I have only attempted to arouse compassion for them.

I wish to warn those people who would never read this book from any interest in the questions of which it treats, but who may perhaps infer from its suppression, that it contains all sorts of piquant and scandalous things. This class of readers is hereby warned that this is not the case. If they spend their money upon this supposition they will be disappointed. The Vienna committee thus commits an intentional or unconscious fraud upon the public. I, at least, will have no share in it.

Feb. 10, 1884 The Author

MENE, TEKEL, UPHARSIN

CHAPTER I.

"Man never is, but always to be blest," and perhaps at no time was he so far removed from the actual attainment of happiness as at present. Culture and civilization are spreading and conquering even the most benighted regions of the globe. Those countries where darkness reigned but yesterday, are to-day basking in a glorious sunshine. Each day witnesses the birth of some new, wonderful invention, destined to make the world pleasanter to live in, the adversities of life more endurable, and to increase the variety and intensity of the enjoyments possible to humanity. But yet, notwithstanding the growth and increase of all conditions to promote comfort, the human race is to-day more discontented, more irritated and more restless than ever before. The world of civilization is an immense hospital-ward, the air is filled with groans and lamentations, and every form of suffering is to be seen twisting and turning on the beds. Go through the world, and ask each country you come to: "Does contentment dwell here? Have you peace and happiness?" From each you will hear the same reply: "Pass on, we have not that which you are seeking." Pause and listen at the borders, and the breeze will bring to your ears from each one, the same confused echoes of contention and tumult, of revolt and of oppression.

In Germany Socialism with myriads of tiny teeth, is stealthily gnawing at the columns that uphold the structures of State and society, and nothing, not even the allurements of State and Christian Socialism, nor the countless traps set for it by the laws and the police, nor the state of siege in the capital, can disturb for a single instant, the secret, noiseless, untiring work of this insatiable subterranean destroyer. The Antisemitic movement was merely a convenient pretext for the gratification of passions which do not venture to show themselves under their true names—among the poor and ignorant it cloaked their hatred of property owners, among those who enjoy privileges inherited from mediæval times—among the aristocratic classes, it disguised their jealous fear of gifted rivals in the race for influence and power, and the romantic idealizing youth saw in it a means of satisfying a certain extravagant and false ideal of patriotism that longs not only for the political unity of the German Fatherland, but also for an ethnological unity of the German people. A secret longing that has been hinted at a thousand times but never fully explained, drives thousands upon thousands away from their homes to cross the ocean. The stream of emigrants pours forth from the German sea-ports like the life-stream from a deadly wound in the body of the nation, jet after jet, in constantly increasing volume, and the Government is powerless to arrest or control it. The political parties are waging a barbaric war of extermination upon each other; the prizes for which they are contending are the conditions of the Middle Ages and an absolute monarchy on one side, and on the other, the Nineteenth Century and the right of popular suffrage.

In Austria we see ten nationalities arrayed against each other, each seeking to injure the others by all the means at its command. In every state, even in every village, the majority are trampling the minority under foot. The minority succumbs when resistance is no longer possible, and counterfeits a submission which conceals a secret intensity of rage that makes them long to compass the destruction of the Empire, as the only possibility of relief. In Russia there is such a condition of affairs that we can almost describe it as primitive barbarism. The Government is deaf to every suggestion of mutual rights and advantages; the public official has no care for the interests of the country and of the people that are confided to him, but thinks only of his own, which he shamelessly promotes by robbery or theft, and by corruptibility and prostitution of the laws. The cultivated classes in their despair have grasped Nihilism as their weapon against the present insupportable state of things, and risk their lives again and again, with dynamite and revolver, with the dagger and the torch of the incendiary, to precipitate the country into that bloody chaos, which, in their delirium, they imagine must precede the establishment of a new system of society. The statesmen who are called upon to devise a cure for this horrible disease propose the most astonishing remedies. One guarantees a cure if the Russian people be declared of age and invested with the right of legislative representation; another has confidence alone in a decisive leap backwards into the slough of Asiatic intolerance, and demands the eradication of all European innovations, with an extension of the power of the sacred and inherited despotism of the Czar; a third believes in the efficacy of a counter-irritant, and recommends a brisk, merry war against Germany, Austria, Turkey, or the whole world combined, if need be. The dark mass of the people however, entertains itself by plundering and killing the Jews, during these tedious consultations of its physicians casting greedy glances at the castles of the nobility, while it is destroying the taverns and synagogues of the Hebrews.

In England the ground appears solid and the structure of State firm, to a superficial observer. But if he lay his ear to the ground, and listen to the muffled strokes of the subterranean giants as they hammer away at the weak points in their dungeons; and if he examine the walls closer, he will see that underneath the varnish and gold plating, dangerous cracks extend from top to bottom. The Church and the Aristocracy of rank and wealth, are well organized and firmly allied to uphold each other, with a true appreciation of the identity of their interests. The middle classes bow submissively to the written and unwritten laws of the dominant caste, are outwardly eminently respectable, show reverence to titles, and swear that those things only are seemly which the upper ten thousand approve, every thing else being low and vulgar. But the laborer, the tenant, stand outside the bonds of this conspiracy; they demand their share of capital and land; they form clubs of free-thinkers and republicans; they shake their fists at royalty and aristocracy, and he who seeks to read the future of England, not in the tea-grounds, but in the eyes of the English working-man, will find it dark and threatening. Of Ireland I need not speak. The revolution against landlordism is in full swing there, murder rules the highways, and if the English Government does not succeed in drowning out the inhabitants in a sea of blood, it will be obliged to witness the forcible depossession of the land-owners in favor of the landless class, which will present an example that would speedily be imitated in England, and afterwards in many other countries.

In Italy a feebly rooted monarchy holds its own with difficulty against the rising flood of Republicanism. The Irredenta sets before the young men of the country, a new ideal to long and work for, to take the place of the old ideal of Italian unity which has now become a reality. The secret sufferings of the masses are revealed by isolated but dangerous symptoms, such as the Camorra and Maffia in the south, while in Tuscany, they assume the form of religious fanaticism, and of the communistic principles of primitive Christianity.

France at the present moment can congratulate herself upon the best condition of political health of any European country; but how many incipient symptoms of disease are to be seen even there,—the germs of coming evils. On every street corner in the large cities, excited orators are preaching the gospel of Communism and violence; the masses are preparing to get possession of the government and drive the ruling bourgeoisie out of the snug offices and sinecures which they have enjoyed since 1789, and to take their places in the legislative assemblies. The parties of the old regime see the day of this inevitable conflict approaching, and strive to prepare for it by half-hearted plots and counterplots, jesuitical, monarchical and military, but without energy, without hope and without combination in which alone there is strength.

There is no need to speak of the smaller countries in detail. The name of Spain brings up before us a vision of Carlism and petty insurrections. In Norway every one is absorbed in the conflict between the present Government and representative legislation, within which lurks a future republic like the stone in a peach. Denmark has its Peasant Party and chronic ministerial crisis, Belgium its armed Ultramontanism. All countries, the weak as well as the strong, have their own special ailments for which they vainly hope to find relief, by sacrificing countless millions year after year upon the altar of the military, like those persons in mediæval times who hoped to ensure their recovery from some dangerous disease by presenting their wealth to the church.

CHAPTER II.

The lack of harmony between government and people, the deadly animosity between different political parties, the fermentation going on in certain classes of society, are only manifestations of the universal disease of the age, which is the same in all countries, although its symptoms are characterized by various local names in different places, such as Nihilism, Fenianism, Socialism and the Antisemitic or Irredenta movements. Another and by far more dangerous form is the depression, uneasiness and breaking away, which characterize the mental attitude of every fully developed man who has attained to the heights of modern culture, irrespective of his nation and allegiance or non-allegiance to party or state. This pessimism is the keynote of our age as a delight in mere existence was of the classic ages, and ultra piety of the mediaeval period. Every man of culture feels this sense of irritating discomfort which he ascribes to some slight, casual cause, inevitably the wrong one, unless he analyzes his feelings with unusual care—it leads him to criticise and harshly condemn the varying phases of our modern social life. This impatience upon which all outside influences seem to exert an exciting and even exasperating effect, is called by some nervousness, by others pessimism, and by a third class, skepticism. The multiplicity of names describes but one and the same disease. This disease is visible in every manifestation of modern culture. Literature and art, philosophy and positive knowledge, politics and economy, all are infected by its taint. We discover the very first traces of its existence in the literature of the latter part of the last century, as any disturbances or changes in the conditions of mankind are detected first by the delicate perceptions of a poetic temperament. While the upper classes were following an uninterrupted round of corrupt gayeties, making their lives one prolonged orgy while the self-sufficient bourgeoisie saw nothing beyond the length of their own noses and were stupidly content with the way things were going, of a sudden Jean Jacques Rousseau lifted his voice in a ringing appeal for deliverance from his surroundings which yet had so many attractions. He preached to the world with enthusiasm, of a return to a state of primeval nature, by which he was far from meaning a return to primitive barbarism, but only a change to something diametrically opposed to the actual state of things. His cry awoke an echo in the hearts of all his contemporaries, as when a certain note is struck, all the chords in the instrument which are attuned to it, are set vibrating—a proof that Rousseau's longings pre-existed unconsciously in those around him. Rakes and Philistines alike began to cultivate their yearnings for primeval nature and life in the wilderness; they formed a comical contrast to the ardor with which they still sought and enjoyed all the super-refinements and gilded vices of the civilization they professed to despise. German Romanticism is descended in a direct line from Rousseau's longings for primeval nature. It is however a feeble Rousseauism, which did not have the courage to go to the end of the path upon which it had entered. Romanticism does not go as far back as the prehistoric epoch, but stops at a more accessible point, the Middle Ages. The Middle Ages as painted by the Romantic School in such glowing colors, are however t as far removed from the actual Middle Ages of history, as Rousseau's primeval nature was from the actual times of prehistoric man. In both cases their ideal world was to be constructed in the same way, with everything now existing replaced by its opposite; in both cases their ideas betrayed a conscious or instinctive fundamental conviction that any change from the present must prove an improvement upon the present condition of affairs. By tracing further the genealogical line of this literary tendency, we arrive at French Romanticism, which is a daughter of the German school; and later we come to the Byronic disgust with the world, which forms a separate branch of the same family. From the Byronic line are descended the German pessimistic poets, the Russian Puschkin, the French Musset, and the Italian Leopardi. The family trait in their mental physiognomies is their tragic discontent with the realities of life, which one vents in pathetic moans, another in bitter scorn of self, and a third in enraptured yearnings for different and more perfect conditions of life.

And does not the literature of our own generation, the literary productions of the two last decades, betray an attempt at escape from our age and its disappointments? The public demands novels and poems that treat of the most distant countries and epochs. It devours Freytag's and Dahn's sketches of life among the ancient Germanic races, the mediæval poems of Scheffel and his imitators, and the novels of Egyptian, Corinthian and Roman times by Ebers and Eckstein, or if it bestows its favor upon a book that announces its subject as modern, it must recommend itself by a certain false, sickly, sentimental idealism; it must be an attempt to clothe human beings like ourselves, with certain attributes that make them as our imagination delights to picture them, but as no one ever saw them in reality. The light literature of England has long since ceased to be a faithful mirror of real life. When it is not describing with gusto, crimes and scandals of all kinds, murders, burglaries, seductions or testamentary frauds, it portrays a model society, in which the members of the nobility are all handsome, dignified, cultivated and wealthy; while the lower classes are honest God-fearing people, devoted to their superiors, the virtuous among them being graciously praised and rewarded by Sir This or Sir That, while the wicked are locked up by the police—in short, a society which is in all respects an absurd idealization of the dilapidated, tottering structure of society as it exists in England at the present day.

The literature of France does not seem to fit into this frame at the first glance; but a second convinces us of our error. It is true, it limits its field of observation to the present and real in life. It denies itself any suggestions or longings for the past or the future, for any better or any different ideal. It is founded upon a principle of Art, that is called Realism or Naturalism. But let us examine closer: is Naturalism a proof of satisfaction with the present, and in this sense, in opposition to the pseudo historical and fanciful idealization which I have just described to be a powerful manifestation of disgust with the actualities of life, and of longing for their improvement? What are the themes which Naturalism portrays with a partiality for which it has been reproached so often? Does it ever depict any lovely or pleasing phases of this mortal life? No. It describes exclusively the most loathsome and hideous traits of civilization, such as are found mainly in the large cities. It takes especial pains to portray corruption, suffering and moral weakness, human beings sick unto death and a society at its last gasp, and as we finish a work belonging to this school, a plaintive voice seems to murmur with monotonous repetition. "You see, tormented reader, that this life which is here described with an inexorable fidelity to nature, is really not worth living." This is the fundamental conviction which every production of the Realistic school in literature silently proclaims; it is the starting point, it underlies the whole and forms the closing moral of each work, and is identical with the convictions upon which the false Idealism of England and Germany is based. The two paths, far from leading in opposite directions, conduct the wayfarers to the same goal. Naturalism lays down the premises, Idealism draws the conclusion from them. The former says: "The present conditions of life are intolerable," the latter adds: "Therefore away with them; let us forget them for one brief moment, and fancy ourselves in that ideal, perfect world which I can call up before my readers by my magic." The poet who sings in inspired verse of Arcadian simplicity, whose maidens are all beautiful and gay, with love in their hearts and lilies in their hands, living in romantic castles perched upon picturesque mountain peaks tipped with gold by the rising sun, who is called "a noble poet," by the admiring public, is only the brilliant co-worker of that other author who dips his pen like a shovel, into the mire, and for whom the public can not find language strong enough to express its disgust.

I have lingered upon this subject because the literature of a country is the most complete and many-sided form in which the intellectual activity of any age reveals itself. But all the other manifestations of human thought of the present time allow us also to discern the same traits as those in the physiognomy of modern literature. All around us we notice a general sense of uneasiness and a mental irritation, which assumes in one mind the form of grief or anger at the unbearable state of affairs in this world, and in another, produces a decided longing for a change in all the conditions of modern life.

The aim of the creative arts in former ages was the reproduction of the beautiful. The painter and the sculptor seized and perpetuated only the pleasing scenes that life and the world offered them. When Phidias was at work upon his Zeus, and Raphael was painting his Madonna, their hands were guided by a naive admiration of the human form per se. They experienced a delight and satisfaction in reproducing nature and when their delicate artistic taste recognized some slight imperfection in her, they hastily and discreetly toned it down, with an apologetic and idealizing touch. The art of to-day knows neither their satisfaction nor their naive admiration. It examines nature with a frowning brow and a keen, malicious eye, skilled in discovering faults and blemishes; it portrays under the pretext of fidelity to truth, all the imperfections in the visible form, involuntarily exaggerating them and giving them undue prominence. I repeat, under the pretext of truth, for truth itself does not lie within such means. The artist naturally reproduces his model as he sees and feels it himself; Courbet's ugly Stonebreaker is as far removed from absolute truth, as Lionardi's lovely Mona Lisa, from which Vasari drew his inspiration on account of its supposed fidelity to nature. And even when modern art is compelled to recognize the beautiful and pay unwilling tribute to it by perpetuating it, the artist contrives to suggest a flaw in it, by smuggling in a hint that the noble and glorious form is used for base purposes and is consequently contaminated. The of the nude female figure is destroyed by a vague insinuation of sensuality and wantonness, which mars every modern painting of this class. It is sure to exert upon the susceptible observer the same kind of influence as the "If you only knew what I know!" whispered by some malicious, old scandal-monger into the ear of her neighbor, when the virtues of some acquaintance are being praised. Ancient art is characterized by a pleased enjoyment of nature; modern art by a self-tormenting dissatisfaction with her. One glorifies her, the other complains of her. One is a constant ode in her honor, the other an incessant, harsh and unfounded criticism. The point of view of the former was that we are living in the most beautiful of all possible worlds, and of the latter, that our world could hardly be more hideous than it is.

Pessimism is also the fashionable coloring of thought now in philosophy, not only in the established philosophies taught in the universities, but also in the private systems of philosophical thought and enquiry, which every person of culture has built up for himself around the important problems of the day. In Germany, Schopenhauer is God and Hartmann is his prophet. The Positivism of Auguste Comte is making no progress either as doctrine or sect, for even its followers have acknowledged that its methods were too circumscribed and its aims not sufficiently high. The philosophers of France are confining their investigations to psychology, or, to be more exact, to psycho-physiology. English philosophy has lost its right to the title of metaphysics, as it has abandoned its higher task, that of seeking a satisfactory view of the world, and is only occupied by questions of secondary importance, John Stuart Mill is studying logic alone, that is to say, the doctrine of forms for human thought; Herbert Spencer is busy with social science—that is, the mental and moral problems which arise in social life; Bain is devoting his time to theories of education, which include the study of psychology and moral philosophy. Germany alone has a living school of metaphysics, but it is dismal and hopeless. Good Dr Pangloss is dead and he has left no heirs behind him. Hegelism, which provided a sufficient cause for every thing and allowed its followers to convince themselves that whatever is, is logical and necessary, has followed its predecessors to the store-room for old and worn-out systems of philosophy, and the world is now attracted by that philosophy which proclaims that this intolerable universe will finally sink again into nothing, owing to the wish of all created beings and things for complete annihilation.

This same disease of the age shows itself in the realms of political economy in a different but no less significant form. We seek in vain among the rich a feeling of security in regard to their wealth and of simple enjoyment of it; neither do we find among the poor that patient acquiescence in the poverty which appears so inevitable and unchangeable to human eyes. An undefined fear of approaching danger haunts the man of wealth; he sees a menace in the present condition of men and affairs, indistinct but none the less real, so that he has come to look upon his possessions as a loan that can be demanded from him, without reprieve,, from one moment to another. The poor man in consumed by envy and greed for the wealth of the privileged few; neither in himself nor in the existing arrangement of the world and society, as he has learned to understand it, does he discover any convincing reason for the fact that he is poor, and hence excluded from the table of life's pleasures. He listens with fierce impatience to a voice within him which whispers that his rights to the blessings of this life are as good as any man's. The rich man is dreading; the poor man is hoping and working to bring about a change in the present condition of property ownership. The faith in a continuance of its present state has been rudely shaken in the minds of all, even in those who will not acknowledge their secret doubts and anxieties.

What do we learn from the domestic politics of each one of all the civilized countries of Europe? The contrasts are becoming sharper all the time, the struggles between the political parties more and more violent. The Conservative adherents of the existing state of affairs are gradually dying off, and one of these days there will be none left upon the surface of the earth. In vain will a Quietist leader be sought to demonstrate that the present arrangements of state and society should not be disturbed but maintained as they are. There are no more Conservatives. This title would have to be dropped from the political nomenclature of the day if it were applied according to its strictly literal meaning. A Conservative is one who wishes to maintain existing institutions. Nobody nowadays confines himself to this platform. Fighting on the defensive is all out of date; only the offensive systems of political warfare are practiced. There only remains Reaction or Reform—that is, revolution forwards or backwards. The former wishes to recall the past, the latter to hasten the future. The Reactionist hates the present fully as much as the Liberal. This universal mental restlessness and uneasiness exerts a powerful and many-sided influence upon individual life. A dread of examining and comprehending the actualities of life prevails to a frightfully alarming extent, and manifests itself in a thousand ways. The means of sensation and perception are eagerly counterfeited by altering the nervous system by the use of stimulating or narcotic poisons of all kinds, manifesting thereby an instinctive aversion to the realities of appearances and circumstances. It is true that we are only capable of perceiving the changes in our own organism, not those going on around us. But the changes within us are caused, most probably, by objects outside of us; our senses give us a picture of those objects, whose reliability is surely more to be depended upon, when only warped by the imperfections in our normal selves, than when, to these unavoidable sources of error is added a conscious disturbance in the functions of the nervous system caused by the use of various poisons. Only when our perceptions of things around us awake in us a feeling of positive discomfort, do we realize the necessity of warding off these unpleasant sensations, or of modifying them, until they become more agreeable. This is the cause of the constant increase in the consumption of alcohol and tobacco, shown by statistics, and of the rapidity with which the custom of taking opium and morphine is spreading. It is also the reason why the cultivated classes seize upon every new narcotic or stimulant which science discovers for them, so that we have not only drunkards and opium eaters among us, but confirmed chloral, chloroform and ether drinkers. Society as a whole, repeats the action of the individual, who tries to "drown his sorrows in the flowing bowl." It seeks oblivion of the present, and grasps at anything that will provide it with the necessary illusions by which it can escape from real life.

Hand in hand with this instinctive self-deception and attempt at temporary oblivion of the actual world, goes the final plunge into eternal oblivion: statistics prove that the number of suicides is increasing in thy highly civilized countries, in direct proportion to the increase in the use of alcohol and narcotics. A dull sensation of irritation, sometimes self-conscious, but more often only recognized as a vague, irresistible discontent, keeps the aspiring in a state of gloomy restlessness, so that the struggle for existence assumes brutal and desperate phases, never known before. This struggle is no longer a conflict between polite antagonists who salute each other with courtesy before they open fire, like the English and French before the battle of Fontenoy, but it is a pell-mell, hand to hand fight of rough cut-throats, drunk with whisky and blood, who fall upon each other with brute ferocity, neither giving nor expecting mercy. We lament the disappearance of characters. What is a character? It is an individuality which shapes its career according to certain simple, fundamental moral principles which it has recognized as good, and accepted as guides. Skepticism developes no such characters, because it has excluded faith in fundamental principles. When the north star ceases to shine, and the electric pole vanishes, the compass is of no further use—the stationary point is gone to which it was always turning. Skepticism, also a fashionable ailment, is in reality but another phase of the universal discontent with the present. For it is only by becoming convinced that the world is out of sorts generally, and that everything is wrong, insufficient and contemptible, that we arrive at the conclusion that all is vanity, and nothing worth an effort, or a struggle between duty and inclination. Economy, literature and art, philosophy, politics and all phases of social and individual life, show a certain fundamental trait, common to all—a deep dissatisfaction with the world as it exists at present, From each one of these multitudinous manifestations of human intelligence arises a bitter cry, the same in all cases, an appeal for a radical change.

CHAPTER III.

The question here arises: Is this picture true of modern times alone? Does it not also represent the characteristics of all previous ages?

I am far from being an enthusiast on the subject of days that are past. I am no believer in any Golden Age. The life of man has always been more or less of a struggle; he has always known discontent and unhappiness. Pessimism has a physiological basis, and a certain measure of suffering is entailed upon us by the nature of our organism. It is by suffering that we first become conscious of our Ego. Our Ego is first brought to our consciousness by a perception of its limitations; and this perception of its limitations is never awakened save by its coming in contact, more or less rudely, with something outside of it.

As, in a dark room, a person has the fact of the existence of the walls brought to his mind, only by knocking his head against them. Man purchases his consciousness therefore with the sensation of pain, and he only learns by repeated discomfort the difference between the subject and the object. But if it is true that mankind has always suffered and complained, that it has experienced in all ages, the sad contrast between desire and possession, between the ideal and the real, it is none the less true that discontent was never so deep nor so universal, nor was it ever manifested in so many directions, nor did it ever present itself in such radical forms as at present.

As we turn the pages of history we find them filled with records of party struggles and revolutions. It often seems to a superficial observer as if the selfish ambition of some party leader, to which the multitudes were wholly indifferent, were the sole power that set some of these revolutions in motion. But I do not believe in the justice of thus identifying these movements with their leaders. Parties are formed and flock to their standards, because they fancy they recognize in their battle-cries the expression of their own indistinct aspirations; and even if the ambitious leader manipulates the passions of the masses, applying them to his own use, as the manufacturer compels the forces of wind, water and steam to do his bidding, he will not be successful in the end, unless he pretends to be working for the accomplishment of certain popular wishes. Party struggles are to a people, what change is to the hod-carrier, as he shifts his hod from one shoulder to the other, a temporary but not a genuine relief, and revolutions are freshets intended to equalize the ideals of the people and the actual conditions of life. They are never arbitrary, but obey certain physical laws, like the cyclone, which re-establishes the equilibrium of air, disturbed by violent changes in the temperature, or like the waterfall, which is constantly striving to bring two bodies of water to the same level. As often as there is found to be too great a difference between the wishes of the people and the actual reality of things, in obedience to the laws of nature a revolution takes place; it may be dammed up artificially by the organized powers for a while but not for long. Revolutions are consequently the only witnesses of history which allow us to draw conclusions from their extent and aims as to the degree and the causes of the preceding popular discontent.

Until the most recent times, revolutions were all of comparatively small extent, and directed against a limited number of abuses. The political contests among the republicans of ancient Rome were caused by the struggle between the patricians and the plebeians. What were the aspirations of the latter which assumed corporate form in Catiline and the Gracchi? They wanted a fair share in the public lands and they demanded a voice in the discussion of state affairs. In the ancient communities the individual citizen had a remarkably highly developed sense of respect and responsibility for the welfare of the commonwealth, and also for the duties and privileges arising from his connection with it. He seemed to think that taken alone, he was a contemptible fragment, but fitted into his proper place in the structure of the state, he became a complete and rounded whole. The Roman plebeian looked upon himself as the unjustly despised and disinherited son of a wealthy house, and merely demanded his seat at the paternal board, and his share in the family discussions—the thought of rebelling against the surrounding conditions of political and social life, never occurred to him. He was proud of them, and paid them willing and delighted homage. He looked up to the patrician on account of his rank and neither envied him his lineage, nor the outward symbols of his exalted position. He contentedly took that position on the scale of social rank which the accident of his birth had assigned to him, and although he glanced with reverential awe at the aristocratic and senatorial families above him, he could experience a sensation of self-esteem and satisfaction when he looked down upon the multitudes of slaves and freed-men beneath him.

Far deeper was the discontent of those slaves who rose in insurrection again and again, during that corrupt age when the republic was being merged into an empire, protesting with their life-blood against the existing arrangement of society, in battles whose tragic pathos is beyond description. In those nameless multitudes who form the living pedestal for the grand figure of Spartacus, we discover for the first time, traces of that burning doubt whether everything that is, must of necessity always remain so. This doubt never seems to have entered into the minds of the burden-bearing Egyptians, whom we see represented in such long, silent, dreary processions on the walls of ancient tombs and temples. Neither has it touched with its poisoned tip the two hundred millions of India, who in silent acquiescence bear the yoke of the English, as for centuries, they bore that of Caste. But the followers of Spartacus were neither radicals nor pessimists, according to our ideas. They attacked the goad, not him who wielded it. Their anger was not directed against the regulation of the world, but only against their position in it. Did they recognize the fact that reason refuses to sanction the degradation of men with will and judgment into mere property, like cattle and inanimate things? By no means. They accepted the institution of slavery without question, only they did not want to be slaves themselves. Their ideal was not the abolition of an unreasonable form of social life, but simply an exchange of roles. These insurgents would have been easily pacified. A victory would have transformed their despair into contentment, and converted the rebels into model pillars of society.

The uprisings of the Middle Ages possess a deeper mental significance. The iconoclastic movements, the Crusades, the fanaticism of the Albigenses and Waldenses, reveal a condition of deep mental uneasiness. The magic fascination of that mysterious land beneath the rising sun, would not have been felt by an uncultivated nature, unless it had already been experiencing an incoherent longing for change from its surroundings. The hundreds of thousands who flocked to Palestine from Europe, were not following so much the banner of the Cross, as a bright vision which floated on before them, visible only to their mental eyes, whose name was the Ideal. He who was thoroughly contented did not leave his happy fireside to trudge through unknown perils to the Holy Sepulchre; it was only the restless and uneasy mind that welcomed change and the possibility of improvement. Neither were those thousands contented with their lot who gave themselves up to torture and death for the sake of their religion; who, to maintain some doctrinal point, marched placidly to the stake, or, in their fanaticism, exterminated entire peoples. For to him who is exercised by such a feverish anxiety for the salvation of his soul and for the terms upon which he can secure future bliss, who spends this life in preparing himself for the next, by such incredible sacrifices, struggles and sufferings, to him this world can not have appealed with any convincing attractions.

Thus we see that mankind during the Middle Ages was also disturbed and discontented; what restrained it from any open revolt against the then existing conditions of life, was the fact that it found in its religious faith a comfort and peace which made it bear all earthly ills with ease and even delight. He who is confidently awaiting some great happiness close at hand accepts with facile resignation a passing discomfort and in fact is hardly conscious of it.

But mankind developed and the consolation of Religion began to wane. The moment arrived when religious faith ceased to be the reliable safety valve for the rebellious tendencies of the discontented. That moment was critical. A trifle more, and the skepticism and tearing loose from old traditions, which characterize the present age, would have broken out four hundred years ago. The people did not allow themselves however, to be robbed of their cherished illusions without resistance, and made great efforts to retain them. This struggle for a consoling ideal is called in history the Reformation. It had the effect of postponing for centuries the awakening of the world from its pleasant dream. But even then there appeared certain isolated symptoms of the evolution of a pessimism which the faith in a happy hereafter could no longer entirely stifle. The Peasants' war in Germany was the last resort of despairing men, to whom an eternal Paradise did not seem a sufficient indemnification for misery in this world. They wanted to force a payment on account, on the sum of happiness coming to them in the future.

It is not until as late as the French Revolution that we find a people to whom the existing state of affairs appeared so entirely unsatisfactory that they were willing to make any sacrifices, pay any price, to have it changed. For the first time in the history of mankind, we see an extensive, popular uprising not directed against single abuses, but against the general conditions of things, in their entirety. No poor people were clamoring for a share in the ager publicus, like the Roman plebeians,—no disfranchised were struggling for their rights as human beings, like the slaves led by Spartacus,—no special class was fighting for certain privileges, like the cities in the Middle Ages,—nor was it an insurrection of visionaries, eager to bear arms in behalf of their religion, like the Waldenses, Albigenses, the Huguenots and the protestant reformers. All these elements, with a thousand others, combined to form the French Revolution. It was at the same time material and intellectual. It denied all faith in Religion, and questioned the established form of individual possession of property. It attempted to reconstruct state and society upon a new foundation and according to a new plan. It wished to create new and more favorable conditions of existence for body and mind. It was an explosion which took effect not only upon isolated weak points, but upon the whole surface exposed to it, and brought down in ruins the entire structure of society. It is true that the incongruity of the then existing circumstances must have been felt with fearful intensity by all, and have caused intense suffering, to have produced such an attempt at complete annihilation, yet we notice in this great Revolution, one trait which makes it impossible for us to look upon the mental attitude of man at that period as so wretched as at present. This trait is the prevailing, inexhaustible optimism. Indeed, the men of the great Revolution were entirely free from any taint of pessimism. They were filled with hope and assurance to overflowing. They were firmly convinced that they possessed unfailing means for ensuring absolute happiness to mankind; and with this conviction it is impossible to be unhappy. They were in the mood of spring-time and dawn, such as inspired Uhland when he exclaimed: "Die Welt wird schöner mit jedem Tag—Nun muss sich Alles, Alles wenden!" This youth fulness, even childishness, of hope and illusions, this delight in the outlook into the future, is perhaps the most remarkable phenomenon connected with the great Revolution.

We learn from our rapid scanning of the past centuries, that the present tone of thought is without precedent. History contains the record of but one moment that reminds us of our own in this respect, and this is the period of the death agony of the ancient world. This resemblance has been shown repeatedly. The people had outgrown the old ideas, and new ones to replace them, had not yet been discovered. They believed no longer in the doctrines of paganism, nor in the teachings of the philosophers. The theories upon which their lives had hitherto been based were found to be erroneous, and consequently the latter had become illogical and without meaning. A weariness and hopeless dejection had consequently crept into the hearts of men; they could find no relief in their own resources nor in anything around them. They lost even the last vestige of faith in a possible improvement and committed suicide by thousands, unable to resist the ravages of the moral epidemic. That dismal time when the Roman Empire was tottering to its fall, and paganism in its death throes, is the only period in which we meet with the same depression, the same restless spirit of investigation and fault-finding, the same skepticism in superficial and pessimism in deep minds which characterize our own highly civilized age. But after all, there is a difference between the two periods; this hopeless despair of the future only attacked the aristocracy of mind, comparatively a few in ancient Rome, while the masses lived out their existence in stolid unconcern, looking upon the great tragedy of the age merely as an exterior, material misfortune. But in our time this pessimism lowers like a dense, black cloud over the vast majority of cultivated human beings. The difference therefore is more in extent than in kind—but extent is the very point that distinguishes an epidemic from a disease.

CHAPTER IV.

Whence comes this mental distress common to all civilized peoples? To what cause can we trace the development of this unparalleled irritation and embittering,, which prevails with such alarming severity among all the tinkers of an age which seems to offer even to the poorest, a wealth of material and intellectual pleasures, such as no monarch of former times was able to procure. The cause? It is identical with that which flooded the hearts of the later Romans with such utter disgust at the emptiness of life, that they sought refuge in self-destruction to escape from it. It is owing to the opposition between the world as it is, with all its phases of individual, social and civil life, and the way in which we now comprehend the significance of the universe. Every one of our actions contradicts our convictions, flouts them, gives them the lie. An impassible chasm separates that which we know to be truth, and the actual conditions of life under which we are compelled to live and carry on our individual and social existence.
Our view of the world, that accepted consciously or unconsciously by all cultivated minds of the present day, is from the standpoint of natural science. We look upon the universe as a vast aggregation of matter,

possessing the attribute of motion which reveals itself to us under the form of various physical laws, some of which we have discovered, defined and proved, while we are as yet only on the track of the rest—these laws we accept as immutable and without possibility of exception. The problem of the beginning and final destiny of things we have given up as impossible to be solved with the means of our organism. As a matter of convenience we have accepted as a provisory conclusion for certain trains of thought, the hypothesis that matter is eternal. The acceptance of this theory, the only purely arbitrary one in our system, serves to explain to us all the various phenomena of nature, while it does not contradict our comprehension of physical laws. It excuses us from accepting any theory in regard to an eternal will or intelligence, or as man has always designated it, God, which would have the disadvantage of forcing upon us, if we accepted it, a whole series of similar hypotheses, such as prophecy, the soul and immortality, all of which are incapable of proof, and can not be sustained by our reason, while at the same time they are in direct opposition to all the laws of nature, which we know to be fixed and unyielding facts. If we descend from the universe to our race, to man, we see in him, as a necessary consequence of our conceptions of material nature, merely a living being, fitting perfectly into its allotted place in the ranks of living organisms, and governed in all things by the common laws of the organic world. We can discover no proofs of any special favors or privileges granted to man more than those enjoyed by every other animal or vegetable organism. We believe that the development of the human as well as of all other races, was perhaps first made possible by sexual selection, and certainly promoted by it; and that the struggle for existence, using the term in its most comprehensive sense, shapes the destinies of nations as well as of the most obscure individual and is the foundation for all forms of political and social life.

This is our conception of the universe, our belief. Upon this base are founded all our principles, and our conceptions of justice and morality. It has become an elementary constituent part of our civilization. We inhale it with the air we breathe. It has become impossible to close our intellects against it. The pope who denounced it in his encyclical, was under its influence. The Jesuits try in vain to save their pupils from its taint, by bringing them up in an artificial atmosphere of mediæval theology and scholastics, as a marine animal is kept alive in an inland aquarium, by salt water brought from the distant sea; but they are already filled with it, they take it in as they read the posters on the walls, as they notice the manners of their associates, as they read their pious magazines and books, when they are buying a breviary—their whole mental and moral life is unconsciously permeated and colored by it; they have involuntary thoughts and perceptions, such as the man of the Eleventh Century never imagined, in vain do they try to perform the impossible—they cannot help being the children of this modern age and of its specific civilization.

And, with this belief, we are obliged to live in the midst of a civilization, which allows one man, by the accident of his birth, to assume the most extensive rights over millions of his fellow-men, his equals in every respect and in many cases, his superiors; which pays homage to another who repeats words without any sense and makes purposeless gestures, as the visible incorporation of super-natural powers; which forbids a maiden in a certain station of life, to marry a handsome, blooming, powerful individual, but mates her with some unattractive, feeble and crippled being because he is her equal in rank, while the former belongs to a so-called lower class; which permits a healthy and strong laboring man to go hungry, while some sickly and incapable idler is surrounded by a superfluity which he is unable to enjoy. We, who believe that the human race has been evolved from some lower form of life, who know that all individuals without exception, are created, live out their lives and pass away, all in accordance with the same organic laws—we are obliged to kneel before a king; we are expected to reverence in him a being set apart from all ordinary laws and conditions, and are forbidden to smile when we read on the coins and in the official decrees of the Government that "by the grace of God," he is, what he is. We, convinced as we are, that every occurrence in this world is the result of certain irresistible and unchangeable physical laws, are yet compelled to look on while the Government pays certain priests, whose official duty it is, to conduct ceremonies with the declared purpose of exerting an influence upon events in this world, which can only take effect by a suspension or revocation of nature's laws; we are expected as occasion offers, to take part in some imposing mass or church service to beg for special favors from some mysterious, supernatural power, whose existence both nature and physical science refuse to recognize as possible, and we award a high rank in state and society to those persons who preside at these inconsistent mummeries. We believe in the powerful and beneficent effect of sexual selection, and yet we defend the modern conventional marriage, which, in its present form, directly excludes it. We acknowledge the struggle for existence as the inevitable foundation for all law and morality, and yet, every day we pass laws to uphold and perpetuate conditions which absolutely prevent the free exercise of our powers, and deny to the strong and those worthy of the fullest life, the right to make use of their strength, and we stigmatize their inevitable victory over the feeble, as a capital crime. Thus our whole system of life is based upon false principles which we have inherited from former ages, which are in direct and flagrant opposition to every one of our present convictions. The form and the spirit of our life as citizens are at constant and open variance. Every word that we speak, every action, is a direct lie against that which we acknowledge as truth in our hearts. Thus we are always parodying our own selves, and acting a perpetual farce, which wearies us to death, in spite of our being accustomed to it, which requires a constant denial on our part of every one of our most cherished beliefs and convictions, and which, in moments of introspection, fills us with disgust and contempt of our own conduct and of everything around us. We assume at every opportunity a costume that looks to our own eyes like a fool's jacket but which we wear with apparent satisfaction and a thousand airs and graces; we counterfeit out-ward reverence for certain persons and things, which appear to our innermost hearts, as absurd in the highest degree, and we cling like cowards, to certain conventionalities, whose utter incongruity we feel with every fibre of our being.

This perpetual conflict between the existing conditions of the world and our secret convictions, has a most tragic reaction upon the inner life of the individual. We seem to ourselves like clowns, who set others to laughing by the jokes, which to them are so flat and stale. Ignorance is easily combined with a kind of animal sense of comfort, and we can live happy and contented, if we accept all our surroundings as necessary and right. The Inquisition, in rooting out doubt with the sword and the stake, intended to benefit humanity in its own way, by saving to man his pleasure in existence. But as soon as we recognize the fact that the hitherto cherished institutions have lost their vitality and are all out of date, that they are empty, foolish phantoms, partly scarecrows, partly theatre properties, we experience the horror and longing for escape, the discouragement and disgust, which would fill the mind and heart of a living man locked in a vault with the dead, or of a sane man imprisoned with lunatics, obliged to humor their vagaries, to escape physical violence.

This perpetual conflict between our ideas, and all forms of our civilization, this necessity for carrying on our existence in the midst of institutions which we consider to be lies—these are the causes of our pessimism and skepticism. This is the frightful rent that goes through the entire civilized world. In this insupportable contradiction we lose all enjoyment of life and all inclination for effort. It is the cause of that feverish sense of discomfort that disturbs the people of culture in all countries today. In it we find the solution of the problem of the dismal tone of modern thought.

It will be the task of the following chapters to set forth in detail the different phases of this discordant strife between the principal conventional lies of our civilization, and the truths they deny, based on natural science, which we have adopted as our conceptions of the universe.

THE LIE OF RELIGION

CHAPTER I.

Religion is the most powerful and widely extended of all the institutions bequeathed to us by the past. The entire human race comes under its ban. It binds with the same fetters the highest and the lowest races alike, and its connecting links render the negro of Australia the brother in sentiment and neighbor in civilization of the English lord. Religion penetrates all forms of political and social life, and faith in its abstract dogmas, is the avowed or unexpressed foundation for the rightfulness, or even the possibility of a whole series of actions which form the degrees of critical development, or the turning points, in any individual existence. There are still great many civilized countries, where everyone is obliged to belong to some religion. No one is asked about his faith, his convictions, but every one is obliged to conform to some established form of worship. The world has progressed somewhat since the days of the Anti-reformation under Bloody Mary, of Spain during the Sixteenth Century, and of the Puritan rule in New England, when every citizen was obliged, under the most fearful penalties, to take part in the established worship; but the progress has been slight, taken as a whole. The State no longer drives every individual to mass and confession, it has abolished the penalty of being burnt at the stake for negligence in church attendance; but it requires, at least in some European and American countries, every one to be enrolled on the list of members of some religious community, and by means of its organization exacts contributions from all sides.

Religion receives into her arms at its birth the infant of civilized life, she becomes its unyielding, implacable companion throughout its entire existence, and will not relinquish her claims even upon its death-bed. A citizen is born—the parents are obliged to present him for baptism, as a refusal, in some countries, would render them liable to a fine arid prosecution by the State. He wishes to get married—this he can only do in the church, with the co-operation of the minister. Many countries recognize a civil marriage as legal, it is true, but, in the first place it is only introduced into a comparatively small number, in the second, where it is already introduced powerful influences are at work undermining it, and, in the third place, social customs have not kept pace with the law, consequently in those countries where the civil marriage is a recognized, permanent institution it is not considered as a complete marriage. He dies—a minister follows his corpse to the grave, and he is laid to rest in consecrated ground, surrounded by the tokens and symbols of Religion. In many cases he can only advance his most authorized interests by taking an oath, based upon religious ideas. He is willing to serve his country, by shedding his life's blood at her command—he can not do so unless he takes the oath of allegiance before God; he applies to the legal authorities to maintain his rights—he is straightway called upon for an oath. He can not give his testimony before his fellow-citizens without an oath; neither can he without first having taken the oath of office, uphold the rights of the people, nor enter into possession of any public office. A passionate resistance met and overwhelmed the recent attempt in England and France to substitute a formal assurance of honor and conscience for the customary religious oath. Through out the whole length and breadth of the civilized world there is not a single nook or corner to be found, in which the autocratic yoke of Religion has been shaken off.

We learn from history that the family, property, State and Religion are the forms in which civilization has developed. Well, none of these four forms includes such a large number of individuals as the last. There are many persons standing outside the pale of family life—such as foundlings, and the street arabs of large cities, although in later years they may found a family by marriage or concubinage. Habitual criminals and the very poor, do not recognize the principles of property. In the midst of our highly regulated civilization, with its multiplicity of laws, its governmental machinery and its army of public officials, there are isolated groups,—the gypsies for example, in almost every country in Europe—who do not join the organization of the State; their births, marriages and deaths are never recorded, they never pay taxes, nor serve out terms of military service; they are without a fixed place of residence, or political nationality, and, even if they desired it, would experience no little difficulty in entering upon a normal civil life, because they could produce none of the be-sealed and besignatured documents, without which the son of modern civilization, numbered and ticketed, can not receive an official recognition of his life, nor of his death. But the case is different with Religion; the number of those without the fold, is exceedingly small. A society of freethinkers was founded in Germany which offered to those who had thrown off the inherited fetters of Religion, the opportunity of declaring their emancipation. It numbers hardly a thousand members after several years, and even of these, many are officially claimed on the records of religious communities^ A law was passed in Austria to legalize the act of withdrawing from the church, but less than five hundred persons have availed themselves of its privileges and of this number, the majority were not persons constrained by their sense of honor to bring their outward lives into harmony with their inward convictions, but were either persons of different religions who wished to be united in matrimony and met on neutral ground by mutually renouncing the religion in which they had been brought up, or else Jews, who fancied they could escape from the popular prejudice against their race, by proclaiming officially the fact that they had renounced the faith of their fathers. This latter motive came into play so frequently that the terms Jew and "creedless" became almost synonymous in Austria, so that the secretary of the Vienna University used to remark good-naturedly. "Why don't you say right out that you are a Jew?" when some candidate for admission to the University, replied. "Creedless," when asked to what religion he belonged—one of the usual questions put to candidates. France is the country where liberty of thought has obtained from the laws, but not from society, the most extensive concessions from the yoke of Religion. But even in France, a large majority of the freethinkers remain in the bosom of the church to which their parents belonged, they go to mass and confession, they are wedded before the altar, they bring their children to be baptized and confirmed, and they summon the priest to the bedside of their dying friends. The number of those who bring up their children without baptism or confirmation, is very small, and still fewer express a wish for a so-called civil funeral. In liberty-loving England the laws and public opinion allow us to belong to any sect or religion we choose, we can be Buddhists, or worship the sun with the Parsees, but we are not allowed to announce ourselves as atheists. Bradlaugh had the audacity to proclaim his atheism. He was in consequence spurned by society, turned out of Parliament and involved in an incredibly expensive law-suit. So powerful is the influence of Religion upon every mind, so difficult is it to break loose from the habit of belonging to some church directly or indirectly, that even the atheists who are trying to substitute for the ancient faith, a new ideal more in accordance with our view of the universe, are so wanting in courage that they retain for their new conceptions founded upon reason, the title of Religion, which is so connected with the follies of the human race. There are some associations of freethinkers in Berlin and in other places in northern Germany, who have found no better name for their communities, than "the Free Religion

Societies" and David Friedrich Strauss calls an ideal belief, whose essence is the non-existence of any religion not perceptible by the senses, the "Religion of the Future." Does not that recall to mind the anecdote of the freethinker who exclaimed: "By the Almighty, I am an atheist."

CHAPTER II.

This is the place to anticipate misconstructions of my meaning. When I call Religion a conventional lie of civilized society, I do not mean by the word Religion, a belief in super-natural, abstract powers. This belief is sincere with most people. It still exists unconsciously even in men of the highest culture, and there are but few children of the Nineteenth Century, who have become so convinced of the inevitable necessity of viewing the world from the standpoint of natural science, that this conviction has penetrated into the farthest recesses of their minds, where moods, sentiments, and emotions are evolved, beyond the control of the will. In these mysterious depths ancient prejudices and superstitions still maintain their supremacy and it is incomparably more difficult to drive them out, than it is to frighten away the owls and bats from the nooks and crannies of a steeple belfry.

In this sense, that is, as a partially or entirely unconscious clinging to transcendental ideas, Religion is in fact a physical relic of the childhood of the human race; I go still further and say that it is a functional weakness, caused by the imperfectness of our organ of thought, one of the manifestations of our finiteness. I shall take pains to explain this assertion so that it may be perfectly comprehended.

Philology and comparative mythology and ethnography have already made numerous contributions to the history of the evolution and development of religious thought, and psychology has been successful in its attempt to distinguish those qualities in the soul which compelled primeval man to the conception of the supernatural, which is still retained by the man of culture of today.

It was not until centuries of civilization and untold generations had passed away after the days of those comprehensive thinkers, Pythagoras, Socrates and Plato, that a reflecting man awoke to the consciousness that certain conceptions are not essential, but only forms or divisions of human thought. At the first dawning of a brighter day for the intellect, the new ideas would overthrow the entire structure of thought built up by primitive man, with a violence which the child of modern civilization accustomed to abstractions and unable to appreciate the enormous effort of mind required to abolish the old and receive the new. is unable to comprehend. To the savage, time space and causality are as real and material as the things themselves, which surround him, and of which he can take cognizance by his coarsest sense, that of touch. He imagines time to be a monster that devours his own children; space seems to him to be a wall built around the horizon, or else the union of the visible earth with the heavens, which he looks upon as a vast roof or dome, and causality appears to him so necessary and inseparable from appearances, that he gives it the simplest and to him most reasonable form: tracing effects to their causes by ascribing them to the direct action of some being like himself. If a tree falls in the forest, some organic being must have thrown it down; if the earth trembles, somebody below must be shaking it, and as this vague generality of "somebody" is not easily grasped by his undeveloped mind, he gives it the convenient form of a human being. This identical process of thought is called forth by all the phenomena which take place around him. Unresisting slave to his conceptions of causality, he tries to discover the cause of every effect he notices, arid, as he recognizes his own will as the source of his own actions, he applies this experience, the result of his individual observation, to nature in general and sees in every one of its phenomena the operations of the arbitrary will of some being like unto him-self. But now arises for the first time a cause for perplexity and astonishment. When his wife starts the fire by rubbing two dry sticks together, when his companion kills an animal with his stone hatchet, his senses apprehend the causes of the blaze and of the animal's death. But when the storm blows over his hut, or he is bruised by the hail, he can not see the Being that is maltreating him in this fashion. He can not doubt that this Being exists and is somewhere close at hand, for there lies his hut in ruins, and the cuts made by the hail-stones are bleeding, and somebody must have done it and done it intentionally. But as he can not find this malevolent Being, his mind is filled with that horrible dread which is always aroused by unknown danger, against which we are not able to defend ourselves—this sentiment is the beginning of Religion.

It is a well-known fact that all travelers who have had opportunities for observing savages, are unanimous in saying that the sentiment of Religion among them is expressed exclusively as superstitious fear. And naturally so. Unpleasant occurrences are not only more frequent, but more forcible than pleasant ones, and they produce a deeper and more violent internal and external effect than the latter. An agreeable sensation is borne stolidly and passively; the intellect is not called upon to define it; muscles and brain can remain at rest. But a disagreeable sensation forces itself at once upon the consciousness and makes necessary a series of actions of the intellect and will, to discover and remove its cause. Hence it comes that primitive man was aroused to a perception of the malevolent powers of nature before he became aware of those which are his benefactors. He devoted no thoughts to the facts that the sun warmed him and the fruit supplied him with food, because he could eat the fruit and lie down in the sunshine, without any effort of mind, and he only exerted himself to think, when compelled to do so. Dangers and calamities on the contrary, roused him to intellectual and psychical activity and peopled the world of his imagination with enduring figures. It was only at a far more advanced stage of intellectual development that man became distinctly sensible of the pleasures that life offered him, and instead of enjoying them instinctively, appreciated them with his consciousness. The next step was to trace them to the beneficent will of some Being possessing the attributes of humanity, and love, and gratitude and admiration were the necessary results. Until this comparatively late period of civilization, his only sentiments in regard to the invisible and unknown power, which stormed, thundered and lightened, and overwhelmed him with all kinds of misfortunes and pains, were of unmixed dread and horror.

Upon this sentiment of fear are based all the primitive forms of religious worship. Care was taken not to provoke the invisible, powerful enemy and the lively, childlike imagination of prehistoric man, his trains of incoherent reasoning, made it easy for him to see in any circumstance a possible source of annoyance to his great enemy. If he was provoked, no pains were spared to appease him. His avarice was gratified by spreading presents before him, offering him sacrifices. His vanity was flattered by singing his praises, and glorifying his virtues. Man humbled himself before him, tried to touch him by prayers and supplication, and even occasionally to frighten him by threats. Prayers, sacrifices and vows are thus expressions of the same sentiment, which Darwin in his work "Expression of Emotions in Man and Animals," claims to be the cause of the wagging and crouching of the dog, the purring of the cat, and the bowing and removal of the hat by civilized man—acts of submission to a more powerful being. To condense these details—causality, which is one form of human thought, was conceived of by primitive man as something necessarily material and concrete. He sought for every circumstance which disturbed him, some cause near at hand. His incapability of carrying on abstract thought confined him to concrete conceptions which appeared to his imagination in the form of accustomed figures. He thus became an anthropomorphite, that is, he imagined all forces, everything capable of producing a phenomenon, in the form of a human being, with consciousness, will and organs to perform the bidding of the latter, his mind being unable to comprehend a force independent of an organic body. Causality thus led him to the acceptation of a necessary cause for all phenomena, his incapability of abstract reasoning, to anthropomorphism—to his peopling nature with a personal God, or with personal gods and goddesses, and his fear of these, who appeared to him as enemies, to propitiatory sacrifices and prayers, that is to an external worship. This is one of the roots of Religion in primitive man and it is still imbedded in the heart of the man of our civilization. Even intellects of high culture, sufficiently advanced in reasoning, to be beyond considering time and space as material existences, are yet in the habit of looking upon causality as something essential; they have not yet climbed to the height of abstract reasoning, from whence causality appears no longer as a concomitant to the phenomenon, but as a certain form of thought. And as to anthropomorphism, it is still carried on today; not only by the child who enjoys fairy-tales, in which the wind and the trees converse together and the stars fall in love with each other, but also by the grown up man, in the secret intimacy of his inner life, which is never entirely freed from the results of his childhood's habits. Is it not remarkable that the fashionable philosopher of our own day, with a curious return to primitive ideas, has built up his system upon the same hypothesis from which were evolved the rudimentary conceptions of the cave-dwellers of prehistoric ages, as well as those of the natives of Australia of today, viz. upon the acceptation of a will as not only the necessary condition preceding every phase of activity, but also of the very existence, of every object. This ascribing certain faculties, which we know by experience to belong to us, to surrounding inanimate objects, this effort to attribute their material form to the pre-existence of some will-power in them, because it is impossible to separate the actuality of a human being from the necessarily accompanying will, with its arbitrary and constantly exercised power—is certainly a return to the very first stage of the intellectual activity of the human race. Schopenhauer has succeeded in sublimating and super-refining his system and clothing it in technical, scientific terms, which give it a fine and dignified appearance, so that he can present it with a good grace to people of culture, but its kernel is, notwithstanding, the most astonishing case of atavism which is to be found in the whole history of philosophy—a history which is. pre-eminently a record of remarkable returns of the human intellect to ancient follies and dreams long since out-grown and supposed to have been consigned to oblivion. When we find that a profound thinker like Schopenhauer, standing upon the height of modern culture, can attribute to inorganic things a will-power like that of man, in order to comprehend them, although even in man, many things are constantly taking place, beyond the influence of the will, such as change of matter, growth, etc., when we see that this system receives a cordial welcome from large numbers of the most cultured and intelligent members of modern society, we are enabled to comprehend in all their details, the ideas of the mammoth-hunter of the quaternary period, who in generalizing the petty experiences of his own limited personality, could only conceive of nature by imagining behind every phenomenon some compelling power like himself, made after his image, only more powerful and awe-inspiring, with a larger stone hatchet and a more violent appetite, and this was the germ from which Religion was developed later.

The conception of a will-power as the cause of the phenomena of the universe, that is, the faith in a personal God or gods, is however, but a small part of Religion. Religion did not confine its transcendental investigations to nature alone, but carried them on to man, and to his position in the universe. To the number of religious conceptions must be added the faith in a soul and its immortality after death. This belief in the immortality of the soul, first rounded the preconceived ideas in regard to God, into a comprehensive system, capable of forming the foundation for a structure of society and morality as it supplied an exact definition of good and bad, and a distinction between vice and virtue. In its promises of future reward or punishment, which presuppose the immortality of the individual, with his most essential attributes, sensibility and conception, it found means to bring man into agreement with its views and acceptation of its theories. This belief in the soul and its immortality, was not evolved from causality and anthropomorphism, but from other psychological sources, for which we will proceed to search.

Specialist enquirers have discussed extensively the question whether the belief in an immortal soul preceded or followed the belief in a God, and whether all ideas of Religion were not evolved from the doctrine of the immortality of the soul, after passing through the intermediate stages of demon-worship. That many ancient races and modern savage tribes consider the belief in the immortality of the soul a more important factor of their religion than the belief in the existence of a God, is shown forcibly by the worship paid to the dead by the ancient Egyptians, the honors offered to the Lares among the Romans, the drinking the blood of slaughtered enemies among the ancient Celtic and Germanic tribes, and the cannibalism of certain tribes in Central Africa and the South Sea Islands. The savage does not drink blood nor eat human flesh, merely to appease his hunger, as a superficial observer might imagine, but from a superstitious hope that the virtues of the slaughtered enemy may descend upon him who eats or drinks a part of his body. It is however, a question of secondary importance whether the belief in God or the soul is the most ancient. One thing is certain and acknowledged, that the two beliefs were conceived and accepted by the mind of man at a very early period. He became convinced of the fact that there was something within him, distinct from the body, which caused life, and which would survive the destruction of the visible frame. An incorrect observation and a mistaken comprehension of the laws of nature by prehistoric man, led to the belief in a personal God, and the belief in the soul was caused by observation of the difference between a living and a dead being. In the former lie could feel the heart beat, and the pulse throb, mysterious actions of which the will was not the controlling force. In the dead man all was silent and still. The important role attributed to the heart as the seat of the affections and sentiments in the usage of language to this day, is a silent testimony of the intense interest aroused in the mind of primitive man by the astonishing movements of the heart. Nothing is easier to an untrained mind than to accept any two succeeding phenomena as cause and effect.

In the dead human being nothing is stirring; therefore that which was beating and hopping in the living man, must have been the cause of life. When the man was alive, it was there; when he died, it vanished, it forsook the body. But what can it be? To this question the fanciful imagination of primitive man produced several answers, giving to this principle of life, this soul, the form of some creature. Some called the soul a dove, others, a butterfly, and those capable of more abstract conceptions, imagining it to be a shadow, or a breath of wind. The disquieting and inexplicable phenomena of sleep and dreams, were capable of an explanation by the acceptation of such ideas, which was perfectly satisfactory to a primitive mind. The soul, that material and organic inhabitant of the body, that kind of parasite on the living organism, experienced at times a desire to forsake its cage. When this happened, the body was left in a condition very similar to that which followed its final abandonment by the soul: it knew and felt nothing, it did not move: it slept. The soul went somewhere; it did and experienced many things, of which an indistinct recollection was retained after its return, and these were the dreams. Grimm tells a story, taken from Paulus Diaconus, that describes how a certain King Gun tram lay down to sleep when out hunting one day, and the servant who accompanied him saw a little animal resembling a snake, crawl out from his mouth and hasten to the brook near by, which it was unable to cross. The servant noticing this, drew his sword from its scabbard and laid it across the brook. The little animal crossed over upon the sword, and after an absence of several hours, returned in the same way, and crawled back into the king's mouth. The king then awoke and told his companion how he had dreamed of coming to an immense river, which he had crossed upon an iron bridge, etc. Grimm relates another legend of the same kind, about a maid out of whose mouth crept a little red mouse after she had fallen asleep; some one then turned her over upon her face, so that when the little mouse returned, it was unable to enter her mouth, and as a consequence she awoke no more. But where was this mysterious inhabitant of the human body, the cause and explanation of the great phenomena of life and death, of sleep and dreams, where did it live before the birth of its landlord and where did it go at the death of the latter? It had occupied other bodies before this, and would go into still others afterwards; this was the doctrine of transmigration of souls. Another theory was that it was born with the body, but lived after it, remaining always in its vicinity; this was the theory believed by the ancient Egyptians, which led to their careful preservation of the dead body. In no case did primitive man conceive of it as ceasing to exist with the living body. And this is quite natural; absolute non-existence is an idea beyond the reach of the human intellect; it is even entirely opposed to human thought. We can not expect a machine to exert an amount of power beyond the strength and capacity of its constituent parts. The conception of absolute non-existence is an effort beyond the power of human intellect. We say that Nature abhors a vacuum; human processes of thought have the same horror vacui. That which thinks in man, is his I, his Ego; it is the foundation, the necessary presupposition of the act of thinking; without the Ego, no thought, no conception, not even sensibility—the idea of non-existence is conceived by the Ego, but while it is trying to represent the idea of absolute non-existence to itself, it has at the same time the full consciousness of its own existence, and this coincident impression prevents completely any real, distinct conception of the actuality of non-existence. In order to grasp this idea clearly and convincingly, the Ego would be obliged to suspend its consciousness of existence for a few moments, cease to be conscious, cease to think. In this state of course, it would not be capable of conceiving of non-existence. This is the circulus vitiosus which man, owing to the nature of his thinking apparatus, is not able to pass. As long as he thinks, his Ego is fully conscious of its existence and not able to grasp the idea of non-existence; but on the contrary, if his Ego loses consciousness of its existence, it has ceased to think and can thus grasp nb ideas at all.

By a miracle of abstract reasoning, the philosopher of India conceived the idea of Nirvanah, the absolute Nothing, the absolute non-existence of matter and motion The human mind is capable of comprehending this conception of an absolute Nothing, when universe and Ego alike can cease to exist. But it is incapable of grasping the idea of an annihilation of the Ego, while the world lives on. How can these things around us, which are only there, because we are cognizant of them, whose existence outside of our perceptions would be absolutely inconceivable, how can they continue to exist if that which first gave them their existence, our Ego, which perceives them, has ceased to exist. It is inconceivable. We can grasp the idea of a Nirvanah, when the entire phenomena of the universe and the Ego, would cease simultaneously to exist; it is not only possible, but in a certain sense would prove a source of egotistical consolation to some minds. But that the Ego can cease to exist, while the world lives on, is an idea which can not enter upon our field of thought, bounded as it is, on all sides by the limitations of the Ego. We can be swept off our feet by a torrent of technical words and phrases, we can compose all sorts of philosophical formulas and definitions, and argue ourselves into a state of apparent conviction that we are conveying the ideas clearly and forcibly to our brains by constantly repeating certain definitions and axioms. But in reality, we can no more conceive of absolute non-existence, than we can of eternity, and neither of these terms conveys any exact idea to our minds. The fact that a few master-minds have succeeded in gaining a kind of dim suspicion of their meaning, too illusory to be described in words, is one of the greatest triumphs of the human intellect. If it were possible to carry on a train of thought independent of the consciousness of the Ego, it would be in the nature of a raising ourselves out of and beyond our actual selves. Of course primitive man was incapable of such super-human mental effort. Centuries of intellectual discipline have only prepared us to formulate the problem. The immortality, the continual existence of the Ego, was recognized as an inherent necessity, in the earlier stages of mental development. And this conception was refined from its first crude form, the corporal resurrection and continued existence of the dead, into the belief in the immortality of the spiritual or intellectual attributes of each individual.

This is what I meant when I said above, that Religion was a functional weakness, caused by the imperfectness of our organ of thought, and one of the manifestations of our finiteness. Man arrived at his belief in God by the operations of causality and the incapability of imagining any forces or causes, except in organic forms, such as he was accustomed to see around him. He arrived at his belief in the soul, by a false and illogical observation of the phenomena of life and death, of sleep and dreams, and at his faith in the continued existence of the soul, by the impossibility experienced by his Ego, of imagining itself as non-existing. The theory of a continued existence after death is nothing more than a certain manifestation of the impulse for self-preservation, as the impulse for self-preservation itself, is nothing more than the form under which our vital energies, that have their seat in every single cell of our organism, manifest themselves to our consciousness. Energy to live is identical with the wish to live. Any one who has had the opportunity of seeing many people die, will acknowledge the fact that people become easily resigned to death when weakened by disease or old age, but that there is a terrible struggle before the end is accepted as inevitable, by a strong and promising nature, stricken down by some accident at the opening of life's career. Suicide appears to be a contradiction to my assertion; it certainly pre-supposes an extremely powerful will, which is as certainly, only the outgrowth of an equally powerful vitality; hence it seems as if in suicides, the energy to live is in direct opposition to the wish to live. But in reality, suicide, except in those cases where it is due to some temporary aberration of the intellect, is merely an inconsiderate act to protect one's life against certain dangers that threaten it. The suicide throws himself into the arms of death because he dreads some impending physical or emotional disturbances; he would not have resorted to this extreme measure unless he had still prized life, for otherwise he would hare had no reasons for fearing any disasters, that even at their worst, could only have deprived him of life. Every suicide is an example of the same frame of mind which impels the soldier to commit suicide before the battle, for fear that he may be shot during the day—consequently a proof, not of weariness of life nor of indifference to death, but of exactly the opposite sentiments. The axiom that the wish and the energy to live are identical, is thus proved to have no exception, and this wish to live continues in the very presence of death.

Every organic being, conscious of its life and vitality in every cell, finds it impossible to realize the idea of a complete cessation of its rich and delightful material activity. We can conceive of the death of some one else as probable and possible, but we consider our own existence as eternal and our own death as some remote and improbable contingency. Only by the aid of the most advanced intellectual culture, by accumulating a vast number of abstractions and analogies, and using them like the rounds of a ladder, do we climb to a height in which our intellectual and our emotional natures are able to realize the fact that the succeeding generations are merely a continuation and development of those that have gone before, and to find a consolation in the permanence and evolution of the human race as a whole, for the perishableness of the individual.

The causes which led to the growth of transcendental ideas in prehistoric man have the same effect upon the civilized man of today, although sometimes they exert their influence in the sphere of the Unconscious. Anthropomorphism has still an influence upon every mind which does not watch over the conception and growth of its ideas with the strictest severity; it is so convenient to clothe abstract thoughts in familiar expressions, and all of us can recall many occasions when we represented to ourselves or to others some spiritual, immaterial idea under the form of some circumstance or appearance that had come under our observation in the animal or vegetable world. And the incapability of realizing any possible non-existence of the Ego, is as marked now as it ever was. The superstition of primitive man, which we have inherited direct, exerts a powerful influence upon us as we enter the realms of the Unconscious. The French philosopher T. Ribot, observes that heredity is to the race what memory is to the individual—that is, heredity is the memory of the species. Every man carries in his mind the ideas of his ancestors, usually unconsciously and but dimly recognized; some external disturbance however occurs, and they blaze up, casting a light as bright as day upon the entire inner world of intelligence and emotions. Heredity is a curse from which we can not escape. It is impossible for us to change the shape of our features or of our bodies, and in the same way it is impossible for us to alter the mental physiognomy of our thought, bequeathed to us with the former by our ancestors. This explains the trait of superstition which is often absolutely beyond the control of the reason or will, and which we notice with such surprise in ourselves, and in others of the most extensive culture; it also explains that exaltation of religious sentiment to which persons of poetic temperament are so liable, because they are particularly susceptible to the influence of heredity. This source of superstitious ideas, heredity, can be only controlled and done away with by the accumulated efforts of many generations. Centuries will be required to produce a human being, who from his birth up, is prepared to comprehend life and the universe from the point of view of reason and natural science, without prejudice or superstition, because a hundred generations before him had been convincing themselves of the correctness of this point of view.

We on the contrary, are predisposed to look upon the phenomena of this life and the world, from an irrational and superstitious standpoint, owing to the fact that not hundreds, but hundreds of thousands of generations before us, have been in the habit of carrying on a false and mistaken habit of thought and theorizing. Among the causes which led to the conception of Religion and its continued existence in the human mind, are some which, although not capable of producing by themselves the ideas of God, the soul and immortality, were yet powerful in impressing and perpetuating them upon the heart of man. One of these accessory causes of the continuation of religious sentiments, is the natural cowardice of man; he dislikes to cut himself loose from any powerful organization, to stand alone, only supported by his own will, with no invisible helper or protector to come to his assistance. The human race rarely produces an individual who, realizing his power, and upheld by an exalted self-appreciation, is prepared to enter alone upon life's battlefield, on which he must wield his sword and shield with might and skill to come out as victor or even alive. These exceptional men, who offer the finest and most perfect types of our race, become party leaders, conquerors, rulers of the people. They look with contempt upon the beaten paths, and open new highways for themselves. They do not accept with patient resignation what destiny offers them, but hew out for themselves a new destiny, even if they know they will perish in the attempt. But the great multitude of mankind has not this independence. The average individual prefers to enter upon the struggle for existence, supported by hundreds of others, and turn a close, serried front to the enemy. They want to feel an armed comrade behind and at each elbow, and in front too, if possible. They like to listen to the words of command, and have their movements determined by a higher authority. Such men cling to Religion as to a weapon and a consolation. What a comfort to imagine that in the midst of the tumult and smoke of the battle, a protecting shield is held up in front of them by a watchful God or guardian angel! The humblest tailor or day-laborer can have the satisfaction of sharing the privilege of Achilles who was protected by the invisible shield of Pallas Athene during the battle on the plains of Troy. And what a sense of strength fills the mind of him who feels that at all times and in all places, he is armed with a powerful weapon—prayer! It is difficult to despair when one believes that a word, a supplication, will remove any disturbing element from his path. To take an extreme case,—an aeronaut falls from the car of his balloon, a thousand feet high. If he is a freethinker, he knows that he is lost and that there is no power on earth that can prevent his body from being smashed to pieces on the ground beneath, in less than ten seconds. But if he is a believer in God, he retains during the entire extent of his fall, or at least until he loses consciousness, a hope that some superhuman power, to which he offers up supplications of intense fervor as he falls, will, to save him, suspend the laws of nature for a few minutes and deposit him gently and softly upon the ground. As long as he retains consciousness the impulse of self-preservation maintains its sway, and he clings obstinately to a visionary, superstitious possibility, even against such an irrevocable sentence of death as has been passed upon him. The human heart has no more precious possession than illusion. And what more beneficent and consoling illusion could there be than the self-deception of faith in God and prayer? In consequence of this fact the majority of mankind will continue to seek refuge from life's pains and griefs in conceptions founded on a childish superstition, until they become so impressed by and convinced of the necessity of viewing the world from the standpoint of natural science, that they learn to consider the death of an individual, even although it be their own, as a circumstance of the most trifling importance for their race and the — universe not until the solidarity of mankind has become so generally and firmly organized that each individual will turn instinctively for help to his fellow-men in any disasters that befall him, and not to an incomprehensible, supernatural power.

Another one of these causes of the continuation of Religion, which I have designated as accessory, consists in the necessity for an ideal that is experienced by all human hearts, even the rudest and most uncultivated. What is this ideal? It is the remote type towards which mankind is developing and perfecting itself; not only the type of physical perfection, but the type of the inner life, of the mode of thinking, and of the constitution of society. The impulse towards this ideal, the longing to attain to it, are implanted in the breast of every intellectually and physically normal man; it is something organically inherent in him, of which he is not necessarily conscious, and in which even in the deepest and closest thinker, there is always much that is unconscious. In building a railroad embankment, a row of wooden stakes is first driven into the ground, of the same height and extending as far, as the embankment is to be; then the workmen shovel dirt upon the stakes until they are entirely covered up and lost to sight. Every living being contains within itself a law for its growth and development, which fulfills the same purpose as the stakes in the embankment; it grows and developes in accordance with this law, trying to fill out the invisible but none the less real framework which it has built up for itself, as the embankment grows and finally covers up the stakes. If an organism developes so that it coincides at all points with the figure which represents the extreme limit of its capacity for development, it has reached perfection and fully attained to its ideal. Usually each individual being remains far behind the ideal of its type, but its effort to reach it is the mysterious compelling force of its instinct for self-preservation and development, that is, of all organic activity. The race as a whole, has also its standard of development, and everything within it to raise it to this standard, as well as the individual. Like the individual every species has its law of growth. It arises, has that within it which impels it to attain to a certain standard of size and strength, and last a certain length of time, it grows to a certain point, and then retrogrades and vanishes from the face of the earth, making way for a more elevated form of life, to which it served as a stepping stone, or, I might say as a sketch or design. Paleontology makes us acquainted with a long list of animal species, who lived during one or more geological periods, and chen became extinct. The same is also true of the human race. It forms one zoological entity taken as a whole, and is governed by one law of life. It had its origin in a certain geological age (whether this was in the beginning of the Quaternary epoch, or in the middle or latter part of the Tertiary period is a matter of little moment), according to analogy, it will become extinct in some other geological period in the future. We can only guess at the forms of life that preceded it, and those that are to follow it are even beyond our imagination. But as long as the human race lives upon earth, as long as it has not attained to the summit of its development, it will continue to struggle earnestly to fill in the invisible framework of its preordained culture and progress and this struggle for the realization of its ideal, the growth to the height of its unseen standard, is felt and experienced by every single member of the human family, with the exception of idiots, although of course most men perceive it only dimly and without comprehending its true import. This dim perception becomes consciousness in cultivated minds. In others, less cultivated, it remains in the stage of an indistinct, impelling longing, which we can call an impulse towards higher things, or a yearning for the ideal, as we may prefer, and which under either name, is nothing else than an intense longing to emerge from our individual isolation and feel more distinctly our unity with our fellow-men. The chain that unites all men of one race into a race, and binds the species itself into one zoological entity, making of it one individual of a higher order, presses upon every human heart, and is felt by all distinctly as a solidarity. This solidarity is constantly seeking expression. Once in a while every man feels the need of knowing that he is a fragment of a mighty whole, of convincing himself that the great current of race development is flowing through his veins side by side with the current of individual self-development and that his individual existence is but a trivial episode in the grand total of human existence. In this consciousness of his identification with a majestic, supreme organism that is living, flourishing and developing more gloriously from day to day with no saddening end in view, he finds an unspeakably deep and tender consolation for the narrowness, limitations and brevity of his individual span of existence. The man of culture finds a thousand opportunities for satisfying this need without leaving his library or his drawing-room. Study of the development of the human race during the centuries described by history, self oblivion in the works of the great thinkers and poets of all ages, or enjoyment of the harmonies of the universe made audible by science, or if these solitary means are not sufficient, social intercourse with minds of wide and liberal mental horizons,—these opportunities are offered to him, and grant him an outlook and an escape from his own individual and isolated existence into the magnificent realm of humanity. But how is it with the man on a lower social scale? Where does he find an opportunity to merge his separate existence into that of collective mankind? When is it proved to him that he is justified in and capable of elevating the conditions of his life above those of the cattle that feed, beget their kind, and pass away? When does he ever find the time in his struggle for his daily bread, in his constant and weary efforts to keep himself supplied with the bare necessaries of life, when does he find an opportunity for communion with his inner self, for raising his thoughts to higher things, for taking observations of his true position in regard to the human race and nature? Until the present day the working man has only attained to a higher existence by means of Religion. The ideal only appeared to him in the disguise of religious belief. The Sunday was not only a day of physical rest to him, but an opportunity for the development of all the blossoms of his mind. The church was his drawing-room, the minister his more elevated intercourse, God and the Saints, his distinguished friends. When in the cathedral he realized that he was in a grand, magnificent structure, that yet belonged to him as much as the wretched hovel that sheltered his poverty from day to day. In the worship of God he found himself taking part in a service that had no direct influence upon the questions of food and clothing, but was entirely separate from his every-day life with its purely physical interests. Surrounded by other true believers he felt himself an authorized member of a great community, and the connection between himself and his neighbors, was expressed openly to his senses by the external symbols of worship, kneeling, rising and making the sign of the cross, which all performed in concert. The sermon was the only elevated discourse which he ever had the opportunity of hearing, and it aroused him somewhat, even if very slightly, from his customary train of dull, rudimentary thought. This is the reason why he continues to cling to Religion with such fervor, and it will remain a powerful and influential obstacle against his acceptance of modern ideas, unless the new culture offers him some substitute for the emotions and satisfactions of his human self-consciousness which he has hitherto found in Religion.

This substitute will be provided; it is even now partly suggested. Intercourse with the poets and thinkers of all ages, through their works, will supersede the sermon; the theatre, concert hall and assembly room will render the meeting-house unnecessary. The germs of future formations are already perceptible on all sides. In those countries which enjoy political freedom, the uncultivated masses meet at certain times and discuss or listen to discussions, concerning the common interests of the place or of the country, finding in such meetings their Sunday rest and recreation On election days, in places where universal suffrage prevails, the working man is filled with a proud self-esteem as a complete man, even more than that he experiences in the common observance of religious worship. Many societies have been formed for ethical and literary culture; in some of them essays or extracts from works of poetry are read aloud, and in these meetings a more human and liberal intercourse prevails than was possible with the minister. It is only to be regretted that these societies have not yet penetrated to the lowest scales of our social system, where they are needed the most. But* these germs are developing. A time is coming and is perhaps near at hand, when we will see a civilization in which men will satisfy not transcendentally, but according to reason, their need for rest and recreation, for elevation of their ideas, and their longing for emotions; when a solidarity of the human race will be the worship of a progressive and enlightened age. By a return to primitive customs, such as history has often had to record, the theatre will again be the place of meeting and worship, as it was two and a half thousand years ago among the Greeks. But not the theatre of today with its indecent plots, its street-song melodies, its idiotic laughter and its semi-nudity, but a theatre where we will see in beautiful, corporate forms the passions struggling with the will, and personal greed conquered by the capability for self-denial, and where with every word and action, like grand accompaniment, we will hear a continual reference to the collective existence and development of the human race. The unity of benevolence will succeed to the unity of worship. And what different emotions will be aroused in man by these future festivals of all humanity! The mysticism of the priest can not rival the clear, rational beauty of poetry. An intellect expands as it follows the scenes of human passion in some noble drama, while it remains passive during the mysterious symbols of a church service, with no reason nor meaning in it. The discourse of a scientist as he explains the phenomena of nature, the speech of some distinguished politician discussing the questions of the day in regard to the State and the commonwealth, have a much more vivid and direct interest for the listeners than the monotonous repetitions of the preacher, as he relates worn-out myths, and dilutes orthodox doctrines for his flock. The adoption of orphans by the community, the distribution of clothing and other presents among destitute children, testimonials of honor to deserving fellow-citizens on suitable occasions in the presence of the public, accompanied by songs and music and carried on with order and dignity— such observances as these would surely give each participant a very different idea of the mutual duties and responsibilities of citizens and men and of their unity, due to the ties of mutual interests and privileges, in short, of their solidarity, than dipping their dirty fingers simultaneously into a basin of holy water, or praying and singing in concert. Such is my idea of the civilization of the future. I am convinced that the day will come when even the humblest man will find his individual life merged into the fuller life of the community, and his isolated, circumscribed horizon broadened by means of festivals of poetry, music, art, thought and humanity, until it coincides with the horizon of the entire human race, thus leading him on to nobler standards of development and setting before him the grand ideal of a perfected humanity. Until this picture of the future becomes reality, however, the masses will continue to seek the ideal exaltation which they find no-where else, in Religion, or rather in its external forms, the lofty cathedral buildings, the vestments of the priests, the organ's tones, the anthems, and all the other mystic accessories of worship.

CHAPTER III.

The foregoing explanations make my meaning clear that the longing experienced by man for a higher intellectual growth and an ideal, for a consolation always ready at hand and even for the self-deception of a powerful and mysterious protector in all emergencies, is no false pretension, but a genuine and ineradicable sentiment. We have also seen that this sentiment necessarily found its gratification in the belief in God, the soul and immortality, impelled thereto by historical, physiological and psychological reasons. The continuation and perpetuation of these transcendental ideas is no conscious intentional fraud in most men, no voluntary self-deception; it is ar honest weakness, a habit which they can not break, a poetical sentimentality which they piously defend from the ruthless attacks of rational analysis. This is not what I mean by the conventional lie of Religion. By this term I wish to express the reverence paid by men, even of the most advanced culture, to the positive, external forms of Religion, its dogmas, doctrines, observances, festivals, ceremonies, symbols and ministers.

This reverence is a lie and a fraud, even in those who are most deeply sunk in transcendentalism, unless they have remained completely uninfected by the views and culture of the present day. It is a lie and a fraud, and it would certainly bring the blush of shame to our cheek, if we had not fallen into the habit of doing so many things without reflection, without enquiring into their significance at all. Owing to the force of habit we go regularly to church, bow reverently to the minister, and take up our Bible with solemnity; we assume mechanically an expression of awe and inward reflection when we are taking part in a church service, and we avoid any exact comparison of its outward observances with our convictions, taking especial pains to close our eyes and minds to the disgraceful treason which we are committing by these acts against all our knowledge, our convictions, and everything that we recognize and cling to as truth. Historical investigations have revealed to us the origin and growth of the Bible; we know that by this name we designate a collection of writings, as radically unlike in origin, character and contents, as if the Nibelungen Lied, Mirabeau's speeches, Heine's love poems and a manual of zoology, had been printed and mixed up promiscuously, and then bound into one volume. We find collected in this book the superstitious beliefs of the ancient inhabitants of Palestine, with indistinct echoes of Indian and Persian fables, mistaken imitations of Egyptian theories and customs, historical chronicles as dry as they are unreliable, and miscellaneous poems, amatory, human and Jewish— national, which are rarely distinguished by beauties of the highest order, but frequently by superfluity of expression, coarseness, bad taste and genuine Oriental sensuality. As a literary monument the Bible is of much later origin than the Vedas; as a work of literary value it is surpassed by everything written in the last two thousand years by authors even of the second rank, and to compare it seriously with the productions of Homer, Sophocles, Dante, Shakespeare or Goethe, would require a fanaticized mind that had entirely lost its power of judgment; its conception of the universe is childish, and its morality revolting, as revealed in the malicious vengeance attributed to God in the Old Testament and in the New, the parable of the laborers of the eleventh hour and the episodes of Mary Magdalen and the woman taken in adultery. And yet men, cultivated and capable of forming a just estimate, pretend to reverence this ancient work, they refuse to allow it to be discussed and criticised like any other production of the human intellect, they found societies and place enormous sums at their disposal to print millions of copies of it, which they distribute all over the world, and they pretend to be edified and inspired when they read in it.

The formulas used in public worship by all established religions are founded upon ideas and customs which originated in the most ancient barbaric periods, in Asia and northern Africa. We can see the traces of the worship of the sun by the Aryans, of the mysticism of the Buddhists and of the worship of Isis and Osiris by the Egyptians, in the observances and prayers of public worship and in the festivals and offerings of Jews and Christians of the present day. And the people of the Nineteenth Century assume a reverent and solemn expression as they repeat the kneelings, gestures, ceremonies and prayers invented thousands of years ago, on the hanks of the Nile or the Ganges, by the miserable, undeveloped human beings of the stone or bronze ages, to manifest in some material was their conceptions of the universe, its origin and its laws—all, conceptions of the rankest heathenism.

As we study this disgraceful comedy, the more we expose to view the grotesque contrast between the modern tone of mind and the established religions, the more difficult does it become to speak calmly and dispassionately on this subject. The inconsistency is so superhumanly nonsensical, so gigantic, that the arguments set forth in detail against it, appear as inadequate and inefficient as a broom to sweep out the sands of Sahara; only the satire of a Rabelais or the inkstand of a Luther thrown against it, could do it justice.

It is impossible to describe all the details of this sham structure of Religion. We must be content to accept a few of the most significant. Diplomatists make use of all possible means and threats to induce the Cardinals to elect a Pope to suit them; but after the tedious and obstinate intrigues have been led to the wished-for conclusion, these same diplomatists, who have been pulling the strings of the puppet show, manifest a sudden and fervent reverence for the Pope's authority and person, which is founded upon the fiction that the Holy Ghost had selected him as the successor of St. Peter. This election of a Pope is regarded by thousands upon thousands of people as a solemn and important occurrence who would laugh at a description of the ceremonies attending the installation of a new Grand Lama in Thibet, upon the death of his predecessor, and yet these ceremonies bear a striking resemblance to each other. The Governments of various countries maintain diplomatic relations with a man whose importance is due to the fact that he supplies God with new saints, and can guarantee to men celestial privileges and blessings, and liberate sinners from the torments of being burned after death; they conclude diplomatic treaties with him and set forth in laws and decrees that the Pope has great influence with God, and consequently that a person standing in such intimate intercourse with the Supreme Being, and sharing his infallibility to such an extent, should receive reverence and homage beyond that which any other man on earth is entitled to. And yet, these same Governments send out expeditions to the Soudan, and laugh at the pretensions of the black Prophet there, who forbids their emissaries to enter into his domain, and declares that he will strike them, if they disobey him, with the anger of the Supreme Fetish, whose prophet and favorite he is. Who can point out to me the difference between that poor negro and the Pope at Rome? Each claims to be the high priest of God, whose thunder and lightning he can control, with the privilege of recommending certain people to God's favor or vengeance, who acts upon their suggestions. Where is the logic of the cultivated European who looks upon one as an absurd pretender, and the other as an imposing figure worthy of all reverence?

Every separate act of a religious ceremony becomes a fraud and a criminal satire when performed by a cultivated man of this Nineteenth Century.

He sprinkles himself with holy water, and expresses by the act his conviction that the priest who said certain words over it, accompanied by certain gestures, had conferred some mysterious virtues upon it, changing its nature in some way, although a chemical analysis of it would show that it differs in no respect from any other water, except in being a little more dirty. He repeats prayers, kneels, goes to church services with all their ceremonies, and thus asserts his conviction that there is a God, who enjoys prayers, gestures, incense and anthems, if the prayers are in certain stereotyped words, the gestures in certain prescribed forms, and the ceremonies presided over by persons in odd clothing, with robes and capes of such peculiar colors and shapes as no sensible man would ever dream of wearing. The fact that a liturgy or form of public worship once established, is observed with painful minuteness, can only be explained to a rational mind somewhat in this way: the priests learned from some good source, and acted upon this knowledge, that God not only had the vanity to insist upon praises, compliments and flattery being offered to Him as well as glorifications of His goodness, His wisdom and His greatness, but combined with this vanity was the whim that He would only accept these praises and glorifications when they were offered according to a certain formula, never to be deviated from. And the men of our age of natural science pretend to reverence these liturgies, and will not allow any one to speak of them with the contempt they deserve.

More revolting and insufferable even than the lie of Religion as acted by the individual, is the same lie of Religion as acted by the community. The individual citizen although he belongs ostensibly to some established religion, and takes part in its ceremonies, often makes no secret of his disbelief in its superstitions, and refuses to be convinced that a certain form of words, repeated in concert by the congregation will suspend or alter the laws of nature, that the devil is driven out from an infant when sprinkled with holy water, or that the chanting and speech of a man in a black or white robe beside a corpse, will open the gates of Paradise to the soul of the dead man. But, as a member of the community and of the body politic, this same citizen does not hesitate to declare necessary all the points claimed by the established religions, and he offers up to them all the substantial and spiritual sacrifices which the salaried minister of this superstition, recognized and supported by the State, may demand. The same Government that builds universities, schools and libraries, builds churches too; the same Government that pays salaries to professors, supports the ministers also; the same code of laws that compels children to go to school, forbids blasphemy and any expression of scorn or defiance of established religions. What do these incongruities mean? This is their meaning: we say that the earth stands still and the sun revolves around it, although science has proved the contrary beyond a doubt; that the earth is only about five thousand years old, and no monuments from Egypt or anywhere else, known to be thousands of years older, will be accepted as contradicting this fact. We are not imprisoned in lunatic asylums for asserting these incongruities to be reconcilable truths; we are not declared incapable of filling office and carrying on our business, although we have certainly given the most striking proofs of mental imbecility, and that we do riot possess the intellectual qualifications for looking after our own affairs, much less the destinies of the country entrusted to us. As private citizens we assert that we do not believe in the existence of God, that the God of the established religions is the outgrowth of childish and undeveloped minds; but as members of the body politic, we declare any one holding such views to be guilty of blasphemy before the law and incapable of holding office. And this, notwithstanding the fact that no scientific or rational proof has ever been offered in evidence of the reality of God, that even the most enthusiastic theologian can produce no testimony to prove the existence of God, that approaches in clearness and convincing force, that offered by the archæologian and geologist to prove the antiquity of the earth and its inhabitants, or by the astronomer to convince us of the revolution of the earth around the sun; notwithstanding the fact that a man is excused, even from a theological standpoint, much more readily when he doubts the existence of God, than when he questions the results of scientific investigations, which are capable of such over whelming demonstration. Besides this, the State appoints professors and pays their salaries out of the government revenue, bestows upon them authority and is always ready to help them enforce it, and these professors are commissioned to teach and to prove that the occurrences of this world are regulated by natural laws, that physiology recognizes no organic difference in the formation of all living beings, and that twice two are four. But in addition to these professors of the exact sciences, the State appoints professors of theology, who are commissioned likewise to teach, but necessarily not to prove, to assert however, that the newborn babe is cursed with original, inborn sin, that God dictated to certain men a book to be reverenced as holy, that on numerous occasions the laws of nature were suspended as a favor to certain human beings, that by murmuring certain words over some dough it is changed into flesh, and this flesh is part of the body of a human being who died almost two thousand years ago, and that three persons are one, and one, three. When a law-abiding citizen listens in succession to a lecture on science delivered by some professor appointed by the Government, and then to a sermon preached by some professor of theology, also appointed by the Government and armed with the same authority—his mind must be in a curious predicament between the two. One tells him that after death the organism is resolved to its constituent elements; the other describes how certain persons not only remained uncorrupted by death, but awoke again to life. And both doctrines are presented to him under the authority of the State, the taxes he pays are applied on their salaries, and the teachings of both are declared by the Government to be equally true and necessary. Which professor is the unlucky citizen to believe? The theologian? Then the State is taxed to support a willful liar as professor of physiology, his theories and assertions must be arbitrary deceptions, and yet he is commissioned to educate the young men of the country. Or is he to believe the scientist? Then the theological professor is the liar, and the Government pays for deliberate lies as in the other case. Would it be a matter to cause surprise if the loyal citizen between the horns of this dilemma, should lose more or less of the respect he had hitherto felt for the Government?

And even this is not all. Those old women who get the hard-earned money away from servant girls, under the pretense of giving them a love-philter to win back the hearts of their inconstant sweethearts, are arrested and fined by the authorities; but at the same time those men are paid fine salaries and upheld by the authorities, who obtain the money of the servant girls by the no less false pretense of getting their defunct relatives out of the fires of purgatory, by some hocus-pocus arrangement. Custom has it that we treat the clergy and the high dignitaries of the church, the bishops and cardinals, with excessive reverence, and men accept this custom and bow before it, who in their hearts, consider these men as cheats or simpletons, not superior in any way to the medicine-men of the red skins, who have their established forms of worship too, their ceremonies and their prayers, and are held in veneration by their tribes as possessing supernatural powers. If we find it proper to ridicule these medicine-men, why should we not be permitted to laugh at the ceremony of kissing the slipper of the Pope or the hand of a priest?

The newspapers have occasionally recorded the fact with humorous comment, that the Chinese Government had been threatening a certain god with deposition, if he should fail to fulfill the prayers of the people; if, for example, he did not send the rain they had been soliciting, or had not secured the victory to the imperial army, etc. But these same newspapers publish in the most prominent place, governmental decrees—as for example, in England, after the battle of Tel-el-Kebir—appointing a day for the people to assemble and give thanks to God, in a regularly appointed formula, for that He had been graciously pleased to grant them the victory. What is the essential difference between a decree of the Chinese

Government depriving the national god of some portion of his offerings, because he had permitted an epidemic to scourge the land, and the decree of the English Government, acknowledging the indebtedness of the people to God because He had taken good care of the political interests of England in Egypt, and shown Himself the true friend of the British and the enemy of the Arabs. Both decrees are founded upon the same ideas, only the Chinese are more courageous and consistent than the English, who in case of a defeat, would not venture to express their disapprobation of His indifference to the duties He owes to the nation that worships Him so zealously, as in case of a victory, they award Him the honor and praise.

As I remarked before, it is impossible to describe this gigantic imposition of Religion in all its details; I must confine myself to some of its leading points in order to avoid incessant repetitious. This fraud penetrates and demoralizes our whole public and private existence. The State is guilty of imposition when it sets apart special days for prayer or thanksgiving, when it appoints ministers and calls the higher clergy into the House of Lords; the community is guilty of the same lie when it builds churches; the judge is acting a lie when he is passing sentence upon some person who has been blaspheming or insulting God or the church; the minister, imbued with the modern tone of thought, knows that he is guilty of deception when he takes pay for repeating dogmas and conducting ceremonies, which he is fully aware are nothing but nonsensical frauds,—the enlightened citizen knows that he is a hypocrite when he affects an outward reverence for the man of God, when he goes to communion or presents his child for baptism. The continued existence and growth of these ancient, partly prehistoric forms of worship in the midst of our modern civilization is a monstrous fact, and the position accorded to the minister, the European equivalent of the Indian medicine-man and the African almamy, is such an insolent triumph of cowardice, hypocrisy and mental indolence over truth and courage of opinion, as would be sufficient, taken alone, to characterize our civilization as a complete imposition, and our political and social conditions of life as necessarily temporary.

THE LIE OF A MONARCHY AND ARISTOCRACY

CHAPTER I.

If we were able to consider the existing institutions of our civilization from an artistic, esthetic point of view alone; if it were possible for us to study and criticise them with the abstract, impersonal interest of that Persian Prince Uzbek, described by Montesquieu, who travelled in foreign countries merely in search of amusement and shook their dust from his feet when he had left them behind him, we would not hesitate to accept the present arrangement of society as skillfully and consistently constructed, forming an harmonious whole. All the constituent parts are arranged in order, and are necessarily evolved from and dependent upon each other, ascending from the lowest to the highest, in an unbroken, logical sequence. When the grand gothic structure of mediaeval state and society was erected, it presented an imposing appearance, and was regarded as a magnificent and comfortable place of refuge and safety by those whom it sheltered. Today only the ornamental façade remains; the useful, habitable portions of the building have long since fallen into decay, so that any one seeking for shelter in it now, finds it impossible to discover a single nook or corner, in which he can be protected from the wind or rain. But the façade still retains its former beauty and grandeur, and arouses admiration in the beholder for the genius and skill of the architect. Nothing but one wall is left standing today of what was once a fine and solid structure. But this wall is an architectural work of art in which all the details are skillfully and harmoniously subordinated to the general design. Of course we should not examine this architectural monument from the heap of ruins behind it; but if we approach it from the front, keeping far enough away to get the effect of the perspective, and studying it merely as an artistic creation, we can not help acknowledging that the architect has produced a master-piece.

A monarchy owes its existence and perpetuation to Religion. The latter in its present and historical form was the necessary foundation of the former. An established religion however, is not necessarily dependent upon a monarchy but can be recognized by a government, whatever its constitution. Theoretically this needs no demonstration. It has been practically proved by the republics governed by the Jesuits among the natives of South America, and the United States of North America, whose constitution is based upon the principles of Religion. An hereditary monarchy on the contrary, is impossible and inconceivable without the foundation of Religion. We can imagine how a powerful and talented man might usurp the supreme command in a country and retain it by stratagem or force of arms; he could conquer the nation by some coup d'état, and support his authority by a crowd of selfishly interested dependents, whom he could attach to his fortunes by material advantages and honors, and an army of whose devotion he could make sure by a succession of victories and opportunities for plunder, by frequent gifts of money and titles; he could call himself king or emperor as he chose, dictator or president, and his authority be recognized as supreme because he would have the power to enforce it. It is even possible that the majority of the people might accept willingly the yoke placed upon them by his ambition, not only because it is a fundamental trait in human nature to be so dazzled by the sight of success that the power of judgment is temporarily suspended, but also because the average citizen would find it to his interest and advantage to sustain the existing state of affairs, and because the ruler, if a man of genius, would govern so wisely that industries and trade would flourish, the laws be administered with justice, and the masses, whose interests are centered in their material needs, find their table more abundantly supplied, and the hoard of savings laid by for a rainy day increasing. Such an usurper might venture to hold his own without the aid of Religion. He might find the sword sufficient for his support and not need the cross. He would have no cause to fear the criticism of reason, because he could oppose material force against its deductions. The logical reasoner might say to him: "You are a human being like the rest of us; as we did not appoint you voluntarily to be a ruler over us, we are surely not bound to pay homage to you and obey your commands." To which the tyrant could reply: "Your argument is indisputable, but so is my army. You will obey my commands not because they are rational and convincing, but because I will compel you to do so." In such a case the ruler could dispense with God's aid; his strong arm would be sufficient. He would not feel the need of the anointing oil or the blessing of the church, as he would have plenty of powder and his bayonets to convince the subservient multitudes of his supremacy, as efficacious as any mystic or gorgeous coronation ceremonies. But circumstances might change, even for such a despot as this, if he had a son for instance, to whom he wished to ensure a continuance of his authority after his death. Then he would place self under the ægis of Religion. He would recall to mine! the fact that during the Middle Ages, the churches were an asylum of refuge, and he would hasten to seek protection at the foot of the altar from the pursuit of reason The blade of the sword alone is no longer sufficient, he must have the cross welded to it for a handle.

The sources of the tyrant's power are too clearly visible to all, he must make them fade into indistinctness by enveloping them in a cloud of incense. The hard facts of history are softened in a mist of legendary lore, and the priest is called upon to reply to the question: "Why should the feeble son, who never could carve out a throne for himself, why should he inherit the power of his father?" by a simple: "Because God so wills it." This is the rock upon which young dynasties will strike and go down. The sons of the Nineteenth Century can not see God in the fire of a fusillade as Moses saw Him in the burning bush; neither can they accept a street-barricade skirmishes a manifestation of His will.

It is a tedious task to throw a halo c sacredness around the prosaic proclamations which form the certificate of birth of a dictatorship and if the inheritor of it is not strong enough to uphold it by force of arms it will not help him much to draw the right to govern from heaven. The catholic church has strictly forbidden the canonization of any person until at least four generations have passed away since his death. The believers must be allowed time to forget his human frailties; for even with the best intentions, we find it hard to believe that the John or Harry, who sat next to us at school has got angel wings now, and is one of the most distinguished soloists of the celestial choir. The church was even wiser on this point than those monarchs who had it proclaimed that they were demi-gods, before their contemporaries had time to forget their unpaid bills and their boots run down at the heel. The fact that the Bonapartes were not satisfied with being the absolute rulers of France, but insisted upon a grand, religious coronation ceremony before the altar of Notre Dame, was their great political blunder. The 18. Brumaire and the 2d of December made the religious coronation superfluous. The dove of the Holy Ghost ought not to have been associated with the imperial eagle.

If it is possible for a dictator to dispense with Religion, this is far from being the case with a legitimate monarchy. Religion is its natural and indispensable foundation. In the majority of cases, the monarch is endowed with rather less than more than the average of human, natural gifts. Very rarely do we find a prince who is what would be called in every-day life a capable man, and only once in centuries does a dynasty produce a man of commanding talents or of genius. Among the reigning princes of civilized countries there are some who lay claim to being great generals, others to being authors, painters, musicians, scientists or legal authorities. They take great pains to master the special branches of learning or art, to which they are most attached, and their productions in this line can be looked upon as tests of their ability. But what is the result? If we examine these productions, not from the point of view of a court hanger-on, but as an impartial critic, we are obliged to come to the conclusion that unsupported by the prestige of royalty, they would never have attained to even a moderate rank in the departments they have chosen. This prince who pretends to be such a fine soldier, would never have received promotion for his military talents; this one who is coquetting with jurisprudence, would not have been able to win many suits; this other, the would-be astronomer, would never have been appointed to even the most insignificant professorship, the would-be dramatist would never have seen one of his plays produced, nor would the painter have sold any of his paintings. If their names had been Mayer or Durand or Smith, they would have been distanced by a large majority of their competitors. It is a matter of doubt whether any one of them, as a private citizen, would have been capable of supporting himself and founding and maintaining a family. We must even make some concessions to imagine them with their actual endowments, but of course, different training, as capable of making good tradesmen, grocers, petty government officials or non-commissioned officers. Some of them at least, are gifted with some social and personal attractions. They are handsome men. They have grace in conversation. They could turn the heads of wealthy heiresses, and make brilliant marriages, which also requires a certain talent. But many of them are without even these qualities, which, if somewhat unimportant, are yet agreeable. They are far from handsome, are weakly and predisposed to disease and too unintelligent to keep even the flattest society conversation afloat for even a short time, and too desperately commonplace to ever awaken the love of a true woman for their own selves alone.

Each one of these princes in his own country holds the same exalted position among his contemporaries: Frederick the Great, the same as Ferdinand VII of Spain, Joseph II, as Ferdinand of Naples, called Re Bomba, Leopold I, of Belgium, the same as Louis XV of France, or George IV of England. They are all equally sacred, equally privileged and equally infallible. Their names shine with the same lustre upon the decrees of State; their commands are equally powerful and receive the same obedience. Every one bows in reverence before them, gives them the same title of Majesty, and calls them without distinction, gracious, illustrious and exalted. Human reason and intelligence revolt at such a spectacle. They exclaim: "You cowardly, incapable creature, how do you come to be at the head of a great army? You ignorant blockhead, who are unable to spoil your own mother-tongue correctly, why are you the high and mighty protector of the academies and universities? You criminal, why have you the right to award sentence of life or death upon those accused of crime? You fickle glutton, why are you the rewarder of virtue and merit? You weakling, why are the destinies of a nation in your hands? Why? Why?

As there can be no rational answer to this question, there is nothing left for the monarchy to reply but: "Why? Because God has so ordained it!" This stereotyped reply is used to repel any indiscreet inquisitiveness or inconvenient criticism. The majesty of God heralds everywhere the arrival of his own majesty. Whenever the monarchy wishes to assert its privileges it points to the divine source from whence they issued; "by the grace of God," we read on the coins, "by the grace of God" in laws, decrees and announcements. "The grace of God" is a kind of reference given by the monarchy when questioned as to its credit. In order to have this reference satisfactory, the one to whom it is given must believe in God; consequently the monarchy has no more important and pressing interest than to preserve in the people, by all possible means of strategy and force, an unswerving belief in God. Confirmed monarchists are completely right in bitterly opposing any change in Religion, or its separation from the State. They are consistent when they preach: "the people must have a religion!" when they oppose the foundation of non-sectarian schools, and still more consistent when they declare that the divorce of Church and State would be equivalent to removing the pillars that support the entire structure of State. Their demand that the State must be Christian, is a necessary result of their point of view. They are not quite sincere however, when they add: "—for without Religion there is no morality, and the State when it ceases to be Christian, will become a field of evil passions, vices and crimes." This addition should be: "—for Religion is the only foundation of an hereditary monarchy; a declaration of independence in regard to Religion, would lead at once to the sovereignty of the strongest or most capable person or persons, that is, to a dictatorship or to a republic." It is only another proof of the falseness of our age that even the most confirmed royalists have not sufficient courage to acknowledge the true reason why they want to drive the people back into the fold of the church. They ought to say boldly: "we need Religion as a shield for the monarchy." That would be honest and courageous. It is a piece of cowardice in them to assert that they support Religion in the name of law, order, morality and the wish of the people.

Our century has produced nothing more repugnant to common sense than the liberal, constitutional monarchy. It is an attempt to unite two separate political forms, two opposed views of the world, which are completely incompatible. It is fortunate that society is not governed by logic, but by indolence and passive endurance of that which is, or, to be more exact, that logic only awakes at long intervals, otherwise this form of government, so contrary to reason, could not have existed an hour. How comes it that a monarchy founded by God and perpetuated by Him, is content to share its privileges with common mortals? The monarch allows his prerogatives to be limited by the representatives of the people, ordinary men, and yet these prerogatives are the direct gift of God! Does he thus acknowledge that ordinary men have a right to interfere with God's will as manifested in him? Is such a thing possible? Is it not an insult to God, a crime? And can a God-fearing monarch decree that a crime of blasphemy, such as this amounts to, is to become one of the laws of the realm? This is the way such a constitutional monarchy appears from the stand-point of the monarchy "by the grace of God." Viewed from the standpoint of the sovereign people, the constitutional monarchy appears fully as unreasonable. Constitutionalism is founded upon the theory that the people has the right to decide its own destiny. From whence did it obtain this right? From Nature herself. It is one form of man's vital energy. The people has the right to govern itself, because it has the strength to do so, just as an individual has the right to live, because and as long as he has the strength to do so. But if this idea is correct how came man then to yield to a monarch who had inherited his authority, whose single will has as much power as the will of the entire people, who even has the right to oppose the will of the people, as the people have the right to oppose his will? If the people should rise in their sovereignty and depose the king, or do away with the institution of monarchy altogether, would the king submit? If the king should rise in his sovereignty and abolish the Parliament altogether, would the people submit? If not, what does the sovereignty of either amount to? Two sovereignties in one state are as impossible as two Gods in nature, that is, two Gods with the attributes which Christians ascribe to their single God. The prerogatives of the people must appear to the king "by the grace of God," as an infringement upon the omnipotence of God, and the monarchy "by the grace of God," must appear to the enlightened people as a denial of their manifest, national power. A constitutional monarchy can only be accepted by sacrificing one's reasoning faculties. It is, compared to an absolute monarchy, what the protestant is to the catholic church. Catholicism is consistent; protestantism is arbitrary. The former gives its superiors the right to decide upon the articles of faith, and allows no criticism of any of its arrangements. The latter allows criticism of its doctrines, by the medium of the Bible, but forbids any criticism of the Bible itself. The mind is allowed free liberty of thought as far as Revelations. The line is drawn at Revelations, where it must stop. Why? There is no reason. Because it is so, and not otherwise. It is free thought with a limited circulation; it is free criticism, with a thumbscrew, which allows it to go only to a certain point. In the same way a constitutional monarchy lays down certain premises, but forbids any one to draw the conclusions from them. It recognizes the fundamental principle of the nation's right to self-government, but at the same time it denies it by asserting the king's right to govern, to be higher and more sacred. It permits logic to follow in its train, but not until its teeth have been pulled out and its limbs amputated.

I consequently sing the praises of the absolute monarchy, surrounded by the mediæval institutions of slate and society. It satisfies logic, and pleases the senses that appreciate symmetry and harmony. We are only obliged to close our ears to the voice of reason for one moment, to accept but one arbitrary premise without criticism, that is, that the monarch owes his privileges to the special grace of God. This statement once accepted, all the remaining details of an absolute monarchy follow in a symmetrical and logical sequence.

There is then nothing to prevent our acceptance of its fundamental principle, that the king can do no wrong, even if he murders, steals or commits perjury. It follows as a logical consequence that the king can do with his country, his people and every individual subject, just exactly as he pleases, without any human being having the right to interfere. It also follows that his person is sacred, a fragment of the divine Providence in material form. The authorized agent of God is entitled to a position and power far beyond that enjoyed by mere mortals. Thus the imposing edifice of an absolute monarchy is complete in all its details; its symmetry is not impaired by inharmonious additions built on here and there like incongruous excrescences, such as disfigure a constitutional monarchy. It is a beautiful production of the human imagination, on whose noble outlines the eye dwells with satisfaction and pleasure. The subject, born to obey, lives and labors contentedly with the constant regularity of a machine; if he is in comfortable circumstances, he enjoys them in peace; if he is hungry, he consoles himself with the reflection that everything that is, must be right; he need never have any feeling of care or responsibility, for the king thinks for him, and regulates his present and his future life as is best for him. And if at any time a tormenting doubt arises in his mind, whether every thing is arranged for the best, in this best of all possible worlds, the church interposes and satisfies him with the assertion that the apparently inconsistent state of affairs is due directly to God's decree, who of course, knows what is best for him, and that he has only his own short-sightedness and limitations to blame for not seeing and appreciating the supreme excellence of all the existing conditions of life. Monarchy and Religion keep side by side like sworn comrades, and fight faithfully for their mutual interests. The king sends the people to church and the minister bids them kneel before the palace.

The king chants: "There is a God, and I keep prisons and hangmen to take care of those who do not believe in Him." The priest chants the response: "The king was set upon the throne by God Himself, and those who do not believe this will lose their chance of Heaven, to say nothing of punishment on earth." The king maintains that what the priest says is true, and the priest denies any usurpation on the part of the king. Of course it must be truth, what two such important witnesses are constantly repeating and the people accept it with respect, all the more profound because one sits on a throne in purple and ermine, with a crown upon his head, and the other wears gold-embroidered raiment and a cross set with jewels upon his breast. A good judge would not accept the testimony of two mutually interested confederates, but the people have swallowed and believed it for thousands of years.

CHAPTER II.

I am not criticising the monarchical institution in the interests of a republic. I am by no means as enthusiastic as those Liberalists who are carried away by the mere name of a republic, without taking into account the true significance of the term. A republic is the principal ideal of many of the so-called Liberalists, to me it seems very undesirable. A republic, if it is to be a progress and a truth, must be founded upon a number of social political and other institutions, entirely different from those existing at present. As long as Europe continues to live in its present forms of civilization, a republic is a contradiction and an unworthy play upon words. A simple political revolution, which would turn any one of the existing monarchies of Europe into a republic, would be merely imitating the acts of the apostles to the heathen, during the early part of the Middle Ages, who converted the pagans from their false forms of worship, by simply giving their gods, festivals and ceremonies. Christian names. The entire effect of such a revolution would be limited to pasting upon the shop-worn, unsalable goods, a lot of new labels, which would deceive the people into thinking a new stock of goods had been procured. A republic is the last link of a long chain of development. It is the form of government in which the ideal of self-government finds realization — the supreme power residing ultimately in the whole people and directly exercised by them. This form of government, if it is organically genuine, and not merely an external, pasted on or painted resemblance to a republic, is inherently incompatible with hereditary privileges and distinctions, with the enormous influence wielded by accumulations of capital and monopolies, with the power of an army of office holders and with any restrictions to the free liberty of thought, speech and action of the grand masses of the people. But to leave the organization of the State as it is, and merely to change the name of the government from a monarchy to a republic, is like the well-known trick of the publishers who manage to smuggle forbidden works into another country, by substituting for the title-page another, taken from come innocent fairy-tale or prayer-book. What was the Italian republic of 1848, or the Spanish republic of 1868, and what is the French republic of 1870, but monarchies with their thrones standing vacant for a while, monarchies parading under the mask of republicanism. They remind us of a carnival party of members of the nobility, masquerading as a set of gypsies or as a peasant wedding-party. Their clothes and appointments, their actions and speech are those of the class they are trying to represent, but through it all they remain their aristocratic selves, and deceive none of the spectators into a belief in the reality of their pretty comedy. But strange to say, the same people believe in the reality of what they see when the monarchy puts on the costume of republicanism and goes through the figures of democratic dances with a good grace; they accept it as a genuine republic and take delight in it accordingly.

Only one revolution grasped the idea that it was not sufficient to oust the king from the State, and to change its name, in order to make a republic of it. That was the great French Revolution. It annihilated with the king all the component parts of the ancient monarchy, as, when any one dies of the plague, his corpse is not only hurried away from the abode of the living, but his clothing and effects are burned. The French Revolution dug up the monarchy, with every one of its roots, and then ploughed up the soil on which it had grown. It demolished the institution of rank, and destroyed, as far as possible, the causes to which the aristocrats owed their privileges; it leveled their castles to the ground, confiscated their property, and even abolished the expressions Sir and Mr. from conversation, claiming that they were relics of feudal times, when everyone was either master or dependent. It did still more. It tried to recreate the entire intellectual world of the people. It wanted to substitute an entirely new mental horizon for the old, and prevent the ancient ideas which it had driven out by the gate of government decrees, from slipping in again by the window of an indolent and passive habit of thought. Consequently it created a new religion, invented a new calendar in which everything, the beginning of the year, the manner of reckoning time and the names of the days and the months, differed completely from the old methods of computing time, it set apart new days for holidays, arranged a new style of dress, in short, it built up an entirely new world, in which there was no room for even remembrance of the former historical evolution—and yet, what did it all amount to in the end? Clothing and speech could be altered, but the brain could not be kneaded over again. The Jews born in Egypt were not fitted to colonize Canaan. The inbred habits of centuries had more control over the French, than the laws, although they were sustained by the guillotine, When Mme. Dubarry passed in front of citizen Sanson on the bloody platform she said: "Excuse me, Mr. Executioner." After the close of the Reign of Terror, the men who had amassed millions by plunder and theft, taking advantage of the confiscation of the emigrés' property, and of the other opportunities which came in their way, these men acquired an influence, and were paid an outward respect, which only required the titles of nobility that Napoleon soon gave them, to be in all points an exact imitation of the ancient aristocracy, and hardly had the throes of the earthquake of the revolution subsided, than the structure of society rose up again like Aladdin's palace, with a few new beams and foundation stones, but in its general outline and architectural plan, a duplicate of the old, and as mediaeval as before. Nothing is accomplished by disturbing part of the ancient arrangement of things and leaving the remainder intact. The execution of the inoffensive king, Louis XVI, was an objectless crime, if the French people intended to retain their former conceptions of the universe, with faith in a Supreme Being and an all ruling Providence, reverence for the Bible and a ceremonial worship. An exclusively political revolution, changing merely the form of the government from monarchical to republican, and leaving undisturbed the existing conditions of society, philosophy and economy, of which the monarchy is the logical sequence, has neither sense nor foundation. It is a violent, exclusively external disturbance such as would follow the decrees of an insane tyrant like Ivan the Terrible, if we could imagine such a being upon any throne at the present day. The logic of facts is against it from the start, and allows it only a brief period of duration. The phenomenon so often noticed in a cripple, is repeated in the organism of the people. As a man whose leg has been amputated suffers pain in the missing limb, a nation, after the amputation of the monarchy, and the substitution of a republican wooden leg, feels the twitches and agony of the missing monarchical form of government It resembles even a lower form of animal life, some of those rudimentary organisms whose amputated organs grow out again; there is an impelling force within them, that makes such organs indispensable to their existence, and reproduces the missing part in time.

Consequently I take no part in the either false or mistaken worship of a republic as conducted by some Liberalists, who bow the knee and sing hosannahs to the empty title of the republic. This religion whose god is merely a name, does not count me among its followers. In order to have the republic the necessary outward form of the internal organization of the State, the people who wish to be crystallized into this form, must comprehend the universe from the standpoint of natural science, and have swept out all the mediæval rubbish of transcendentalism and the hereditary differences of social station and property holding. A republic with religions recognized by the State, with transcendental formulas for oaths, with laws which punish the expression of contempt for God, with hereditary privileges of rank, and with the preponderating influence of inherited possessions—such a republic is no progress for humanity, and is superior in no respect to a monarchical form of government. In reality it is inferior to it, it fails to satisfy the logical mind and esthetic taste of the observer like the imposing, self-centered and grandly symmetrical structure of an absolute monarchy.

It is evident from the foregoing paragraphs that I understand and admit the historical and logical grounds upon which the monarchical form of government is based. Indeed, a people who believe that the universe is governed by a personal God, that the Bible is the authentic revelation of His will and that the clergy are men appointed by Him to make His meaning clear, are inevitably led to believe in a monarchy; for the king, answerable to no one but himself for his actions, above the jurisdiction of the legal authorities, guiding the destinies of the nation and suffering no interference, is a faithful representation of God, of His position in the universe, and of the way in which He governs. The Bible acknowledges the monarchy as an institution created by God, and the church maintains that the supreme power of the king and the absolute obedience due him by all his subjects, are God-given rights, which God will sustain. And a people who see nothing incongruous in the fact that a man can be born to wealth and rank, and in this way bring into the world with him a clear title to honors, influence and luxury, as a part of his personality like his hair or his skin, such a people shows itself logical and consistent when it admits the fact that a child may be born possessing inherently the right to rule the whole land; wherever this wonderful right may be situated, in the stomach or in the head, it is born with it, and no one questions its existence or authority. This fact is no more unreasonable nor more difficult to conceive, than that several hundred children should come into the world with some inborn organic rights to take precedence in rank and wealth over the millions around them. As an abstract conception the monarchical form of government can be easily evolved from the theological conceptions of the universe, and be defended by them with certainty of success in argument. In the man who accepts them with sincere belief, his reverence for the monarchy is no lie. But to those who look upon the world from the heights of natural science, it appears to be a lie and a fraud. Even to many who believe still in its divine origin, its present forms and practices seem to be inconsistent, and more or less of a lie. For this is the tragic side of our contemporaneous civilization, that the ancient institutions have no longer the courage and self-confidence to maintain their positions before mankind, in the stiff and unyielding forms in which alone they are true to logic and history, repeating the Jesuits' motto: "As we are or not at all." They attempt an impossible compromise between their premises and the convictions of modern times; they make concessions to the latter, and allow themselves to be penetrated by intellectual elements, foreign to their constitution, and sure to disintegrate it. The new ideas to which they are trying to conform themselves are in direct opposition to every one of their fundamental principles, so that they resemble a book containing on the same page some ancient fable with foot-notes criticising, ridiculing and abusing it in every possible way. In this shape these institutions, denying and parodying their true character, seem objects of ridicule and scorn to cultivated minds, and even to the uncultivated, sources of annoyance and painful perplexity.

The monarchical form of government grew from several different historical roots. It is probable that the men of the earliest prehistoric ages were social beings and lived in tribes, as monkeys and numerous other gregarious animals do to this day. Each band had its leader, who guided and defended it, and without doubt was the strongest individual of the tribe. In the early dawn of civilization whose reflection rests upon the most ancient portions of the Bible, the Vedas, and the sacred books of the Chinese, the family was the foundation of society, and the patriarch the natural ruler, judge and adviser of his family and descendants. As men increased in number the families grew until they became tribes. The father of the family was succeeded by the chief who ruled the. tribe; whose authority was founded upon the fiction that all the members of the tribe were of his blood—a fiction which is even at the present day, the foundation of the clan attachments and customs of the Scotch—and partly upon the more tangible and reliable grounds, upon which herds of cattle select their leaders, that is upon his superiority, which might be due to either greater physical force or energy, or to the possession of greater wealth in flocks, pastures, implements or servants. In this phase the difference in rank between ruler and ruled is comparatively slight, and the sources of pre-eminence are apparent to everyone. He is obeyed by his son from motives of affection and respect, by the weak,, because he is strong and inspires fear, and by the poor from hope of gain, because he is rich. The right to inherit this pre-eminence was hardly recognized at this period. The actual possession of the means of power, sufficed theoretically and practically to show his right to it. No supernatural element had entered into these simple relations to complicate them; he ruled because he had the power, and the tribe obeyed because they chose or were obliged to. As civilization developed however, the leader found it necessary to strengthen his legitimate sources of superiority by adding to them the awe of the supernatural. His surpassing energy, wealth or bodily strength did not seem to him sufficient at this stage, to ensure to him the continued possession of his exalted position against the covetousness and ambition of his rivals, consequently he made the gods his mysterious and therefore doubly to be feared, confederates. He assumed the position of chief-priest of the tribe's religion, called the invisible spirits into his service and cultivated the growth of superstition until it became one of the strongest supports of his power. This was the condition of things among all the peoples of the globe, at the moment when they entered upon the field of history. The royal family claimed to be descended in a direct line from the gods. The Pharaohs, the Incas, were the sons of the sun. The Germanic royal leaders claimed to have sprung from the loins of Thor. The Maharadschas of India, traced their origin to Vishnu. The people considered their leader a sacred being, and ascribed supernatural powers to him. In the Orient no one could look upon the light of his countenance without being stricken with blindness. The kings of England and France possessed the power of curing scrofula, St. Vitus' dance and epilepsy, by merely laying their hand upon those afflicted with the disease.

The eternal vengeance of the gods rested on those who laid violent hands upon the person of the king, including their family and their entire tribe. In addition to his human hirelings, the king had all the gods and demi-gods of the heavens as guardians of his throne. The difference in station between the king and the people had already become immense. He was no longer merely the first among his fellows, the patriarch of the tribe, but a being of superior mould, supernatural and beyond the jurisdiction of the laws and customs of ordinary life. There was now no merely human connection between the king and the people; he was unapproachable; he lived on earth it is true, but like a god in disguise, having nothing in common with the masses around him. It sometimes happened that, owing to some inexplicable decree of Providence, he might be deposed from the throne, and some lowly born usurper wrest the crown from him to place it upon his own head. But even when forced to abdicate, the legitimate monarch did not sink to the level of the multitude; and even adorned with the crown, the usurper was without the consecration of divinity. The former remained always a dethroned monarch, the latter a man of the people, who sooner or later was obliged to subside again into the nameless multitude from which he sprang, as an ice-crystal dissolves into the water around it, while the deposed king always retained his distinctive individuality, like a diamond, no matter what his surroundings.

What a curious paradox this phase of the development of civilization presents! The monarchical form of government, which has been able to hold its own from the earliest prehistoric ages to the present day, has long since thrown away as superfluous, those reasons for its existence which could be accepted by the intellect, and only retained those which vanish into nothing at the first ray of rational criticism.

The monarchy of today depends for its authority not upon its actual power, but upon its divine origin. It commands no longer by the strength of its army, but by the "grace of God." An army that is ready and willing to enforce the commands of the king is, even now, a most irresistible argument. But the monarch scorns to make use of it for this purpose. The assertion that the king received the title to his high estate from the hand of God, is believed by no one nowadays, not even the most credulous old woman, to be more than a legend. But the monarch keeps repeating this fairy-tale with energy while the parson and the policeman see to it that the people pay attention and believe or at least appear to.

In ancient times and during the Middle Ages, even up to a late period, as there was then no science of history, and an analysis of origins and development was entirely unknown, the halo of divinity surrounding the king was a material reality to the eyes of the people, during all those years of dawning intelligence. The memory of the nation did not extend more than one or two generations back. The darkness of the past was impenetrable, and it settled down gradually upon the origins of everything. Who could remember the beginnings of a dynasty? It was not difficult for any one to credit the legends sung by the bards, who traced the descent of the monarch to divinities, whose rank depended directly upon the rewards paid for these improvised genealogies. But in our age these ballads and traditions have lost their reliability beneath the broad glare of critical history. We are all familiar with the origin and growth of the European reigning houses, who are today the legitimate representatives of God's will on earth, according to their own statement.

We can trace the Bourbon dynasty, the most ancient and sacred of all the royal houses of Europe, to Hugh Capet, a rebellious landed proprietor, whom some believe to be its founder, or to Robert le Fort, a butcher's assistant in Paris, if we believe the traditions of the people. The Habsburgs of Austria, in whose veins by the way, now very few drops of the blood of the original stock, are the descendants of a poverty stricken Frankish nobleman who served various masters, first in the employ of a bishop, then of a city, like a hired prize-fighter or police-man. The less said about the Romanoffs, the reigning family in Russia, the better. Illegible documents can sometimes be deciphered by the student of history, but to solve the problem as to who was the father of a son of the Empress Catherine II, is beyond the power of any scientific investigator. The Hohenzollerns of Germany have at least a clean record of which they need not be ashamed. They are descended from poor, but honest parents. The burggraves of Nuremberg were undoubtedly good and reliable officials of the holy Roman Empire, and their appointment to be Grand Master of the German Order of Knights, then Margraves of Brandenburg, from there to electoral Prince, King and Emperor, was an honorable and straightforward rising career. The date of every upward step is duly recorded in history where it is shown to be the work of men, requiring no celestial interference. In the reigning dynasty of England we see an astonishing example of the adventurous travels which the royal blood, the bearer of the legitimate sovereignty can undertake through a dozen or more different families, without losing any of its right or title to reign. The curious zigzag line which forms the legitimate stock from the Duke of Normandy to the Duke of Saxe Coburg Gotha, seems to show that the royal blood, like a good man, is always conscious of the straight and narrow way, even when it seems to deviate most from it.

Now where in the history of these families is there room for the intervention of God, by whose grace they claim their privileges? At what point in their career did it put in its appearance? At Hastings, when William the Conqueror won the victory over the Saxon King Harold? Or when Hugh Capet rose in revolt against his lawful king of the Carlovingian dynasty, as Pepin had done against his Merovingian monarch? Or when Rudolph of Hapsburg conquered his rival Ottocar of Bohemia? And what if these three founders of legitimate dynasties had been defeated? If William had been driven back to Normandy, and Hugh strung up for the rebel that he was, and Rudolph had remained dead on the Marchfeld plains, what then? What would have become then of the "grace of God"? Would not those exalted personages, the founders of the three mighty dynasties, would not they in that case have been and remained merely robbers and adventurers? Or was it success that made them divine? Does the "grace of God" consist then only in the fact that a daring and powerful man has fought his way by force to the summit of his ambition? And does his government become legitimate from the moment he assumes the power? That seems to be its only meaning. The people seem to think: when God gives office to a man, he gives him sense to go with it. It is therefore reasonable to suppose that when he gives a crown to any one, he presents him at the same time with a legitimate right to it. But according to this view, every revolutionist becomes a legitimate monarch, if his attempt is successful. Cromwell would then be as legitimate a sovereign as Charles I. whom he beheaded, Barras and Bonaparte as legitimate as Louis XVI. who met with the same fate, Louis Philippe as legitimate as Charles X., and Napoleon III. as legitimate as Louis Phillippe. The royalists would then have no right to resist nor even to disapprove when any one usurps the sovereignty of the State; they would then be obliged to admit that Rienzi, Masaniello, Mazzini, Kossuth and Hecker would have been "sovereigns by the grace of God," if their attempts had been crowned with success. More than this, they would be obliged to acknowledge that Lincoln, the rail-splitter, Johnson, the tailor, and Grévy, the lawyer, were persons equally as divine as a Hugh Capet or a Rudolph of Hapsburg, because they attained to success and possession of power fully as much as the latter. The standpoint of the royalist would then be the same as the frogs in the fable, who accepted with the same blind obedience whatever king Jupiter sent them, whether it was a log of wood or a stork. If success is the proof of the grace of God, then it is the only source of legitimate sovereignty, and the royalists would be obliged to recognize as legitimate rulers, any and every foreign conqueror, president of a republic, governor or potentate of any kind whose ambitious efforts had met with success.

Or has this spring of legitimate sovereignty run dry in late years? Can it be that in ancient times alone, the grace of God was manifested on earth by election frauds, revolt, perjury and the power of might over right? Can it be that the relations between heaven and the royal palace have been altered recently? If this is the case, it becomes a matter of the greatest importance to determine the exact moment when this change took place. The royalists certainly owe us the information of the year, month and day on which it occurred. For, in quite recent times, dynasties have been founded in Sweden and Norway, in Belgium, Servia, Roumania, Greece and Bulgaria. These dynasties claim the grace of God as the source of their power; their subjects acknowledge their right to sovereignty; the dynasties founded centuries ago accept them as their equals; we are thus left in doubt whether these new monarchs obtained their privileges really by the grace of God, or whether they are not bragging of titles and taking possession of privileges upon which they have no just claim. If the Bernadottes, Coburgs, Obrenoviches etc., are reigning by the grace of God, then it is proved that the grace of God is as prompt now, as during the Middle Ages, to confirm might by right, and the royalists must consent to recognize as a legitimate sovereign any socialistic democrat who might by some revolution rise to the summit of power m the German Empire for instance; and pay the same respect to his person and his authority, as they now pay to the German Kaiser. Or, if the reverse is the case, if the grace of God is exhausted like an over-cropped field, then those monarchs of recently created dynasties, are nothing more than swindlers who, by false pretences, deceive the public to their own advantage, a proceeding fully described and provided for in the criminal courts. Then they are impertinent in requiring allegiance from their subjects, and the ancient dynasties become accomplices in the fraud, when they recognize and accept the validity of their claim and admit them to their inner circle.

I hear a protest from the royalists against my arguments. But this protest does not take the shape which a logical mind would expect: viz. that these new dynasties ere invited by the people to assume the reins of government, who thus established their rights and prerogatives voluntarily. The royalists will not acknowledge that the will of the people can make a king, for in that case, the reverse would also be possible, that it could unmake a king and proclaim a republic and that no royalist will admit. No, the protest I hear is different; it says: the men who have founded new dynasties in recent years are off-shoots of ancient royal families who have reigned for centuries; they were born with a certain latent, hereditary, legitimate royal authority, which only waited for favorable opportunity to blossom into a visible crown and its appendages. This can not be asserted with truth the Bernadottes and Obrenoviches, but as it applies to the Belgian Saxe-Coburg, the Grecian Glücksburg, the Roumanian Hohenzollern, and the Bulgarian Hesse, I will accept it and let it pass. Consequently, it is understood and admitted that a legitimate sovereignty is a natural, hereditary quality in certain families; when f royal prince is born he has an innate authority to rule not over any special people, but to rule in general, t vague right to govern, which awaits patiently the appearance of the object, the people or peoples to be governed. A Coburg, a Hohenzollern brings his authority to reign by the grace of God, into the world with him; if the Belgians or Roumanians choose him for their king, they are merely affording him an opportunity to exercise his pre-existing legitimate sovereignty. He is given the grace of God as a medical graduate gets his diploma. With his diploma in his pocket the newly-fledged doctor has the legal right to carry on a practice, but the faculty do not undertake the task of supplying him with patients. And so when a prince is born to some legitimate reigning family, his grace-of-Godness gives him the theoretical authority to govern, but does not supply him necessarily with the country upon which he can exorcise this right.

This idea is imposing and satisfactory. It explains many things that might otherwise have perplexed us. We can understand now how a legitimate king "by the grace of God," can deprive another legitimate king "by the grace of God," of throne and country. Enlightened by this idea we see that the annexation of Hanover, Hesse and Nassau by Prussia, and of Naples, Tuscany, Modena and Parma by Sardinia, are no denials of the principles upon which the monarchies of the Hohenzollern and Savoy families are based. The conqueror does not deprive the conquered monarch of his right to govern, his diploma of legitimate sovereignty, he only takes away the country upon which the latter has been exercising his right. He remains still what he was before, a king "by the grace of God," only he is now a king out of a situation. If he can, he is at liberty to find some other country where he can settle down and rule with undiminished legitimate sovereignty by the grace of God, and if he is successful in finding such a place, his gratitude to the grace of God ought to be exceptionally fervent this time. This distinction between the abstract right to govern and the concrete possession of a country to govern, is a necessary and elementary principle of the monarchical theory. Without this principle, the kings who conquer and annex the countries of other monarchs, would be the rankest revolutionists; without it, they would prove beyond the question of a doubt that their grace-of-Godness is a fraud, even in their own estimation, and they would show their people what they really thought of a legitimate monarch's claims to hereditary sovereignty, and how to go to work to oust such an one from his position. By the light shed by this principle of the separability of theoretical sovereignty from actual government, we are able to comprehend without difficulty how the house of Brunswick could be ruling England with full and legitimate authority, while the no less legitimate Stuarts were living in exile at St. Germain and Rome, and we can also understand how King Humbert can succeed Victor Emmanuel in Italy "by the grace of

God," while Francis II. of Naples, has been amusing himself in Paris as best he can, for almost a quarter century, "by the grace of God."

But enough of these absurdities. It is not worth while to waste any time discussing seriously the divine origin of the monarchy, the only foundation upon which it relies at present, even to enter upon such a discussion would be the height of folly. The general familiarity with the historical facts connected with the beginnings of the different dynasties, some of whom originated hardly more than an hour ago, under the eye of some prosaic newspaper reporter, the spectacle occurring more and more frequently, of the deposition of legitimate sovereigns from their God-given positions, the small amount of respect shown by anointed kings to the supernatural rights of their fellow-monarchs—these facts combine to make it even more difficult for a Christian than for an atheist, to believe that the grace of God placed the crowns upon the heads of the potentates of Christendom. The grace of God can not be intermittent! It can not sustain a king one day and abandon him the next! Such ideas are so frivolous that the cherished convictions of a conscientious believer in God rise in rebellion against them. The entire fiction of the grace of God bestowed upon monarchs seems to an enlightened man like one of those old jokes which the soothsayers of ancient Rome used to repeat to each other with a solemn face, but a wink of sly understanding; to the religious man it is a blasphemous farce. Where the former would have the right to smile, the latter would grow indignant.

Let me now drop this discussion of the origin and legitimate authority of the reigning dynasties. I will continue, accepting as truths all that they claim to be true, and assuming the solemn aspect of a conjurer plying his trade. I accept therefore as demonstrated to be the actual fact, that the king is born with the authority to command me; I, the subject, am born with the duty to obey; God has arranged it thus, and, if I resist, I am blasphemously attacking His designs in regard to the universe. Proceeding from this point I find myself at the very next step in the midst of this grand lie of a monarchical form of government. Russia and Turkey are the only countries in Europe with absolute monarchies, and this, as I have mentioned before, is the only logical form of the monarchical institution. All the remaining European countries, except such as are republics, have combined with the monarchical form of government some constitutional forms which are diametrically opposed to it and in perpetual contradiction with it. A limited monarchy condemns every one who takes part in the farce, to an everlasting hypocrisy, and causes them to act a perpetual lie.

In those countries where the Parliament is a truth, and the monarch is only a figure-head, patiently endured, as in England, Belgium and Italy, the laws and decrees proclaim lies, when they are issued as manifestations of the royal will, for they are the results of the. Parliament's will and take effect whether the king accepts them or not. The Cabinet ministers lie when they make use of the customary phrases; "On behalf of His Majesty we recommend," "By His Majesty's command," "We have the honor to recommend to His Majesty so and so," for they know, and every one knows, that the king has not recommended or commanded any thing of the kind, and that the "so and so" recommended to him, is usually an established fact before they lay it before him, entirely independent of his wish or decision. Every one knows too, that the monarch is obliged in reality to obey without question the designs and decisions of the Parliament and Cabinet. The king lies in every word of his address to Parliament when it assembles, if he speaks in the first person, for the address is not at all the expression of his own sentiments, but a document whose composition is due entirely to others, who place it, when finished, in his hands, and he reads it as a phonograph repeats the sentences that have been spoken into the receiver. The king lies when he accepts the fiction that the prime minister is the man of his choice, in whom he has the utmost confidence, for he is not at liberty to follow the dictates of his own wishes, but must select and conform himself to the person pointed out to him as the man for the place by the majority of the people's representatives, although he may detest him in his heart, and vastly prefer some one else. The king lies again when he signs and allows to go forth as the expressions of his will, the documents, appointments, etc., which are brought to him by the Cabinet ministers merely for his signature, and which are sometimes exactly contrary to his genuine wishes and convictions.

This is all reversed in the countries where the monarch retains his ancient privileges conferred upon him by the grace of God, limited only in name by a Parliament which is merely an ornament attached to the ancient absolute monarchy. Germany and Austria have governments of this kind, and in these countries it is the Parliament, not the king, which lies to the people. The monarch demands recognition as the visible agent and representative of the divine will, and lays claim to infallibility of course, as an authorized agent of the infallible Supreme Being; at the same time he concedes in theory some authority to the people to influence his decisions, thus acknowledging their right to criticise, change or set aside any of the decrees of a being installed and inspired by God. By doing this he exposes God to the criticism of mere mortals, and thus commits a crime which he would punish severely in one of his subjects. But this is the case after all, only in theory. In practice the will of the king is as autocratic and powerful as ever and all these constitutional additions to the monarchy are mere shams. The Government lies to the people when it calls upon them to select their representatives; it lies to the Parliament when it lays decrees and measures before it for discussion and approval, for the choice of the people does not confer upon their representatives the power to enforce the will of the people, and the Parliament has no authority or influence to change any of the decisions of the Government.

In those countries where the will of the people is really constitutionally enforced, the position of the monarch is ignominious, but the fiction of his supreme authority is so skillfully concealed, and the external honors and personal advantages and pleasures directly connected with the maintenance of his royal position, are #o numerous and important, that we can understand how men of self-esteem and little sensitiveness, can condescend to assume the role of a puppet whose tongue and limbs are set in motion by the strings pulled by the members of the Cabinet. But in those other countries where the Parliament is a political imposition, the part of the puppet is played by the representatives of the people, and it is much more difficult to understand how men worthy of the name, can find in the petty gratification of their vanity, any compensation for the humiliations which, as members of the legislature or Parliament they are obliged to endure. We can understand how a king in his magnificent palace, in his becoming uniform, in receipt of his splendid allowance, only hearing the most exalted expressions of respect, "gracious Majesty," "illustrious Highness" and so on, falling like snow-flakes about his ears, surrounded on all sides by luxury and the most exaggerated outward forms of homage, we can understand how he can forget that the will of the people is the actual sovereign, and that his glittering pageant of royalty would vanish entirely if he were to attempt to play the role in earnest. But how can the members of Parliament in a sham limited monarchy consent to make themselves ridiculous by speeches without effect, gestures without purposes and votes without results? This is what we cannot understand. Neither the undisguised contempt of the prime minister nor the calumnies of the press subsidized by the Government, deter them from their task. Can it be that they are sustained by a secret hope that some day the Parliament may become in reality what it now only appears to be? But such a hope or desire is impossible to any one who accepts and believes the fiction of the divine origin of the monarchy.

To any one who despises and condemns the conventional lies and liars of our modern civilization, there can be no more enjoyable spectacle than that afforded by the so-called Liberalist party in the German Reichstag between the horns of that dilemma into which that implacable logician, Prince Bismarck, has driven them, his agents in Parliament and the journalists in his pay keeping the horns of the dilemma constantly before them: either they are rank republicans and are guilty of hypocrisy and perjury when they surpass each other in protestations of loyalty, or else they are sincere in their loyalty to the Emperor, and if so, they must prove it by obedience to his will. This "either—or else" are like hammer and anvil between which the Liberalists are pounded to a jelly that not even a dog would touch. It is intensely amusing to see how these weak-spirited parties in the Reichstag writhe beneath the iron grasp of that pitiless logic. How they long to escape, and yet they cannot! They are devoted to the reigning dynasty, the Emperor has no more attached subjects than they are, a republic would be an abomination of desolation in their opinion, but at the same time, there is the constitution, which His Majesty has condescended to confirm by oath, and with his illustrious permission they would like most submissively, to venture to make use of the privileges so graciously granted, etc. But all this is of no use. The hand at their throats presses them closer and closer against the wall, until they are almost suffocated, while a voice thunders: "Do you acknowledge that the Emperor is commissioned by the Almighty to rule over you? Yes? Then how do you dare to oppose him in the very slightest degree, how do you dare to limit the imperial privileges and authority given by God? Do you doubt the fact that God endowed him with those privileges? Then you are Republicans! There is no middle course. You must be Imperialists or Republicans."

In fact there is no middle course. An absolute monarchy on one hand, a republic on the other. Any compromise is a fraud and a lie, and a government which calls attention to the dilemma deserves the gratitude of all enlightened minds. But it ventures much in doing so. It lays itself open to the attack of some politician who might say: "If logic is trumps, then the Government is the chief liar and hypocrite. If the will of the Emperor is the will of God, how dare you set up a Parliament that even in appearance seems to limit the imperial will by the will of the people! Either you are convinced that the people are entitled to a voice in the management of the country, which means that you believe in a republic, or else you have not the slightest intention of admitting the right of the people to assist in the government, you intend to do as you please in everything, and the Reichstag to be a nonentity in every way as regards the management of affairs; in this case the entire parliamentary elections, discussions, votes, etc., are a conscious lie. Either Republicans or liars. There is no middle course."

This is the gigantic lie of a limited monarchy, the fact that an absolute monarchy can only be changed into a limited, constitutional monarchy, by denying the divine origin of the royal authority, thus removing its entire foundation and leaving it suspended in the air like Mahomet's coffin. During the Middle Ages the authority of the king was often intrenched upon; the nobles rose in insurrection again and again, striving to deprive him of some of his power and prerogatives. But this limitation of the royal authority, these insurrections against the crown were not founded upon any principle that contradicted the divine origin of the royal privileges; they had nothing to do with the sovereignty of the people. The barons acknowledged voluntarily that the king owed his authority to the grace of God, even when they were besieging him in his castle, but they maintained at the same time, that the grace of God had smiled upon them also. This was no denial but merely an ingenious extension of the doctrine of the supernatural authority of those in power. As the monarch asserted that he was king by the grace of God, they declared that they were barons by the grace of God. It was like the monomaniac who imagined that he was God. When another lunatic was brought to the asylum, whose mania took the same form, he began to ridicule the absurdity of the latter's pretensions. "As if that creature could be God!" he cried. "And why not?" enquired the attendant who thought his first patient was almost cured. "Because there can not be two Gods, of course, and as I am God, he can not be." Like this monomaniac the nobles intrenched upon the divine prerogatives of the crown, not in the name of reason, but owing to the vagaries of their own imagination. This made the mediæval belief in the divine authority of the king and also in the privileges of the favored classes, not only possible but sincere, while a belief in the sovereignty of the people and also in the sacred origin of the monarchy directly exclude each other.

In addition to its political side, the lie of a monarchy has also its purely human side, against which reason and truth revolt as much as against the former. The fiction of the augustness and supernatural attributes of the monarch humiliates and degrades in their own eyes all those who come into personal contact with him, for they laugh at it in their hearts. The spectacle of the king's existence has always been a comedy to those who had any share in it. But each one played his part with zeal and apparent conviction of its reality, he never stepped out of his role, and while on the stage, he took every possible pains to present the spectators, from whom he was separated by the fiery barrier of the footlights, with a poetic delusion, which he never allowed to fade, and only the few confidants who were admitted through the small stage-entrance, were allowed to see that the magnificent palaces of the scenery were nothing but old canvas, that the jewels and the gold embroideries on the royal vestments were only paste and tinsel, and that the hero, between two grandly heroic declamations, whispers to some one behind the scenes his longing for a glass of beer. But the modern actors in this comedy are continually forgetting their roles, and ridiculing them, ridiculing themselves and the honorable public.

They are like the honest amateurs in "Midsummer Night's Dream" discussing their programme: "Nay, you must name his name, and half his face must be seen though the lion's neck; and he himself must speak through, saying thus, or to the same defect,—Ladies, or fair ladies, I would wish you, or, I would request you, or I would entreat you, not to fear, not to tremble: my life for yours. If you think I come hither as a lion, it were pity of my life: No, I am no such thing; I am a man as other men are: and there indeed, let him name his name; and tell them plainly he is Snug the joiner."

The royal palace, a sacred place in the good old days of the monarchy, into which the common mortal only entered with awe and trembling, now stands open to the reporter. All its scandals, all its criminalities and absurdities are discussed on the street. The most insignificant subject is acquainted with the secret vices of the king, the diseases of the prince, the mistresses of this monarch, the flirtations of that princess, he knows that his king or his emperor gambles at the Exchange, that he is an idiot, he knows all about the king's ignorance, his badly spelled letters are ridiculed and his foolish sayings quoted—and yet the subject prostrates himself in the dust before him, never mentions him publicly except in terms of the most extravagant loyalty, and takes especial credit to himself if he can lick the dust from the august feet more zealously than his neighbor. What a spectacle for an unprejudiced and enlightened looker-on! What a source of perpetual disgust at the nature of civilized man with its inherited instincts of a gregarious animal! The famous artist who has just completed some immortal master-piece, longs for no higher crown of honor than a visit from the king; from the excitement and exaltation of grand conceptions and realization, his mind sinks to the gratification of his childish vanity by the hoped for visit from his sovereign. He is perhaps a Beethoven, a Rembrandt, a Michael Angelo; he will be known and admired when nothing remains of the king but a line in the interminable list of kings' names, which forms the superfluous appendix to the history of the world; he has a complete consciousness of his own ability; he knows that the king will not appreciate his music, his painting, nor his statue, that the king's eye is dull, his ear deaf, and his heart dead to all beauty and harmony, that his criticism is absurd, that as far as regards esthetic cultivation he is about on a par with any street-sweeper—and yet the artist's heart throbs with joy when he sees the king's absent, leaden glance turned upon his work, or watches him as he listens sleepily to his music. The scientist, who has just conquered some new truth for mankind by his intellectual efforts and enlarged the mental horizon of his race, is so ambitious as to set his heart upon decking himself in some fool's jacket, of official style, and appearing thus before the king, to say a few words to him in regard to his world-stirring invention or discovery, it may be something connected with the unity of forces, spectral analysis or the telephone; he knows that the king is incapable of understanding him, that his Majesty can not take the slightest interest in a subject so entirely beyond his comprehension and that he looks down upon science and everything connected with it, with the arrogance of a barbarian, that he prefers a well-grown corporal in his body-guard to all the scientists in creation; he knows also that he has only a few minutes in which he can hurry through what he has to say, embarrassed and stammering, while the king is thinking of other things and allows his face to reveal clearly what a bore he finds such duties, forced upon him by his exalted position, and yet the scientist crawls to the palace, weighed to the ground with these humiliating conditions, and takes his position contentedly behind some diplomate who wishes to announce his arrival in the capital, and in front of some petty officer who comes to the palace to express his gratitude for a decoration. How many poets and authors beg for permission to dedicate their works to the king, knowing perfectly well beforehand, that the book will be placed unread in the back of some library shelf, where genealogical almanacs, plates, diagrams and works on titles and heraldry fill up the front row.

The hereditary aristocracy is naturally more humble, more reverent to the king—if such a thing be possible—than the aristocracy of intellect. This hereditary aristocracy which surrounds the king constantly, which sees the night-cap under the crown, the flannel under the purple mantle, which is the author of all the stories and caricatures about the royal family, which ridicules his weaknesses, and acquaints the people with his vices, this aristocracy has notwithstanding all this, no higher ambition than to creep or flatter its way into the favor of the king, whether he is a Louis XV. or a Philip IV. It condescends to any dirty trick that will turn the royal glance upon it; it sells to him its wives and daughters; it accepts that disgraceful motto: "the blood of the king does not tarnish." An aristocrat who is too proud to even look at or address his own servant directly, works hard for the privilege of being the king's servant, and on certain occasions to wash his hands, bring his food, fill his glass, run his errands, and perform all the menial services of a waiter, lackey and messenger-boy, even if they are only symbolical. It is a well-known anecdote, but not therefore necessarily true, that Peter the Great when on a visit to Denmark, wishing to convince the king of the implicit obedience paid him by his subjects, commanded a cossack in his suite to leap from the top of a high tower. The cossack crossed himself and sprang into the air without a moment's hesitation. There is not any doubt that the majority of courtiers, even at the present day, would respond in the same way to a similar test. Why? From heroism? These same heroes would never run the risk of catching cold by attempting to save a drowning man. From the hope of reward hereafter? This hope may have made the sacrifice of his life easier to Peter the Great's cossack, but the aristocrats of these days are in many cases the disciples of Voltaire, and think far less of the joys of paradise than of those lying within their grasp which this earthly vale of tears has to offer them. I can not explain this wonderful phenomenon of a devotion and veneration, capable even of self-destruction, for an individual who perhaps is not distinguished by any intellectual, physical or natural attractions, and who is perhaps of an exceedingly repugnant and despicable temperament. Münchausen relates a hunting adventure: he went hunting one day with a female hound, big with young, when he started up a hare, also big with young; his hound pursued her out of sight, and when he came up with them he saw to hip astonishment, seven little hares running along with the mother-hare, and seven little hounds chafing them with the mother-hound; both of the animals had been delivered of their young on the way, And each one of the latter had at once taken their places in the chase. Something similar seems to take place between a monarch and his subjects. The subject is from the moment of his birth, devoted to the king for life and death, as the little hounds from the moment of their birth began to chase the hares. I mean this seriously, although I express it rather lightly. Only the phenomenon of atavism can account for this loyalty to a monarch surpassing the sentiment of self-respect, dignity as a man and even the instinct of self-preservation. It is evidently a return t prehistoric ideas, an indistinct trace of habits inherited without interruption for thousands of generations, when men experience or pretend to experience, an affection for an individual that they do not know personally, perhaps have never seen, who certainly will never reciprocate their sentiments, and when they let this affection surpass that which they feel for their own families or even for their own selves.

It is certainly one of the most deeply rooted characteristics of man's nature to prostrate himself in the dust before any one whom the multitude has acknowledged and set up as pre-eminent. I say: whom the multitude has set up as pre-eminent, not: who is by nature pre-eminent. Man as an animal, was born to live in herds, and has all the instincts of a gregarious animal. The principal one of these instincts is the habit of subordination to a leader. But he only is leader who is accepted and endured as such by the entire herd. Only a small group of enlightened minds are able to judge a personality by its inherent qualities; the majority of mankind judges it by the effects of those qualities on others. A cultivated intellect examines and tests the individual, uninfluenced by his relations with other men; the man of the masses asks only for the position and situation accorded him by the world, and experiences an irresistible compulsion to accept as his own the views of the majority. This explains why every famous man, even if he is only well-known, or sometimes merely notorious, meets with an attention and devotion which are refused to the man of real worth who, indifferent to the world and its popularity, has lived in contemplative solitude. It is not necessary to be a king, to be surrounded by a court. Notoriety alone is sufficient. Actors, conjurors and circus clowns have their courtiers. There are people who force their way to notorious criminals and boast of their intercourse with them. Acts of self-abasement are being daily performed before Victor Hugo, which surpass any thing of the kind in the court of the Czar of all the Russias or of a Grand Mogul. His admirers are filled with ecstasy at every word he speaks, at the utterances of an intellect enfeebled by age, almost approaching imbecility. They crowd to kiss his hand. They reverence and admire his old mistress and esteem it an honor to follow her funeral to the grave. They extend the worship of the ancient poet to his grandchildren, of whom we know nothing except that they are exceptionally spoiled and affected children, victims even in these early years of a mania of greatness. What is it which causes men to commit such follies? What was it that surrounded Beau Brummel and Cartouche with a court like that of any great artist or scientist? The answer lies close at hand and has been often given: Vanity; but it is a superficial answer. Wherein does the gratification to one's vanity lie, in belonging to the crowd surrounding some famous personage? What pleasure can there be in hustling around in the throng paying court to some well-known man? It lies in the fact that by so doing man is gratifying his instinct as a herding animal, the instinct of subordination to a leader. Snobbishness has an anthropological foundation, and this fact Thackeray forgot when he entered the lists to do battle with it, inspired by such bitter hatred. But loyalty, in the sense in which royalists understand the term, is the highest and most perfect manifestation of snobbishness.

It will be seen that I am trying to find ameliorating circumstances for Byzantinism. I would very much like to convince myself of the genuineness of the sentiments towards kings and princes, which so many people parade. 1 am ready to admit that the Russian peasant is not playing the hypocrite when he kisses the hem of the Czar's garment, and that the German soldier is not lying when he declares that to die for his Emperor would be the highest happiness that could befall him. But anthropology and atavism and heredity, all the fine words which I have called upon to aid me in defending the loyalty of the ignorant and uncultivated, all these leave me in the lurch when I come to the Byzantinism of cultured and enlightened minds. Their Byzantinism is and remains, a conscious lie. It has no root in the character. It is a farce in which each one is working for pay; some for offices and wealth; others for titles and decorations, a third for some political reason, because the monarchy seems to him necessary, for the moment, to the welfare of the people, or for the interests of his caste,—all are working for an immediate or indirect personal advantage. And this is what makes the lie of the monarchy so much more repulsive than the lie of Religion. The enlightened man who bends the knee in church and murmurs prayers, does it from mental indolence or indifference, or from a cowardly acquiescence in custom; even if he is a hypocrite, and is trying to win the favor of the priests and their powerful influence by his counterfeit piety, he only humiliates himself before a symbol and does not kiss the hand from which he expects the reward. But the sycophantic courtier, the citizen illuminating and decorating his house with garlands of flowers, the poet composing odes in honor of royal marriages and the births of princes, they are all only working for the pay which they will presently receive, and are in no respect superior to the demi-mondaine, intent only upon coining money with her smiles.

Many persons who consider a king as a human being like all the rest, only more insignificant and less talented, who laugh at the preordained divine mission of the reigning dynasties, and admit that they are acting a lie when they testify to their submission, reverence and love of their monarchs and the royal families, are constantly trying to excuse their falsehood and lack of fidelity to their convictions, by maintaining that the accepted fraud of royalty is a harmless deception.

The monarchy, at least in honestly constitutional countries, is merely a bit of theatre scenery. The king has really less authority than the President of the United States of North America. England, Belgium and Italy are in reality republics with kings for the figureheads, and the inherited external forms of submission by which the crown is surrounded are mostly matters of habit, and prevent in no way the free action of the will of the people, and of the will of the people alone. This is a grave mistake which will prove fatal in many cases to the destinies of nations.

The power of the king is still immense; their influence even in such countries as Belgium and Roumania, England and Norway, is all-powerful, even if it does not affect directly the form of government, but acts with and through it. We have the moist reliable testimony of this fact. The right honorable Mr. Gladstone, who is certainly competent authority, expressed his opinion most significantly on the influence of kings in an early number of the Nineteenth Century. Certain publications of recent times throw sufficient light upon this subject, especially Martin's Life of the. Prince Consort, with the correspondence between Prince Albert and Prince Wilhelm of Prussia, afterwards King and Emperor, and the relations between Napoleon III. and the English Court, Baron Stockmar's Notes and Reminiscences, and many reliable portions of Schneider's and Meding's Memoirs. We learn from them how the web-work of intimate relations between the different sovereigns is spun over the heads of peoples, Parliaments and ministers; how the kings consult with and advise each other direct; how they pass judgment on every political occurrence from the point of view of the interests of their dynasties; how they turn a solid and united front to the movements tending to arouse the people to a recognition of their strength and rights, and how they allow themselves to be influenced by petty whims, by personal friendships and dislikes, in the most important decisions, involving the destinies of millions. Public orators, abound in phrases, the representatives of the people declaim in Parliament; the Cabinet ministers make public the result of their discussions with solemn gravity; they are all convinced that they alone have the power to guide the destiny of the nation; but in the mean while the king is smiling contemptuously and writing confidential notes to his royal friends across the border, concluding with them informally, all sorts of alliances and exclusions, wars and treaties of peace, conquests and renunciations, limitations and concessions to freedom, and when the plan is all decided upon, it is carried out, the Parliaments can say what they please.

They experience no difficulty in finding plenty of tools to do their work in the correct, constitutional way; a hundred where they need but one, are at their disposal, and in case of necessity it does not require very much of an effort to change the currents of public opinion. Thus it happens that the sovereigns who are supposed to fill only an ornamental position in the state, limited by the constitution to a mere existence without any political significance, are the ones who cast the deciding votes in matters of state, at the present time as well as during the Middle Ages, at the present time even more than ever before, for never was the combination between the monarchs of Europe as firm as today, never before did they form such a solidarity, and never before were their natural supporters, the aristocracy and the clergy, so devoted to their authority as today. The cowardliness of men who accept the conventional lie of a monarchical form of government, against their convictions, reason and comprehension of the universe, is revenged upon them, or rather upon human progress. The sly pseudo Liberalists who think they are deceiving the king by awarding him external honors and privileges, when according to their opinion, the actual power does hot go with them, are in reality, the dupes of the king who skillfully adapts himself to their views, but manages to get control of the real authority, so that the sham is after all not the monarchy, but the legislative representation of the people.

CHAPTER III.

The relation between the monarchy and the aristocracy is similar to that between Religion and the monarchy. As Religion can exist without a monarchy, but the monarchy not without Religion, an aristocracy without a monarchy is possible, but a monarchy without an aristocracy could not last at all. There are some kingdoms without an hereditary nobility — such as Greece, Roumania, and Servia — others, like Norway and Brazil, have abolished it. But these are artificial formations, without a future. Either these monarchical states will depose the royal family to the ranks of the nobility and change the form of the government to a republic, or else the next or at least the second generation, will produce an hereditary aristocracy which may not have any legal position or titles, but will have privileges all the more substantial on this account. An hereditary monarchy has a natural impulse to surround itself with hereditary attachments. We know that many kinds of insects provide for their young by depositing their eggs near or in the middle of the substance which is to be the food of the young caterpillars, so that they find the table all spread for them when they emerge from the egg. In the same way every king wants to surround his heir even in the cradle, with a loyalty and submission which he could not obtain without help, and these sentiments he expects to find in the gratitude of a certain number of families whom he or his predecessors, have heaped with honors and wealth. This precautionary confidence of the monarchs is often deceived; in the moment of danger to their nearest personal interests, the living generations of aristocrats are apt to forget the debt of gratitude bequeathed to them by their ancestors along with their possessions and privileges, and abandon the prince to his adverse fate, who ought to find his safety in the dearly bought and paid for fidelity of the aristocracy. It would be a useless task to recall all the examples of such ingratitude recorded in history; it will be sufficient to mention the attitude of the English nobility towards William of Orange and George I., the relations between the legitimate aristocracy of France and the two Napoleons and Louis Philippe, and between the Napoleonic nobility and the reinstated Bourbon dynasty. But kings cling nevertheless to this untrustworthy pledge of the future, and lull themselves into a deceptive dream of security when they see themselves surrounded by a numerous set of nobles, as the soldier on the field of battle seeks shelter behind some cover which he knows at the same time, would oppose but little more resistance to the enemy's bullet than the air alone.

A strange spectacle, arousing astonishment and indignation, incredulity and ridicule, this mediæval comedy in the very midst of our modern civilization! One class of human beings assumes the airs of ancient Egyptian or Indian caste, in the midst of our Caucasian humanity. It lays claim to titles which once signified certain offices, but today have no sense whatever. It paints, engraves and carves upon its carriages, residences and seals, unreasonable and absurd pictures, representing battle-shields, such as have not been used for several centuries, whose obstinate perpetuation affects us like the behavior of a man who should insist upon carrying a flint and steel around with him to strike a light, or one who should tattoo his face after the manner of the ancient Celts. Why should we not laugh when somebody calls himself a duke, which signifies a leader, a commander of the army, when he is some little dude, who has never led anything but a German, or when another boasts of his noble birth, and considers himself an important personage in the nation, when at the same time he is a humpback, with scrofulous tendencies perhaps, and intellectually below the level of any one of his own servants? Our civilization contains hardly any more absurd relic of ancient days than an aristocracy whose only claim to distinction is in empty titles and coats of arms.

I am far from asserting that equality of positions would be a more reasonable formation of society. Equality is a chimera of book-worms and visionaries who have never studied nature and humanity with their own eyes. The French Revolution thought it had condensed the thoughts of encyclopedists when it announced its motto to be: "Liberté, Egalité,

Fraternité". Liberty? Correct. If this word has any meaning at all, it can only be that the obstacles have been removed which had hindered or entirely prevented the free play of the natural powers of the individual and of society, obstacles usually in the form of laws which owed their existence to the superstition and folly of short-sighted men. Fraternity? Oh, this is a sublime word, the ideal goal of human progress, a presage of the condition of our race at the time when it attains to the summit of its fullest development, a time still very remote. But equality? That is a mere creature of the imagination for which there is no room in any sensible discussion. In justice to the period preceding the French Revolution it must be said that it never discussed and proclaimed social equality, but merely personal equality before the laws. But the authors and leaders of the great Revolution did not publish this distinction; they sought for a striking and an appealing word, and in their famous motto, sacrificed accuracy to brevity. Thus "Egalité", without any modifying term, appeared in the triad of the revolutionary programme, and the multitudes, who are apt to repeat party cries without reflection, adopted the term as meaning equality in the sense in which it is accepted by the democrats of the Parisian beer tunnels. Equality even before the laws, is possible only in theory, in reality it is impracticable. It is true that if a machine administered the laws they would be carried out with mechanical exactness, without prejudice or partiality, but when a living human being undertakes the task, inequality is unavoidable; the most conscientious judge, armed at all points against external influence, is yet unconsciously to himself, biased by the personal appearance, the voice, the intelligence, the cultivation and the social position of the parties before him, and the point of the law wavers and turns from favor to severity in his hands, as the magnetic needle is turned by the electric current. This source of error in the enforcement of the laws can be reduced to its minimum, but never entirely done away with.

Equality before the laws is difficult, but social equality is absolutely inconceivable. It stands in opposition to all the laws of life and development that govern the organic world. We, who stand upon the firm foundation of the scientific view of the world, we recognize in this very inequality between living beings the impulse towards all development and perfection. The struggle for existence, that inexhaustible source of the beautiful variety and wealth of form and appearance in nature, is nothing else than a perpetual demonstration of inequality. A better equipped being makes his superiority felt by his fellows, he deprives them of part of their share of the repast spread before them by nature, and prevents the possibility of the full display of their individuality, in order to attain more space for the manifestation of his own. The oppressed inferiors revolt, the oppressor overpowers them. In this struggle the powers of the weak grow stronger and the faculties of the strong attain to their highest possibilities.

The appearance of any especially endowed individual in the species, is, in this way, a benefit to the entire race, advancing it one or more steps. The most imperfect individuals are destroyed in this struggle for the first place, and vanish. The average type becomes continually nobler and better. The generation of today, taken as a whole, stands where the exceptionally endowed beings stood in the last generation, and the generation of tomorrow will aspire to the rank of the leaders of today. It is? an endless progression, always forward. The masses are trying to raise themselves to the level of the distinguished men and the latter are pushing forward to maintain the inequality now existing between them and the masses, and even to increase it. Continual exertion of the various faculties, untiring effort on both sides, and the result, a constant progress towards the realization of the ideal. The superior men call the struggle made by those beneath them to attain to their level, envy; the inferior call the efforts made by the superior to maintain their supremacy, pride. But these are only manifestations of that natural property of matter, inertia, which causes it to consider every effort, even if it be necessary and salutary, as unpleasant for the moment, and the apparent discontent with the compulsion to effort, can never be accepted as a proof against its usefulness.

Inequality is therefore a law of nature, and upon this fact an aristocracy founds its rightfulness. That the aristocratic position should be inherited, is also a claim which our reason can not dispute. If there is one observation whose truth can not be doubted, it is that the qualities of the individual are inherited by the offspring. If the father was fine-looking, strong, courageous, healthy, the probabilities are that the son can congratulate himself upon the possession of the same qualities, and if the former had through these qualities won his way to a distinguished station in society, there is no reason why the inheritors of his blood should not maintain it. It might be better however, for them and society, if they were obliged to fight their way up to the coveted positions and win them anew for the family; this would prevent any deterioration and retrogression in them; the chances are that even in a free-for-all race, the sons of superior men would form the majority of the victors.

An hereditary aristocracy is not only natural, it has moreover its advantages for the common welfare. In a democracy founded upon the mistaken equality of the French Revolution as its ideal, only men of a ripe age could attain to the positions in which they could first begin to exercise an influence upon the development of the people. Only in cases of the rarest occurrence would young men succeed in finding opportunities to be victorious over their rivals, and rise to the positions of legislator, party-leader, secretary and president. Such examples as the generals of the first French republic, the Bonapartes, Washingtons, Gambettas, prove nothing against my assertion. They rose to the summit of the nation in consequence of sudden revolutions. Their unexpected elevation was not due to general capability, but in the first place, to the chance that they happened to be close at hand ready to fill the positions, when the positions were ready to be filled, and in the second place, to the forbearance of their numerous and authorized rivals who would not stoop to use force to get the power into their hands at such moments of confusion. Revolutions can promote young men to the first places it is true. But revolutions are exceptional cases, occurrences which will not continue repeating themselves for ever. They are not the normal evolution of a democracy. When it has finally settled down into established forms, and is living according to rule under its natural conditions, then it has no room for the meteoric career of a Washington, Bonaparte or Gambetta. But it is of the greatest importance for the progress of humanity, to have young men take now and then a prominent part in the discussions for and against matters concerning the State. Old men are not accessible to new ideas, and have not the energy and capability necessary to grasp new principles. The physiological law according to which nerve sensations have the tendency to travel along the most accustomed paths, and only enter upon new ones with difficulty, is most important in its application here. It reveals to us the fact that an old man has become an automaton whose entire organic functions are ruled by habit, and whose thought and sensations are hardly more than reflex activity, in which the intervention of the consciousness is hardly necessary. How can we expect then novel forms of effort from these stiff, old organisms? How can we compel their trains of thought to leave the smooth, easy, accustomed track and go bumping along over newly broken ground? Where a youthful intellect has only to grasp the new idea, the old intellect has first to do the same, that is, comprehend the new thought, and secondly to conquer the tendency in his mind to formulate the idea in question in his old, accustomed way. He is thus required to make a twofold effort, and his powers far from being stronger than those of the young man are considerably weaker. This is the physiological explanation of the so called ossification of old people. They find it too much trouble to escape from the habits into which they have fallen; their central nervous system also, is often incapable of generating impulses of sufficient energy to conquer the resistance of the nerve sensations to enter upon untried paths. Consequently a community governed by elderly men degenerates into mere routine, and has the inherent tendency to become a museum of ancient traditions. But new ideas meet with a cordial welcome where young men are at the helm, making and administering the laws. All innovations are quickly accepted and the established customs have to prove at all times their title to superior excellence, or be swept away, for there is no body-guard of habit to protect them. The inexperience and rapidity of decision of young leaders are the disadvantages accompanying their youthful energy, but they can never do very much harm, on account of the fact that the machinery of the State is so complicated that it is a long way from the mental initiative to its actual realization, and the number of wheels which have to be set in motion, use up the energy of the first impulse, so that the final result is only a very small portion of the original force. Only by means of an established, hereditary aristocracy is it possible in normal times, for a number of talented men to attain to positions of trust and responsibility at the very blossoming-time of their life. For the aristocrat has over the obscure mass of the nameless multitude, the advantage of notoriety, which he finds in his cradle when he is born, while the unknown son of the people is usually obliged to devote the best years of his life to the task of winning it by a grievous waste of vital energies and deterioration of character. In the natural course of events the position won by the plebeian as the result of his life struggle, is the same as that where the patrician begins his career, and consequently the latter enters upon the fulfillment of its duties with all his youth and energy unimpaired, while the former has lost all his in the effort to get there.

Still another advantage to the commonwealth is derived from the existence of an hereditary aristocracy. The possession of an illustrious and honored name is usually a guarantee that the person to whom it belongs will have a surer and more correct comprehension of duty and a higher ideal of humanity, than an individual of a more obscure origin. Of course this universal rule can not be applied to all cases. A prince or duke of the most ancient pedigree may be a scamp, and the son of a day-laborer, or even some foundling picked up in a city gutter, may be the most brilliant example of dignity of character and self-abnegating heroism ever seen. But the former case is the exception and of the latter I know nothing as long as it is not proved. Suppose there is a position vacant that will require in its incumbent courage, reliability and fidelity to duty. I, with my fellow-citizens, am called upon to elect him. Several candidates present themselves, but I know none personally; one is a descendant of an aristocratic family, the other bears a name which I hear now for the first time. If I in such a case, follow the dictates of a superficial democracy, I shall cast my vote for the plebeian, about whom 1 know nothing, simply to manifest my adherence to the principle of equality; but if on the contrary, the interests of the community are really dear to me, if I am conscientiously anxious to increase at least the probability that the public welfare is entrusted to clean and powerful hands, then I shall vote for the aristocrat. I am not acquainted with him, it is true, but between the two unknown candidates) he is the one who has the strongest reasons for being faithful to his post; the chances are in his favor. Why? Not on account of the usual stereotyped reply: because he has received a better education, and the principles of chivalry were instilled into him at an early age. This is a reply that leaves us too often in the lurch. Aristocratic birth is no guarantee of a good moral training; every one knows examples of princes who grew up amid most deplorable surroundings and became in time not only liars, cowards and cheats, but common thieves or fine thieves, if it makes stealing any finer to steal jewels instead of cotton handkerchiefs. No, the guarantee of a higher moral level in the aristocrat does not lie in his training or education, but in his pride of family, we might call it ancestral self-conceit.

He identifies himself and his fortunes with his family to an extraordinary degree, and merges his own individuality into the higher individuality of his house, more than is possible with the plebeian. The latter is himself, otherwise nothing, hence an entity; the former is the representative of an entire family. He knows that his actions will reflect a lustre upon all the bearers of his name, as their actions and honors are reflected upon him. A member of the aristocracy is a collective individual, in whom the ancestors, contemporary members and future descendants of the family are united, and the securities which he offers are theoretically, and until proof of the contrary is given, in the same proportion to the securities offered by the nameless candidate as the strength of an union of men is to the strength of one. Even if he is personally a coward and a man of low tastes, he will feel himself spurred on to heroic efforts on certain occasions, simply because he bears an historic name, and says to himself: "Even if I fail and go down, my heroism will not have been in vain — the honor of it will be credited to my family, to the men of my blood; I will thus be adding to the lustre of my name, and increasing the positive possessions of my heirs." The average Smith or Jones has nothing of this incentive to heroism. His self-sacrifice could not benefit any special persons, and the welfare of the people is a thought rather beyond the comprehension and self-application of a common mind in moments of danger. It is true that the masses also obey an absolute command. History presents us with abundant testimony of this fact. On the field of battle, Smith and Jones do their duty as gallantly as any Howard or Montmorency. But in the present condition of the development of mankind, it seems to me that the abstract generality of the categorical imperative forms a less firm a priori foundation for my confidence than the palpable interests of a noble family. Especially in those cases where it is a question of sacrificing their lives for the State. That powerful longing for continued individual existence, which T discussed in a preceding chapter, renders the sacrifice of life far more easy to a patrician than it can possibly be to a plebeian. The former is sure of immortality; the latter has usually the consciousness that no cock will crow his name, his heroism to the world, after he is gone. The hero has at the best, only a moment of conscious self-satisfaction before he is thrown into the ditch with the masses; the man of rank during that moment is filled with enthusiasm as he dwells upon the certainty that he will have a noble memorial tablet and an imposing monument in the consecrated ground of history, erected to the memory of his heroism.

I have a firm hope that the recognition of the fellowship of the human race will gradually increase. The most enlightened men have always had a very clear comprehension of it, and as occasion offered, they accepted martyrdom without hesitation for the future welfare of the human race. But, in general, we are still stuck fast in individual isolation and egotism. Only very slowly are our limited perceptions of our immediate interests widening into a comprehension of the identity of the interests of people, species and race, and humanity must make a grand forward stride before the common man will perform an act of greatness, which requires the sacrifice of life, for the reason that he has come to look upon the advantage to the community which would result from it, as a personal advantage to himself, as the man of high rank would have the feeling that he was promoting his own personal interests, when he was bequeathing to his family the memory of an heroic deed. It is therefore of great importance for the State to possess a class of whom it is known with certainty, that it has reasons for placing the fulfillment of duty above life itself. Then in moments of danger the volunteers in the front ranks can be depended upon. Then there will always be some Winkelrieds on hand, ready to sacrifice themselves for the common good, with open eyes, conscious of their purpose and fully aware of the inevitable results.

These advantages of an hereditary aristocracy are counterbalanced by certain disadvantages it is true; this is unavoidable in human affairs. In the first place it can be said that it exerts a beneficial influence only upon the character, not upon the intellect of the people. Promoting intellectual activity, broadening the views of the masses and elevating the level of average intelligence — these are tasks which ought not to be expected from an hereditary aristocracy. The privileged class can be corporeally more finely developed than the masses, because it has better food and lives under conditions more favorable to health, and this physical superiority gained by these conducive circumstances is increased and perpetuated until it becomes a characteristic of the race, and is indelibly fixed upon the offspring. But in the matter of intellect, it will never take the lead, because mental superiority can not be inherited, and, as regards talent, every one must be literally his own ancestor, the architect of his mental fortune. This is a strange fact which has not been sufficiently dwelt upon as yet. Genius and even rare talents, are entirely distinct from genealogy. They have no lineage. They are and remain individual; they appear suddenly and disappear as suddenly in a family; I am not aware of a single case where they have been inherited by the children according to the laws regarding physical traits, in an increased or even equal measure. More than this: men of unusual talents seldom leave any offspring, and when they have children, they are weakly and less vigorous in every way than the average of mankind. We seem to see in this fact the operation of a mysterious law of nature which evidently wishes to prevent the development of beings of too marked a superiority as regards intellectual endowments, in a single species. Consider what the consequences would be if genius could be inherited like physical beauty, muscular development and a fine figure. There would then be living in the world a small class of Shakespeares, Goethes, Schillers Byrons, Molières,—between this class and the great multitude there would be an enormous space; and the difference between them would be constantly growing greater. This small group could not endure the ordinary conditions of existence and would either attempt to have certain special laws enacted for their benefit, thus forming a small state incomprehensible to the masses within the State, or else they would have the common laws adapted to their necessities, which would be ruinous to the people at large, as much so as if they were compelled to live in and breathe an atmosphere of pure oxygen. The higher intelligence always conquers the lower, even if the latter is combined with far superior bodily strength. Where a mentally more developed race comes in conflict with one less developed, the latter invariably succumbs. Perhaps an aristocracy of genius even if small in numbers, would have the same influence upon the people as the whites have upon the red-skins and negroes. But such an aristocracy will never appear in this world. Genius expends so much vital energy in its ordinary activity, that none is left for the propagation of the species. What a strange division of labor there is in the human race! Common men have the task of looking after the material preservation and perpetuation of their race, while to the men of rare talents is entrusted only the work of promoting the intellectual development of the race, as occasion offers. A man can not beget both thoughts and children. Genius is like the centifolious rose, whose vital energies are all concentrated in the blossom, which thus becomes the ideal type of its species, but in this evolution the power of reproducing its kind is lost. Goethe, Walter Scott, Macaulay and Tennyson may be raised to the peerage, but their descendants if they happen to have any, will never represent in aristocratic circles the intellectual giants of the people from which they sprang. And even when a nobleman born, like Byron for instance, has the gift of genius, this does not prove that it was the prerogative of his rank.

Thus we see that the finest intelligences of a nation are not to be found in its hereditary aristocracy, which as members of a caste, are only superior to the rest of the nation by their qualities of body and character. In consequence of this fact it is to their interest to rate these qualities higher than those which they do not possess. They set up an ideal before the man and the citizen, which does not depend for its brilliancy upon intellectual endowments, and where their influence preponderates, intelligence can not count upon being accorded the rank to which it considers itself justly entitled. A second disadvantage of an hereditary aristocracy in a nation, is that its existence leads unavoidably to violations of the right of single citizens. It deprives many of them of their just share of air and sunshine. It has one advantage over the plebeian which increases the obstacles in the upward path of the latter, sometimes closing it entirely. All the laws which assert the equality of the citizens without regard to birth, are powerless in the matter: the conditions being equal between two rival candidates, the one of aristocratic birth will obtain the coveted position, and often in spite of the fact that he is known to be inferior in endowments to the other. And it can not be otherwise. Absolute justice is a theoretical conception which can not be materialized. Justice as we realize it, is the diagonal of a parallelogram whose sides are might and the ideal of right. The constitution of society imposes upon us all certain limitations, and the more favorable station of the aristocrat on the battle field of life is one of them. We must bear it with the rest. We can make the attempt to force our way to the front ranks, and if our shoulders and elbows are strong enough we can succeed. If we have not these natural advantages then our complaints of the privileges of the higher classes are about equal to the kid's complaint of the rudeness of the lion who is about to devour her.

If we view the world from the standpoint of natural science, and admit that the universal laws regulating the organic world are also the fundamental and governing principles of human social life, then we can not hesitate to acknowledge that the institution of an hereditary aristocracy is not only natural, but in some respects even useful in a nation. Whatever philosophical speculation which does not take account of actual facts, may have to say against the existence of a privileged class, it is absolutely certain that such a class is sure to arise wherever more than two human beings combine into a permanent union of interests. The example of all communities founded originally upon the basis of absolute equality, is before us to convince us of this fact. The great republic of North America is theoretically a perfect democracy. But practicably, the slave-owners of the southern states formed an hereditary aristocracy with all its specific instincts and attributes, in the eastern states the descendants of the first Puritan pilgrims and of the early colonists from Holland lay claim to an exclusiveness and social privileges, which they deny to the thousands who came over later and their descendants, and the great financial pirates, who have amassed their wealth by making use of the most objectionable stratagems and influence, have established regular hereditary dynasties, whose members are not only in social life the models for the imitation of the crowd, but interfere in the destinies of the community and of the state with very genuine power. The instinct for equality seems to be exceptionally powerful in the French people. And yet it did not prevent them from erecting a new institution of nobility on the ruins of the old, which does not boast of titles and coats of arms perhaps, but possesses all the substantial attributes of an aristocracy, and whose ancestors—oh, irony of history!— were precisely those most fanatical equality enthusiasts of the great Revolution. I am not referring to the imperial aristocracy formed by Napoleon upon the model of the historical nobility, from the numbers of the regicides, but to those families which have inherited political influence and wealth since the days of the great Revolution, because their ancestors played more or less important roles at that time. If we examine the list of names of those who have, as ministers, senators, representatives and high public officials, governed France during the last four generations, we will find that certain names constantly reappear. The Carnots, Cambons, Andrieux, Brissons, Bessons, Periers, Aragos, etc., have founded powerful dynasties of politicians, and any one who is acquainted with the contemporaneous bearers of these name, will acquiesce in my assertion that they did not owe their first political positions to their own abilities, but to their names. The Ottoman Empire also has a strictly democratic constitution and with the exception of the Osman dynasty, and the disregarded descendants of the Prophet, is without an hereditary nobility. Every day common workmen, or barbers, become pashas, and the caprice of the Sultan, who alone has the right to distribute titles and honors, never enquires into the lineage of the favorite. And yet the country as a general thing, i governed by the sons of these parvenus, the effendis, and although the pasha can not bequeathe his title to his spring, yet he can usually manage to invest him with part of his authority. Nepotism is the very last root of hereditary privileges, which still remains alive, when the democratic hoe has chopped out all the others. It is human nature to favor one's own son or the son of one's friend, instead of strangers, no matter what the merits of the latter may be! The son-in-law of the professor gets the grand scientific title instead of his rival who did not choose a wife with his foresight, the diplomatic career is easily attainable by the son of the Cabinet minister, and all the youthful scions who played about the drawing-rooms and halls of their distinguished fathers' residences, form a ring, a closed phalanx, which the outsider has great difficulty in breaking through, and he who stands nearest to the dish dips his spoon into it first and oftenest.

CHAPTER IV.

I have conceded that an aristocracy is a natural and therefore unavoidable and necessarily permanent institution of humanity and do not oppose the hereditary honors and privileges which are accorded to it; but only upon one condition: that the aristocracy really consist of the best and most highly qualified human material in the nation. If a caste of nobility can show an anthropological foundation for its pretensions, then its existence is justified. It must have been formed originally out of a group of selected human beings, whose natural advantages were perpetuated and increased by sexual selection. This is the historical evolution of all aristocracy. In a people originally all equal, the strongest and finest-looking men, the bravest and most sagacious, rose early to positions of power and influence among their fellows, and their children derived their pride in the family name from these natural endowments of the parents. The son had the feeling that his father did not owe his exaltation to any capricious human favor, but to Mother Nature herself, and he expressed this idea in terms corresponding to his primitive conceptions, so that he boasted of being descended from the gods of his people, or, otherwise expressed, from its ideal types. The ancient Germanic races, the modern Hindoos, and certain primitive tribes such as the North American Indians, have this demi-god nobility. But where on the contrary, a nation has been formed from a mixture of different ethnological elements, where a stronger has conquered a weaker race, the descendants of the conquerors, that is, of the more vigorous and energetic stock, better developed at least physically, form the aristocracy. This was the origin of the nobility in all the European countries, which during the Dark Ages, were obliged to submit to the irruptions of alien, mostly Germanic races. The original aristocratic stock of France was mixed Frankish, Burgundian and Saxon-Norman, of Spain, west Gothic, of Italy, Vandalian, Gothic and Lombard, partly also Suabian, French and Spanish, in Russia, Scandinavian, in England, Norman, in Hungary, Magyar, and in China, Mantchoorian. Everything that I have said in regard to the justification of the existence of a superior social class, can be applied to an aristocracy that was originally composed of the most perfect individuals of the race, or of the conquering nation. Such a noblesse will be fully justified in assuming the places of honor and responsibility, because they will have the strength to seize them and retain them. From the start, better organized and higher-minded than the masses of the plebeians, they will be obliged to practise and increase their strength and valor continually, as otherwise they could not resist the encroachments of the people. By this means their supremacy over the people is maintained. The operation of natural laws leaves them only the alternative of keeping up the advantage they have gained over the rest, or of vanishing into obscurity. They must be heroes, for if they value their lives more than their privileges, the latter will be wrested from them by those who have no fear of death. They must perform their duties as vanguard and standard-bearers in every particular, for if a chance is left for others to press in, they will be overwhelmed and forced to the rear. They can not form an exclusive caste, for in that case they would degenerate, and the moment that their would-be rivals discover that they have ceased to be the better race, they would be pushed off from their pedestals. They can not set themselves up in opposition to the natural laws to whose operation they owe their own pre-eminence. As often as a person of marked individuality arises in the people, giving evidences of great superiority above the average, compelling the masses to acknowledge his higher organization, the aristocracy are obliged to hasten and open their ranks to him and consecrate him as one of their number. This constant infusion of new and vigorous blood counterbalances the unavoidable degeneration which time produces, and this elevation of the fittest, which was the foundation of the aristocracy, should continue unchecked for. all time.

This is the theory of an aristocracy whose right to its claims must be acknowledged by all, whose supremacy must be borne. But does the practice correspond with the theory? Is the nobility which fills up the foreground of the scene in almost every country in Europe, is it an aristocracy such as I have been describing? No one, master of his senses, can answer yes to this question. The so-called nobility, that is, the class which is distinguished by hereditary titles above the rest of the nation, fulfills not a single one of the conditions of a natural aristocracy. The demi-god nobility in those nations which have not been subjected to foreign conquest, and the victor nobility in those nations which were subjugated,— the original noble stock in all has either died out or decayed. Died out or decayed, and that too, by its own fault, because it resisted the operation of those laws of nature to which it owed its own existence, because it became exclusive, and did not understand how to renew its youth. On account of this many families wore out their fruitfulness, so that the day arrived when no heir was forthcoming; in others the descendants of distinguished ancestors became gradually stupid, cowardly and weakly; they were not able to defend either their estates or their positions from the covetousness of those beneath them, more powerful and vigorous than they, and so they have gradually sunk lower and lower into poverty and obscurity, until their blood now flows perhaps, in the veins of some day-laborer or peasant. Their positions left vacant by death or decay, are filled by a miscellaneous set of people who do not owe their elevation to higher organizations, not to nature, but to the favor of monarchs or other distinguished persons. All the aristocracy of the present day—I do not believe there are any authentic exceptions to this rule—is patent aristocracy, and in by far the largest majority of cases, of very recent date. An individual will, not an anthropological law, was the creator of their titles. But how since the Middle Ages, beyond which not a single genealogical tree in Europe spreads its branches, hew did the fortunate man gain the favor of the prince which found expression in the letters patent of nobility? By ideal human qualities, by endowments, talents, which made it desirable to use their possessor as new and fine stock for the elevation of the race? The history of all the noble houses of Europe lies open to us, we have only to read to find the reply to this question. There is hardly a single instance of the elevation to the peerage of a grand and noble nature, which could present to mankind an ideal type of its possibilities. If, as happened once in a great while, a man of genuine merit was presented with a coronet, he must have had combined with his fine qualities, others of a lower and contemptible character, and to the latter alone did he owe the royal recognition of his services. The causes of the exaltation of numerous families are such that they can not be mentioned in respectable society: these families owe their honors to the shame of their female progenitors. Their coats of arms keep in perpetual remembrance the fact that complaisant fathers and husbands and unprejudiced beauties laid the foundations of their high estate. In other cases, the patent of nobility was the reward of some rascality or crime, by which the founder of the house had served his royal master. I must admit however, that unchastity and assassination, although often enough the starting point of brilliant earthly careers, have yet been the means by which only the minority of noble families attained their privileges. The majority gained their pre-eminence in a more ordinary way. We find wealth or many years' service in the army or government, frequent causes of the elevation of men to the peerage. How can men amass wealth sufficient to attract royal notice? By being unscrupulous or extraordinarily fortunate, and the former is of far more frequent occurrence than the latter. During the times of the Reformation they plundered the churches; at a later period they fitted out cruisers, that is, became pirates; then slave-traders or slave-owners; in modern times they become government contractors and defraud the State, or else speculators and wrest the hard-earned savings from the hand of toil, by cornering the markets, or, in the most respectable case, they become manufacturers on a large scale and extort their millions from their hundreds or thousands of wretched pauper-laborers. And what sort of people are those who obtain recognition from the prince for their services in peace or war? They are always, I say always, without exceptions, clammy mollusc-souls, slimy, cringing hangers-on, who spend their lives in stifling every sentiment of manly independence, culling out every trace of pride and self-esteem, abasing themselves before any one superior to them in station and imitating his peculiarities to flatter themselves into his favor, counterfeiting extravagant loyalty to his person, and finally, as a fitting crown for the services of a lifetime, spent in crawling in the mire, they beg for a title of nobility. Men who are made of good, solid, humanized substance, with a stiff back-bone, who can not be peaceful and happy when they are not acting out their true nature, such men will never condescend to deny their own individuality and ape the opinions of those who happen to be above them, flattering, intriguing, begging, and, by these means, the only ones that are sure of success, win the royal good-will. The prince selects such men when he has posts of danger and responsibility to fill, but forgets them when he has favors to bestow. These men press forward and are ready to sacrifice everything when it is a question of serving the country; but they do not turn their hands over to attract the monarch's glance in processions and parades. So that a patent nobility is an institution which is to the human kind, what horse-racing is to horse-breeding. Those who win the race, and are selected to raise a new breed, are however the possessors of qualities which a common father might wish for his son, so that he might make his way in the world, as it is called, but which no poet would dare to ascribe to his hero, because poetry maintains the ideals of humanity purer than laws and customs, because the esthetic conscience still asserts itself, where the moral conscience has nothing more to say, and because we will shake hands with such men, whose success is unquestionable, but we will not allow them to be idealized in poetry and held up as models before us. Those individuals who have been exalted above the multitudes by honors and titles in each generation, are not always the poorest endowed as regards talents. They are not stupid, on the contrary, they are crafty and skillful; in perseverance, tenacity and strength of will, they are also above the average. But that which is certainly lacking in them. is character and independence, and these are the very points in which a natural, that is, a blood aristocracy, would be sure to excel, and which would create alone a social inequality in their favor and to the prejudice of the plebeian, without the intervention of written laws.

I have thus drawn the portrait of the individual by whose elevation to the peerage the family became ennobled. His descendants will usually rise to a higher moral level than their progenitor. It does not require such strenuous efforts to retain as to obtain a title. The nobleman is not obliged to be the unscrupulous egotist, the courtier or the intriguer that his ancestor was to whom he owes his rank. His character improves by the gradual action of the views inseparable from his position, which are based upon the original theory that the aristocracy is the society comprising the best and noblest persons in the State. For although the patent nobility may have nothing in common with a blood nobility, yet it maintains stoutly the theoretical fictions on which the latter is really founded. What has been the anthropological fate of the modern aristocratic families? They have either intermarried in deference to mediæval prejudices and abhorred mesalliances, as they are called, or they have in certain cases allowed these marriages with persons of inferior social station to take place. The result of constant intermarriage is a speedy and inevitable decay of the noble families. This is owing to the fact that they originally sprang from persons not endowed with superior organic strength, as would be the case in a natural aristocracy, descended from better organized individuals, and hence, inbreeding must necessarily result in a rapid exhaustion of the vital capital. This vital capital may be as large as that of any common family, but it is exhausted sooner on account of the greater expenditure of it necessary in the more intensive life inevitable in the higher and more responsible position, without being able to borrow judiciously from time to time from the inexhaustible vital capital of the people. And when a member of the aristocracy does marry outside of his circle, and brings new blood into the family, let us see what kind of blood it is and what the causes are which led to his matrimonial choice. The cases are rare in which a man of rank takes a girl from the lower classes to be his wife on account of her physical and moral superiority. In order to bring about a genuine improvement in the blood of a family, the mother of the new branch should be some woman who possesses in addition to the normal physical organization which we recognize as harmonious beauty, a soundness and equipoise of temperament, qualities which reveal themselves in a calm, or even narrow-minded, morality. Usually a mesalliance is caused by the attractions of wealth or else by some caprice of passion. Let us analyze the conditions under which these two kinds of mesalliances are usually contracted. A man of ancient lineage marries some wealthy plebeian in order to replate his coat of arms, as the saying is. In that case he is either some roué who has come to grief by his extravagances and seeks refuge in matrimony as he might in a charitable institution or else he is some decayed specimen of humanity without vital strength; for a man full of organic energy is proud and enterprising, he will only court the woman for whom he feels an affinity, and is well able to make a good appearance in the world, without the dowry of an unloved wife. The aristocratic bride-groom must be also a man of common character and ignoble views, prepared to dissemble and lie, for rich heiresses as a rule, demand that the coarse appropriation of their wealth should be concealed under the appearance of affection, at least during the honeymoon. She, the wealthy heiress, is also a very inferior type of humanity; she is the daughter of an intellectually limited and worthless father, for no other kind of a parent would sacrifice his child to external show, nor wish to enter into family relations with a society which will always look down upon him and his, and treat them with contempt, as unwished-for intruders. The girl herself, is either contented with her lot, willing to be the wife of a man to whom she is indifferent, in which case she is a creature without heart or character, a vain foolish doll, or else she experiences a longing to love and be loved, and yet resigns herself to the fate projected for her by her family, and this presupposes that she has a nature without strength of will and a spiritless character. The mesalliances which are not contracted for a dowry are yet similar to them in kind. I am not speaking of course of those cases where true and respectful love leads to the union of persons of different social stations. I can pass these by more easily as they do not occur hardly more than once in a century, and have never exercised any appreciable influence upon the improvement of the aristocracy as a race, on account of their rarity. The rule is that when a man of rank marries beneath him, it is usually some theatrical star, circus-rider or clever adventuress, known in all the watering-places and metropolitan drawing-rooms of Europe. Of the couple thus formed, the woman is an abnormal being, who has already given the world to understand that she does not conform to the average type of humanity, that she selected an exceptional, often eccentric and sometimes objectionable life-career from choice, that she tempted fate, and rebelled against the duties which modern society imposes upon its feminine members. The man is what psychiatry calls a "degenerate," that is, an individual m whom will and reason are decayed, the moral sense rudimentary and sexual passion alone, often in a strange state of degeneration, the main-spring of the inner life. Such persons are unable to resist the desire for the possession of a woman who knows how to awaken their love; in order to win her they commit follies, ignoble actions and even crimes, if nothing else will do. If we glance through the novels which close with the marriage of the prince and the actress, we will find almost without exception that the man is a "degenerate" in the technical sense, a weak, sensual and impulsive nature. The mesalliance therefore, as experience shows that it is usually contracted, is very far removed from being of any anthropological benefit to the aristocracy; on the contrary, it seems as if it were a fiendishly shrewd plan for uniting the very worst specimens of humanity in matrimony, to produce offspring morally diseased.

This is the origin of the patent nobility, and this is its necessarily consequent fate. The ancestor is an egotist, courtier and intriguer, probably all three combined, the descendant condemned to decay as if by a decree of destiny—either by the exhaustion of the family blood by unfavorable inbreeding in a narrow circle of equally poorly qualified families, or else by contracting misalliances with undeveloped or abnormally developed exceptional types of womankind. These sociological and anthropological facts are open to the eyes of all and are known to all cultivated people. And yet — and here we see another monument of human cowardice, stupidity and hypocrisy—and yet the nobility enjoys a supreme social consideration, accorded by most men voluntarily and even with a certain inward satisfaction. Snobbishness, which so "dearly loves a lord," is at home in all countries, even the most democratic. The Frenchman, who boasts of having discovered equality, is as proud of the acquaintance of a duke or marquis, and as interested in the daily life of his national aristocracy, as any English flunky. The American, who is supposed to adore the Almighty Dollar alone, and pretends to ridicule the differences of social station in the old world, is after all, inwardly enraptured when he can adorn his drawing-room with a live lord. He who wishes to know the exact price of a title, that is in certain countries, can easily obtain the information. The cost of a princely, or baronial coronet is well-known. We are aware that this ornament is the equivalent of a certain sum of money, and yet we pay a reverence to it which we would never think of awarding to the latter. The following little trait shows the propensity to lying of our civilization better than could be proved by volumes of argumentation. A representative laid before the French legislature a proposition to give to any one who so desired it, a title of nobility upon the payment of a certain fixed sum into the treasury; for $12,000 he could become a duke, for $10.000 a marquis, and so on in proportion, until for $3.000 he could assume the simple title of monsieur de. If this proposition were to become a law, there would be hardly any one who would take advantage of this open, honest, business transaction and buy a title before the eyes of the public as he would a coat or a watch-chain. But at the same time if an advertisement is inserted into some prominent newspaper saying that titles of nobility will be procured for wealthy people without publicity, a hundred replies to it are received by each mail. If the title of duke or marquis of the Republic of San Marino, or of the Principality of Reuss-Schleiz-Greiz, is offered for sale at the same or even higher prices than those proposed by the French legislature for a similar title, a purchaser will soon be found. And yet, in the first case, it would be a correct, straight-forward sale, in the other an underhanded and equivocal one; in the first, the title would have legal weight in a country containing thirty seven millions of inhabitants? and in the other only in a few villages. Yes, but in one case it would be publicly proclaimed that the title of nobility is free to any one who could produce the necessary cash, while in the other, the fiction would be thrown around the sale that the title was presented as a reward for services rendered, and that the newly-made nobleman is a being of a higher mould than the rest of mankind. Consequently people prefer to get their titles of nobility in some underhand way, through the intervention of some equivocal go-between, rather than by the open purchase in court, because they like to keep up, at least externally, the appearance of a nobility founded on genuine merit or royal favor.

The privileges accorded to the aristocratic class not consist of titles and compliments alone, neither are they only of a social nature. Notwithstanding the that all citizens are declared by the laws to have absolutely equal rights and duties, the nobility, in countries with a monarchical form of government, has managed to exert a very genuine and very important influence, which has obtained for it the possession of all the sinecures in the gift of the people and State. I use the word sinecure in its most comprehensive sense. According to the present conditions of holding and acquiring property, we must consider those public offices which have a certain income attached with limited duties, as presents from the State. All these offices, which require no special capability, which any average man could fill if he once got the chance, which must have been the positions referred to in the saying that when God gives a man an office He gives him sense to fill it, that is, the positions of officers, diplomates, beneficiaries, court dignitaries, etc., are all filled by members of the aristocracy. The State thus favors this small group of privileged individuals and presents them with these fine offices, upon which they have not the slightest reasonable claim; it sets the table for them with an abundant and tempting repast, all because, as Beaumarchais says, they took the trouble to be born.

The fraud of a patent nobility which has managed to creep in to all the historical forms and privileges of a blood aristocracy, whose existence had for justification an anthropological principle, because it was composed of the descendants of the most capable individuals of the race, or of a higher race of conquerors, this fraud is endured and even cherished by mankind, although history and reason are constantly holding up before us the evidences of the imposition. It is the cornerstone of the monarchical form of government. We act as if we believe that some narrow-minded, petty dandy, because he is a Sir This or Sir That, were therefore made of finer stuff than the rest of the people. We act as if we believed that a king by scribbling a man's name upon a bit of parchment, could make a noble, superior creature out of a common human being. And, by the way, why is not this miracle possible to a king? The grace of God is at his disposal and by its aid he might well effect this metamorphosis, which would be as comprehensible and conceivable as any of the miracles described in the Bible.

THE POLITICAL LIE

CHAPTER I.

Let us take a specimen man of our modern civilization, and examine the relations existing between him and the commonwealth, a man of the people, without family connections or influence to attract the favorable notice of those in power and thus obtain special privileges. I mean of course, a citizen of one of the regularly organized European states. Some portions of the portrait I intend to draw will not apply to this or that special country. The measure of liberty conceded to the individual varies in different places, and so does the form in which the limitations occur. But in the general outlines, my description will give a faithful representation of the place and conditions prepared by our civilization for the average citizen of any European state.

My specimen typical man is at the age when his parents recognize the necessity of attending to the cultivation of his mind. He is sent to the public school. Before he is admitted his certificate of birth must be produced. One would suppose that in order to share profitably in the blessings of public instruction, all that would be necessary would be to live and to have attained to a certain measure of physical and mental development. But this would be a mistake. A certificate of birth is absolutely indispensable. This respectable document is the key to the secrets of reading and writing. If it is not in his possession, a long and tedious process of red-tape must be gone through with, into whose details I need not enter, to procure a certificate signed by certain persons, recorded and stamped, to prove satisfactorily to the authorities that he was born. The boy is finally duly admitted into the school, and leaves it a few years later to enter upon his business career. His tastes and inclination^ impel him to assist his fellow-citizens in their suits at law, with counsel and mediation. But he is forbidden by the authorities to even attempt anything of the kind until he has procured the permission of the State, set forth in various diplomas. While on the contrary, he is perfectly free to make himself useful in the world by making shoes for instance, although a badly made shoe is sure to cause more suffering than a foolish piece of legal advice. He is now twenty years old and would like to finish his education by travel. This he is not allowed to do. The time has come when he is obliged to serve out his term of military service, give up all claims to his own individuality for several years, which is even more painful than the loss of his shadow was to Peter Schlemihl, and become an automaton with no will of its own. Very well. He owes this sacrifice to his country, which may be threatened some day with invasion. During this time of military service, my Hans — I will call him Hans for convenience — finds leisure and opportunity to fall in love with some young woman. He is a high-minded young fellow and scorns to make love to his sweetheart in the kitchen, according to the usual convenient garrison style. He wishes to get married. Very well again. He wishes to, but he is not allowed to. As long as he is a soldier he must remain a bachelor. Surely it would not interfere with anybody's rights, nor diminish his ability for bearing arms, nor injure any one far or near, if he were a married soldier, but all that is not to the point, he is obliged to wait until he has taken off his uniform for good. This finally comes to pass. Now can ho take his sweetheart home with him? Certainly, if both he and she are provided with all the necessary papers, and a goodly lot of them is required. If even one of them is lacking, it is all up with the wedding. Hans manages to sail around this dangerous reef by skill and good fortune at last, and now he would like to open a wine-house. This he can not do without the permission of the authorities, and they will or will not grant this permission as they happen to think best. He would meet with the same experience in many other trades which he might select, even if they did not interfere in the slightest with the rights of others, nor could possibly be construed as a nuisance, as injurious to the health of others or as immoral. Hans wishes to rebuild his house. He must not stir in the matter unless he has the requisite certificate of permission from the authorities in his hand. This is easily understood. The street belongs to everybody, his house stands on the street—consequently he must submit to the usual regulations. He has also an extensive garden, and in the centre of it, far from the public street, sheltered from all eyes and where no stranger's foot would ever enter, he wishes to erect some building. Even this is not allowable without the indispensable permit from the authorities. He perhaps has a store, and feels no need of a day of rest in every seven. He would like to sell goods Sundays as well as other days. This he must not do, unless he wishes to be arrested by the police and fined or imprisoned. The shop may be a restaurant. Hans suffers from sleeplessness and rather prefers than otherwise, to keep his establishment open all night. The police appoint a time to close and if he attempts to suit his own pleasure he is threatened with punishment. His wife presents him with a child. More bother. He must register the fact at the proper place, or else it will go hard with the little one later. He must also attend to its being vaccinated, although he has noticed that persons not vaccinated resisted the disease, during a small-pox epidemic, while others who had been vaccinated, took it and died.

I hasten by the hundred petty annoyances which Hans meets with during the year. He wanted to establish an omnibus line to run in the streets of his native city; he was not allowed to do so without a license. He took a fancy to a charming spot in the public park, kept up by the money of the city treasury; he was warned to keep off the grass. He undertook one day a pedestrian tour through his province; a few hours after he had started, he met a policeman who began asking him all kinds of indiscrete questions, about his name, his business, his family, trip, etc., and when he replied somewhat cavalierly to this total stranger who had not introduced himself, with the customary apology, he was forced to undergo several annoying indignities before he was at liberty to continue his tour. A neighbor one day coolly appropriated part of his garden and fenced it in for his own use; Hans appealed to the law; the proof of the trespass was clear and convincing; the case dragged along for months. He won the suit, but the defendant proved that he was insolvent, so that although Hans got the bit of his garden back again, he had lost in time and money about twenty times what it was worth, to say nothing of the vexation, which he did not reckon in the account—because he was so used to it from his youth up. He saw in the Museum a beautiful picture of the time of the Renaissance, the clothing of the persons represented in it appeared to him so sensible and graceful that he had a similar suit made for himself. When he appeared in it on the street one Sunday, the police threatened him with arrest, unless he returned home and took off at once, what they called a masquerade costume. He found a few congenial friends and concluded to form with them a club, to meet frequently and express their indignation at the existing conditions of the laws. The police demanded at once a list of the members' names, and after a while forbade their future meetings on account of the political nature of the club. Hans had become somewhat obstinate by this time and he founded a second club, to be an informal savings institution and mutual aid society; however this was at once interdicted by the police because no license had been obtained. Amid all sorts of contrary happenings Hans grew old and gray. When he was in a contented frame of mind, he consoled himself by thinking how much worse off the Russians were in their country, than he in his; when, on the contrary, he was disturbed and annoyed, he dwelt upon the thought of the degree of the liberty enjoyed by the English and Americans. He believed this by what the newspapers said; he had no personal experience in the matter. One day his wife died. He did not want to lose her even in death, so he buried her beneath her favorite tree in the garden. This time he was in a serious scrape. A regular police thunderstorm broke upon his devoted head. Burying a corpse on one's own grounds was strictly forbidden! He had become liable to heavy penalties, and his wife was dug up and carried to the cemetery by the authorities.

Hans was now alone in the world, he lost his spirit and courage, his business declined and soon he sank into absolute poverty. He fell so low that one evening he took up his position on a street corner and begged for alms. He was at once arrested by a policeman. He was taken to the station where he had an instructive conversation with the police commissioner. "You know that begging is strictly prohibited," exclaimed the latter. "I know it is so, but I can not understand the reason," said Hans, "I was in nobody's way, troubled no one, I merely held out my hand silently." "That is idle talk, I can not waste my time listening to it. You must go to jail for eight days." "And what shall I do, when I am set at liberty again?" "That is none of my business. You must attend to that." "I am old and am not able to work. I have nothing. I am sickly." "If you are sickly, go to the hospital!" exclaimed the commissioner impatiently, but then added: "No, you can not go to the hospital if you are only ailing. You must have a serious disease to get in there." "I understand," says Hans, "such a disease as a man either dies of soon, or if he does not, recovers from in a short time." "You are right," replied the official and turned to the next comer. Hans served out his term of imprisonment, and then was so fortunate as to be admitted into a poor-house. Here he had food and shelter, but the former was bad, and the latter rendered insupportable by the fact that he was treated like a criminal and a prisoner. He was obliged to wear a sort of uniform which attracted attention and ridicule on the street. He once met a man whom he had known in better days. He bowed, but the latter did not reply to his greeting. Hans walked straight up to him and asked: "Why this contempt?" "Because you did not understand how to follow the example of respectable people who have become rich," replied the man and passed on quickly, an expression of disgust upon his features.

Hans grew more and more melancholy. All sorts of dark thoughts swarmed in his brain. One bright morning he set out for a walk, and his whole life passed before him in imagination; he began to talk to himself first in a whisper and then louder as he became excited: "Here I am, seventy years old, and how has it been with me? I have never been myself. I have never been allowed to have a mind of my own. As soon as I formed a decision and tried to carry it out, the authorities interfered. Unwarranted people have stuck their noses into my most private and personal affairs. I had to pay attention and respect to everybody, and nobody paid respect and attention to me. Under the pretext of protecting the rights of others, they deprived me of every one of my own, and come to think of it, they deprived the others of their rights too. All my life long I was not allowed to do more than to play with my dog unmolested, and even with him I was dragged before the courts by the Society for the Prevention of Cruelty to Animals, if I ventured to whip him. I can appreciate the reasons for my being forced into the army—but if enemies should invade and overrun the country owing to the lack of an army to repulse them, my private welfare would hardly suffer more than under the blessed authorities; and also for my being called upon for such heavy taxes — the police, which has always had its eye so paternally upon me, must be paid, although it was not exactly necessary to rate me for a business that did not support me, and to punish my insolvency by seizure. But what good were all the other oppressions and vexations? What advantages did I get from the authorities for all the sacrifices of my independence which they demanded? To be sure they protected my property — that was an easy matter, for I have none, and when all that I had, my garden, was taken away from me, I had to stand the annoyance and pay for it all myself, besides. If there were no police every one would do exactly what he chose —well, what then? Then I would have shot my neighbor dead, or he me, and that would have put an end to the matter. The authorities see to it that we have good paved streets—Ugh, I don't know but what I had rather wade through the mud in high boots for ever than have the everlasting police nuisances around. And may the devil fly away with the whole concern!"

And as Hans arrived at this point in his monologue, he turned and jumped into the river along whose banks he had been walking. But the police were on hand as usual, fished him out and carried him to the nearest magistrate, who condemned him to a term of imprisonment for his attempted suicide. But Hans had taken cold in the water; consumption set in, and, I do not know whether to say fortunately or unfortunately, he died in prison. His death gave the authorities their last chance for an official certificate as far as he was concerned.

CHAPTER II.

My poor Hans reasoned like an embittered and uncultivated man. He spoke of the police authorities alone, because they were the only wheels of the machinery of State that were visible to him; he exaggerated the inconveniences of our civilization and failed to appreciate its blessings. But, taken as a whole, he was right: the restrictions imposed by the State upon the individual, are out of all proportion to the benefits it offers him in return. The citizen resigns his independence only for a certain purpose and with the expectation of certain advantages to be gained by it. He supposes that the State to whom he has sacrificed a large part of his rights as an individual, will in return, guarantee the security of his life and property, and apply the combined strength of all to certain matters, to carry out certain undertakings, which will promote the personal interests of each individual, but which alone he could neither have planned nor accomplished. Well then: we must admit that the State fulfills these theoretical presuppositions but very imperfectly, hardly better than the primitive, barbarous communities, which allowed their members an incomparably larger share of individual liberty than the civilized State of modern times. It ought to ensure to us our life and property. This it does not do, for it can not prevent wars, which cause the violent death of a horribly large number of citizens. Wars between civilized nations are no rarer and no less bloody than between savage races, and with all his laws and restrictions to liberty, the man of our civilization does not procure any greater security from the deadly weapon of his enemy than the barbarian, unrestricted by the blessings of a police guardianship. To find any actual difference in security to life and limb between the two, we must be convinced that the death that comes to a man in uniform from the hand of a murderer also clothed in uniform and obeying the word of command, is less of a death than that caused by the tomahawk of some painted warrior, acting according to no manual of regulations. Some isolated minds dream of the abolition of wars and the substitution of arbitration in their place. What will be, will be. I am not speaking of a future that may never arrive, but of the present. All the sacrifices of his personal liberty during times of peace do not relieve the individual from the necessity of defending his own skin at critical moments, the same as the savage in the jungles of Africa. And even aside from war, all our regulations and restrictions do not protect the life of the single citizen any more than the unrestrained freedom of barbarism. Murders between the members of a savage tribe occur no more frequently than in civilized communities. Acts of violence are almost always committed under the influence of passion, and this is entirely beyond the control of our restraining laws. Passion is a relapse into the primitive condition of mankind. It is the same in the highly cultured cosmopolitan as in the Australian native. A man under the influence of passion, will commit violence, and kill, without the slightest thought of the laws and authorities. And it does not benefit much the dead man to have his murderer arrested and punished for the crime—and even this is not always the case, for the jury is very apt to acquit any one who committed an act of violence when impelled by passion or emotional insanity as it is called in the courtroom. And even this feeble and as we have seen, practically insignificant consolation, that the murderer will be obliged to pay the penalty of his crime, is equally the right of the savage and is far more liable to be realized in his case, because the vengeance of the family and tribe is much more difficult to escape from than the pursuit of the detectives, notwithstanding the descriptions and rewards published in the newspapers. Next to the crimes caused by passion come the cold-blooded and premeditated crimes. These are decidedly more frequent in civilized than in savage communities. They are principally the work of a certain class of human beings which owes its origin and development to civilization alone. Science has proved that habitual criminals are degraded organizations, descended from drunken or licentious parents, and usually cursed with epilepsy or other diseases of the nervous system. The extreme poverty of the lowest classes in the large cities stunts both the physical and mental growth to such an extent that the pathological condition of habitual criminality ensues. All the laws in the world are powerless to prevent the crimes which are the consequences of this circumstance due directly to civilization, and the presence of these thieves and murderer-robbers in the midst of our conventional well-regulated society, is a menace whose gravity can not be over-estimated.

We have about the same measure of security in regard to the possession of our property, as of life. In spite of all our laws and regulations we are robbed and plundered, sometimes straight from our pockets, sometimes indirectly, by swindles of various kinds, large and small, individually and as a people. What protection have we against the founder of swindling enterprises who steals the savings of the public, or against the speculators, the bulls and bears, who by some manipulation of the markets destroy or at least diminish, the fortunes of thousands? Does not the man of civilization whose property is in paper, does not he lose his property by these crimes just as completely as the barbarian whose flocks and herds are driven off? The reply is made to my questions: we can protect ourselves against the swindler and speculator; no one compels us to put our money in the hands of the one, nor to buy the artificially inflated stock of the other. To which I reply: Certainly we can. The cautious man, the reasoning man can do so. The multitudes can not. And if it comes to self-protection of what use is the law? Of what use are our sacrifices of liberty and our taxes? Even the savage if he has strong dogs, stout weapons and servants enough, if he is vigilant and strong, can successfully protect his property and that without any police. And the member of our civilized society who has not sagacity, which is one kind of strength and vigilance, will lose his savings out of his chest and his purse from his pocket, notwithstanding the countless numbers of pens scratching away on stamped paper all day long in the official bureaus. And here is another point to be regarded. The man of civilization has not only to look after his own protection, like the barbarian, but has moreover to offer up continual sacrifices of his possessions to pay for the protection that the State ostensibly affords him, but which is adequate only in theory, and these sacrifices are often more considerable than the total amount for which protection might be required in case of need. Of course the man of wealth pays over to the commonwealth much less than the amount remaining to him 1 , but millionaires are the exception everywhere. The rule is that the great majority of people in every country are poor, even in the most favored lands, or at best, only possess the necessaries of life. But every one, even the poor man, pays taxes, and to such an amount that he would be comfortably off at the close of his life, if he had been able to retain for himself the fruits of his labor which he has bee n obliged to pay over to the State. That the barbarian may lose his property is only possible, that the man of our civilization is deprived of his by the State, by means of direct and indirect taxation, is certain. And if anything remains to the latter after his taxes etc., are paid, it can be stolen or swindled away from him, unless he guards it with the same care as the barbarian does his property, for which he has had no tithes to pay. The case of the civilized man is therefore like that of the young fellow in the anecdote, who enquired of the boat's captain what the price of passage between Strasburg and Basle would be, and received the answer: "Four gulden on the boat, but only two gulden if you'll help draw the boat on the towpath." The case of the man of our civilization is even worse than this, for he is not allowed the alternative of choice; he is obliged to help draw on the tow-path and pay his two gulden besides.

There remains the last aim of the State: the combination of the powers of all to execute certain works for the benefit of the individual, which the individual alone could not accomplish. This task is fulfilled by the State s it must be acknowledged. But even this is performed in an offensive and imperfect way. The State as at present organized, is a machine which works with an enormous waste of power. Only a small and constantly diminishing portion of the original force, obtained at such an incredibly high cost, remains for actual production; the rest is lost in overcoming the internal friction or else escapes in the smoke and noise of the steam whistle. According to the way in which all the European states of today are governed, the sums exacted from the citizens are squandered on foolish, frivolous and criminal undertakings. The whims of certain men, the selfish interests of certain small minorities, determine only too frequently the purposes to which the efforts of the community shall be directed. Hence the individual citizen labors and bleeds so that wars may be carried on which put an end to his life or his prosperity, that fortresses, palaces, railroads, harbors or canals may be built, from which neither he nor nine tenths of the nation will ever derive the slightest benefit, so that new offices may be created to make the machinery of State more complicated, to increase the friction between its wheels, in which he will lose still more of his time and leave still another piece of his liberty, so that office holders may be paid high salaries, who have no other aim in life than to lead an ornamental existence at his expense and lay another burden upon his shoulders, in short, he spends his life laboring and bleeding to add with his own hands to the weight of his yoke and the number of his chains and to create the possibility for new demands upon his labor and blood. Only in very small states or in those of extensive decentralization and self government, are the results of the taxation of the people free from unjustifiable waste. Such communities resemble in their constitution and conditions of existence, the cooperative societies in which each member can easily superintend the application of his contributions, prevent unnecessary expenditure, oppose unpromising undertakings and cause them to be abandoned in time. Every benefit and every loss is felt directly by each member, the former compensates him for his sacrifices and he is warned by the latter to take precautionary measures against their reoccurrence. In such communities it is certainly difficult to procure funds to carry on any ideal or distant enterprises which do not promise appreciable benefits or pleasures to each individual member, but it is still more difficult to use the power of the whole to satisfy the caprices of one, or to inveigle money from the members to buy the rods with which they are to be beaten.

To condense the foregoing details: the life and property of the individual are no more protected by the modern complicated machinery of State, by the everlasting writing, recording, office holding, permits and injunctions than entirely without the whole intricate apparatus. For all the sacrifices of blood, money and liberty offered to the State by the individual citizen, he receives in return hardly any other actual benefits than the administration of justice, which is costly and tedious out of all proportion to what it should be, and public instruction, which can not be said to lie accessible to all in the same degree. In order to have these advantages, hardly any one of the restrictions of individual liberty and independence are strictly necessary. The pretext that the liberty of the one is only restricted out of regard for the rights of others, is a bad joke; this pretended regard does not prevent the oppression of the individual and deprives all of the larger part of their natural liberty of action.

The law exerts upon every one alike the same steady and certain pressure, which without the law, would be only exerted in exceptional cases, by single violent natures. It is true that in our present civilization the average duration of life of the individual is longer, his health better protected, the level of general morality higher, the common existence more peaceful and deeds of violence, except those committed by habitual and hereditary criminals, rarer than in a state of barbarism. But these facts are in no way the results of the bureaus and their regulations, but the natural consequences of the higher cultivation and better judgment of the people. The citizen in the chains with which he is loaded down by the State, is obliged to rely upon himself for protection as much as the free barbarian, but is less skillful in it than the latter, because he has forgotten from want of practice, how to look out for himself, because he has no longer the proper sense for the appreciation of his near and distant interests, because from his earliest years he is accustomed to bear with an oppression and compulsion against which the savage would protest even at the expense of his life, because the State has brought him up in the idea that the government officials are to do the thinking for him in all cases, because the law has broken the elasticity of his character, crushed out every power of resistance by its constant pressure and brought him down to such a point that the oppression of the State has ceased to be injustice in his eyes.

It is not true that all our existing police regulations are needed to protect our life and property. In the mining camps of the West and in Australia, the individuals took their protection into their own hands, forming the so-called "Vigilance Committees", and the most model order prevailed without any official machinery. It is not true that all our legal squabblings and janglings are needed to have justice properly administered. In those primitive communities to which I refer, a public and private right was recognized, which ensured to the first possessor his legal title to his "claim" and to all the fruits of his labor, and this without courts, magistrates and records, due solely to the common sentiment of what is equitable and proper, which civilization has developed in mankind. These were the circumstances in those camps formed of the roughest, most passionate and undisciplined individuals of all nations. And the great majority of humanity, the gentle, the peaceable, the quiet-loving members of society, do they require these everlasting leading-strings? If nine tenths of the existing laws and regulations, courts and magistrates, decrees and records were entirely done away with, the security in regard to life and property would remain the same as at present, every human being would continue to enjoy his rights unmolested, not one of the genuine advantages of civilization would be diminished in the slightest, and yet the individual would acquire by it a liberty of action unknown before, he would appreciate and live up to his individuality with a delightful intensity of which he can now form no conception, hemmed in as he is on all sides by the present inherited conditions of existence. Perhaps this emancipation might cause him at first uneasiness and alarm, such as a bird born in captivity, might experience if the cage door were left open; it must first learn to spread its wings, conquer its dread of space, and experiment until it has confidence and courage in every fibre of its being. But on the other hand, the barbarian accustomed to untrammelled self-control and self-guidance could not conform himself without constant and acute suffering to a life in which he would feel a hand upon his shoulder, an eye fixed upon his face and an order resounding in his ear all the time, continually forced onward by outside, foreign impulses, continually obliged to obey a foreign will—this life of external control with its perpetual licenses, would kill him in a short time probably.

Is this condition which I recommend as desirable, is it anarchy? Only an absent-minded or superficial reader could have deduced this conclusion from my preceding remarks. Anarchy, the absence of all government, is a creation of certain minds, incapable of correct observation. As soon as even two human beings settle down to dwell together, a government is necessarily formed, that is, forms and regulations of intercourse and behavior, consideration and subordination, become necessary. The natural condition of humanity is not that of an amorphous aggregation of matter, that is, without crystallization in its particles, but exactly the reverse, a mass whose atoms assume invariably certain regular forms owing to their inherent power of attraction. In every mixed mass of human beings, forming an apparent social chaos, a state is sure to be organizing itself, as crystals are sure to be developed immediately in any solution of crystallizable matter. The rational mind therefore does not demand anarchy, that is utterly inconceivable, but an autonomy, an oligarchy, a government of and for self, of limited extent, with the radical simplification of the present machinery of government, the suppression of all unnecessary wheels, the liberation of the individual from purposeless compulsion and the limitation of the demands of the community upon the citizen to that which is obviously indispensable to the fulfillment of its duties. The individual will thus be freed from what Herbert Spencer calls "The Coming Slavery," while retaining all the advantages civilization has to offer him.

Even in these ideal circumstances the citizen would be obliged to work for the community, in other words, pay taxes, but the public assessments would lose their characteristic of extortion which makes them so odious now. We make no resistance when called upon to pay for our loaves of bread, our tickets to the theatre and our subscriptions to clubs and societies, at the utmost we regret that it is not always easy to make up the sum total. Why is there no resistance in this case? Because we know that we receive the value of what we pay out; because we can not feel that we are being robbed. When a government is so simple in its construction that every citizen knows all about its purposes, can supervise its work and has a voice in the direction of its energy, then he looks upon the taxes he pays as an expenditure for which he receives a direct return. He knows what he is getting with every penny of his tax-money, and the evident equitableness of such a transaction precludes the possibility of discontent. But in the State as at present organized, the taxes are necessarily odious impositions; not only because they are everywhere far higher than they ought to be, on account of the enormous expense of running the governmental machine owing to its defective construction, but also because they are founded upon and surrounded by injustice in every form, due to the historical organization of society and its blundering laws, and principally owing to the fact that the expenditure of the public funds derived from taxation, is regulated by

Fiscalism and not by rational common sense for the benefit of the State. By Fiscalism I mean the organized system of plundering the people, getting the utmost out of them, ostensibly for their own future benefit, without the slightest consideration of the true rational purpose of the State and its political results to the individual. Fiscalism does not ask: "What sacrifices are indispensable to carry on the legitimate and necessary functions of the State!" but: "How can we manage things so as to get the largest possible revenue out of the people?" It does not study and enquire: "How can we protect best the interests of the individual without allowing the community to suffer by our indulgence?" but: "In what way can we revenue drivers get at the money of the people with the very least expenditure of mental energy, attention and consideration for others?" The modern conception of a State is an arrangement to increase the well-being of the individual; the feudal conception on the contrary, sees in the individual only a slave to increase the glory and power of the State. Fiscalism is based upon this latter conception. In its eyes the State is the pre-existing and natural ruler, the citizen the later arrival and the natural object to be ruled. The taxes are not an expense which the citizen voluntarily assumes, voluntarily pays and for which he expects to receive certain benefits in return, but a tribute, such as one would pay to a third person, and for which the third person, the hideous Moloch, State, gives nothing in return but a receipt. We feel that we are members of a free combination for the attainment of certain common ends. Fiscalism recognizes in us merely slaves of the State. We call ourselves citizens, Fiscalism calls us subjects. The difference between the two points of view is expressed in full in these words.

Fiscalism is a necessary consequence of the historical development of the system of taxation. There were no assessments in primitive communities. The chief of the tribe paid his necessarily higher expenses out of his larger income, in wars each man capable of bearing arms supplied his own necessities and the priest alone received contributions from the people. The State had no needs, consequently it required nothing from those belonging to it. But this state of things soon changed everywhere, either owing to the oriental despotism that arose from the acceptation of the fiction of the divine origin of the person and power of the king, or else from the subjugation of the people by some alien conquering race. In both cases the mass of the people became a drove of slaves, the personal property of the king or of the conquerors, and they were obliged to pay taxes, not for any state purpose, but merely to fill the money chests of their masters, who did not feel called upon to do anything in return for the people, but accepted the revenue as they did their income from their lands or herds of cattle. Free races in those days looked upon taxation as a disgrace, a token of servitude, and many centuries of hard pressure were required before the Germanic races, for instance, could be prevailed upon to pay the taxes levied upon them, resembling those they had been accustomed to exact at the point of the sword from the nations they had subdued. The fiction that the citizens are bond-men, obliged to work first for their owner the king, has been the foundation for the rights of the State ever since the Middle Ages, as also for the relations between the subject and the ruler, who in his person represents the entire State. This fiction is still accepted in our times; and in the form of Fiscalism we find it prominent in our modern State, with all its constitutionalism and Parliaments, supposed to embody the sovereignty of the people.

The same fiction is also the foundation upon which rests the organization of the system of public offices and the positions of the officials in regard to the citizen. According to the enlightened conception of the State, the public official is an agent of the people, who receives his support, his authority and his position directly from the people. He must consider himself the servant of the community according to this conception, feel his responsibility and constantly keep in remembrance the fact that he is installed to attend to certain interests of the individual members of the community, who can not attend to them personally with the same convenience and certainty. He ought never to forget that he is not theoretically indispensable to the community any more than a servant to a household; each individual could if necessary, black his own boots and fetch the water for himself, and in the same way could attend personally to the administration of the government, so that a recognition of the advantages attending the division of labor is the only cause of the existence of the office holding public. But in reality the office holder considers himself the master, not the servant of the public. He believes that he owes his authority not to the people but to the ruler, he may be either king or president of a republic. He looks upon himself as the dispenser of a part of the supreme governing power. Hence he demands from the citizens the respect and subservience which they owe to the principle of sovereign authority. The public functionary is a more developed form of the steward or overseer, considered historically. The clerk growling at the citizens summoned to his office is the historical descendant of the commandant or overseer appointed by a tyrant of the Dark Ages to superintend his people of slaves, and to keep them in a becoming state of obedience by his body guard of warriors, with the whip and the goad. As the public functionary is a fragment of the royal grace-of-Godness, he lays claim to some of its infallibility. His position is below that of the head of the State, but it is above that of the masses to be governed. They are the flock, the ruler is the shepherd and he is the shepherd's dog. He can bark and bite and the sheep must bear it. And what is the most remarkable of all: the sheep do bear it! The average citizen, such a man as my Hans, accepts without question the pretensions of the office holder. He admits his right x command and assumes the duty of obedience upon himself. He comes to the public bureau not as to a place where he could insist upon what was due to him, but as if he had come to beg for a favor. Besides it would be very foolish of him to rebel against these paradoxical circumstances for, in any discussion or contest with a public functionary, the latter would be sure to come out victorious in the end, and even in the most favorable case, the citizen would be exposing his interests during the continuation of the contest, to delays, hindrances and disadvantages of all kinds. Fiscalism is rounded into a whole by Mandarinism, and both are logical deductions from the conception of a sovereign by the grace of God and a people subject by the curse of God. The laws are made today the same as centuries ago to favor Fiscalism and Mandarinism. Out of a hundred laws decreed with or without the cooperation of the people, as the case may be, ninety nine are sure to have for their object not the increased liberty of the citizens, nor the amelioration of their conditions of life, but improved facilities for the bailiffs and sheriffs in the exercise of their authority. The people are subjected to a thousand annoyances that the public functionaries may have an easier time. We are designated by letters and numbers like so many cattle, so that we can be counted and compared with less trouble. We are all punished in advance by suspicious restrictions because one of us might some time step over the line. Shall I mention an example? All merchants and bankers are compelled by law to keep their sets of books in a certain prescribed way. Why? Because some one of them might plead bankruptcy fraudulently and the examiner would only be able to discover the fraud by considerable mental exertion, unless the books were kept according to a certain formula and everything set down in its proper place. If there were no books at all the examiner would have a hard time finding his way through the wilderness of business memoranda. In order to save him this trouble in case of a bankruptcy, the law deprives a hundred other merchants who would never think of defrauding their creditors, of their freedom of action. Each one of us is obliged to report his coming and going, at least in the large cities, to the police. Why? Because one of us might happen to commit a crime some day, in which case the police would be obliged to hunt him up. In order to save themselves this trouble, for which by the way, they are hired and paid, they oblige us to take upon ourselves this constant trouble of reporting our whereabouts to them. I could give a hundred such examples if I were not afraid of their monotony. At the same time the restrictions thus imposed by the State upon the citizens miss their aim completely. The laws oppress those only who nave no idea of resisting them; while on the other hand, they have never prevented the consummation of any unlawful act by those who have determined to submit no longer to their control. The bigamist commits his crime in spite of the formalities which render marriage so difficult, expensive and surrounded by such ceremonies to the honest man. The robber has his knife and his revolver in his pocket in spite of the laws forbidding the peaceable citizens to carry weapons. And it is the same in every thing. It is the same system as Herod's although less tragical, who ordered all the children to be killed because there was a possibility that one of them might grow up to be a pretender to his throne and allowed the very one to escape the slaughter who was to become dangerous to him.

The philosophical conception of the State has altered, the relation of the citizen to the State is theoretically that of a member of a society where all have equal rights, every one of the constitutions which have been formed since 1789, being based upon the principle of the sovereignty of the people, but practically the machinery of the State has remained the same. It works today just as it did in the darkest times of the Middle Ages, and if its pressure appears somewhat lighter upon the individual it is only on account of its wearing smoother. The tacit presumption upon which all our laws and regulations are based is now as much as ever before, that the citizen is the personal property of the sovereign, or at least of that impersonal phantom the State, which has inherited all the privileges of the ancient despots, the public functionaries being its visible incarnation. The government official is not the employé of the people, but the agent of the powers of the State, consequently the enemy, overseer and jailor of the people. The laws are intended to give the official the opportunity to defend the interests of his real or ideal master the monarch or the State, against the people, which is credited with a perpetual tendency to rid itself of its task-master. This is the only possible explanation of the respectful consideration and the prominence conceded to the autocratic office holder to . this very day. He is not able to dazzle the public by his rich relations, nor by the brilliancy and luxury of his manner of living; neither can he compel the admiration of cultivated minds by his higher culture or greater talents, the utilitarians can not consider his employment any more useful than the class of direct producers, the farmers, artisans, artists or scientists. But if the position of a public functionary does not mean the possession of a larger income, greater talents nor especially capability, why is it that a government office confers upon its incumbent an importance and respect beyond that of almost any other position? Why? Because the official is a part of the sovereign authority, which the people, unconsciously to themselves, from sheer stress of custom, regard as something mysterious, supernatural, awe-inspiring and terrible The grace of God in which the sovereign basks, illuminates also his employés; a few drops of the sacred oil with which the king is anointed at his coronation, fall upon the brow of the government official. This phenomenon takes place even in those countries which have no monarch nor coronation, nor any grace of God. It has become a reflex action of the people's mind.

CHAPTER III.

And now what about representative legislation? Does it not return to the individual the liberty of which he has been deprived by Fiscalism and Mandarinism and the laws passed in their interests? Does it not change the feudal subject into the modern citizen? Does it not place in the hands of every individual the right to govern and decide the destinies of the State, in conjunction with the rest? Is not the voter on the day when his representative is elected, a real sovereign, exercising even if indirectly, the old royal privileges of appointing employés, passing laws, levying taxes and deciding upon the foreign policy of the Government? In short, is not the ballot the all-powerful weapon with which our poor Hans for instance, can humble the pride of the government official, that even Shakespeare complained of, and by its assistance is he not able to attack and demolish all the regulations which reduce him to slavery?

Certainly. Representative legislation accomplishes all this. But unfortunately, only in theory. In practice it is a lie as enormous as all the other phases of our present state and social life. I must not omit to mention that the lies by which we are surrounded are of two kinds. Some wear the mask of the past, the rest the mask of the future. Some are forms which had once a substance—the others, forms which have as yet no substance at all. Religion and the monarchical form of government are lies because we allow the external forms to remain although we are convinced of the absurdity of the empty sham. Representative legislation, Parliamentism, on the other hand, is a lie because as yet it is only an external form, the internal organization of the State remaining completely unchanged. In the former case it is new wine in old bottles and in the latter, old dregs in new vessels.

Representative legislation is the machinery by which the principle of the sovereignty of the people becomes action. Strictly according to theory, the entire people should assemble in an immense mass meeting, make its own laws and appoint its employés, thus expressing its will directly and carrying it immediately into action, without the loss of power and the modifications it is sure to undergo as an inevitable consequence of repeated transmissions. But as civilization increases, it has a tendency to group the individuals into larger and larger communities, to unite into one nation all those speaking the same language, the entire race, and to enlarge the confines of the States to immense proportions. Consequently the direct practice of self-government by assembling the entire people, has already become a material impossibility in by far the largest number of countries, and in those remaining, it is only a question of time. Hence the people are obliged to transfer their power to a small number of delegates whom they authorize to act for them and exercise their rights of self-government. These delegates in turn are obliged to transfer the power a second time, as they can not govern directly, and they authorize a still smaller number of chosen men, the members of the Cabinet, who in fact, prepare and administer the laws, levy and collect taxes, appoint employés and decide upon peace or war. In order to have the people retain its sovereignty, in order to have its will continue to be the sole arbiter of the destinies of the nation, notwithstanding the repeated transmissions of authority, certain suppositions must be proved to be true. The confidential agents of the people must divest themselves of their personality. The seats in the legislative assembly must not be filled by men, but by mandates, who speak and vote. The will of the people acting through the agent, should not experience any interruption or modification nor be subjected to any personal influence. The members of the Cabinet likewise should be impersonal machines to receive and carry out the intentions and will of the majority of the. legislators. Every neglect of the commission with which the Cabinet is charged by the representatives, and the latter by the people, should be followed at once by the removal of the offender. But the commission must be clearly and unmistakably understood in the first place. The people must be united in their opinions on the laws and the method of administration which they have decided to be necessary for the best interests of the State, and they must require the strictest adherence to these methods and principles from their representatives. They should choose for their representatives such men alone as they know possess character and talent, with the ability to comprehend and carry out the programme laid down for them by the electors, so that they will not deviate from the straight line drawn for them, nor hesitate to sacrifice their time, labor and their personal interests when necessary, to the common welfare. This would be ideal representation; in this way the legislation would be the actual work of the legislators. The centre of gravity of the entire structure of State would be in the ballot box, and every individual citizen would have his visible and perceptible share in the guidance of public affairs.

But now let us turn from theory to practice. What a disappointment awaits us here! Representative legislation even in its most classic homes, England and Belgium, does not fulfill a single one of the conditions I have been enumerating. The will of the citizen expressed in his vote, is entirely Barren of results. The delegates elected act in all cases according to their individual pleasure, and their only sentiment of constraint is in regard to their rivals, not at all in regard to the wishes of the people who elected them. The Cabinet not only rules the country but the Parliament as well; instead of their following a policy prescribed to them, they dictate the policy of the Parliament and nation. They manage all the powers and resources of the nation according to their own discretion, bestow favors and presents, support numerous hangers-on in luxury at the expense of the community and never hear a word of reproof if they remember to send to the majority in Parliament occasional titbits from the royal feast spread for them by the State. In actual practice the ministers are no more accountable than the members of Parliament. They are not punished in the slightest for the hundred acts of arbitrary power, injustice and misuse of their authority, which they commit every day. When a case does occur once in a century, of a minister being called to account for his misdemeanors, because he has proved himself an exceptionally outrageous rascal, or because he has aroused a passionate hatred against his person, the impeachment proceeds in a pompous and imposing manner, but terminates in an absurdly insignificant sentence. The Parliament is an institution for the satisfaction of vanity and ambition and for the furtherance of the personal interests of the members. The people has been for thousands of years in the habit of submitting to a sovereign will and of showing honors to a privileged aristocracy, in whose hands they left all the funds of the State for their personal use. Certain enlightened minds, capable of seeing into the future, gave them a form of government in representative legislation, which permitted them to set up their own will as the sovereign power and to deprive the aristocracy of their control of the public finances. What did the people do? They hastened to put on representative legislation, but on top of their old habits, so that now as much as ever before, they are ruled by an individual will and they are plundered by a privileged class; only this will is no longer called the king, but the leader of his party and the privileged class, not the aristocracy, but the majority in the House. The old relation between the average citizen and the State remains unaltered; my Hans to whom I am always returning, continues to pay taxes whose amount he does not fix himself and whose expenditure he can not control, he must obey laws which he did not impose upon himself and whose utility he fails to recognize, he must take off his hat to the public employé that another's will has set up over him, whether his name be Johnny in England, Ivan in Russia or Hans in the German-speaking countries.

Parliamentism has one advantage; it makes it possible for those who are ambitious, to rise by utilizing their fellow-citizens. I will show that this is a genuine advantage. Every nation, and especially those still engaged in an ascending self-development, inspired by an inexhaustible vital energy, produces in each generation some individual in whom an especially powerfully organized personality clamors for room for expansion. These are men born to rule, who refuse to bear another's yoke or to submit to another's control. They want to have their head and their elbows free. They are only able to yield to the discipline of their own will and judgment, never to those of another. They submit because they choose or think best, never because they are compelled to do so. These individuals never meet with a barrier that they do not demolish or ride over it. Life does not seem worth living to them unless they experience that satisfaction produced alone by the unchecked play of all their capabilities and inclinations. The consciousness that a large part of their horizon is obscured by some alien consciousness, removed alike beyond their influence and observation, destroys their enjoyment of it, they look upon their Ego as a cramped and wretched Ego, incapable of stretching and asserting itself, their very existence appears insupportable to them if they consider it impelled and guided by alien forces. Such individuals require room. In solitude they find it without effort or difficulty. If they are anchorites, if they are hermits or fakirs, Canadian trappers or pioneers of the back-woods, they can live out their lives without conflicts with others. But if they are to remain in the society of man, there is but one place for them: that of leader. They would not remain an instant in the condition of my Hans. They are no soft plasma, but crystals, hard as diamonds. They can not squeeze into the hole which ha structure of State has left open for them, without regard to their shape and size. They must have a special cell, made to fit their angles and planes. They rebel against the laws which do not fit their case, in whose creation they had no share, and they shake their fists in the face of the government official who attempts to give instead of receiving commands. There is no room at all for such natures in an absolute monarchy. This form of government is usually stronger than their power of expansion and they are worsted in their attempt to overthrow it. But before they succumb they shake the State until the king trembles upon his throne and the peasant in his cottage is thrown down by the violence of the shock.

They become regicides, rebels or at least highway robbers or freebooters. In the Middle Ages they wandered through the forests as Robin Hood, or as leaders of a band of brigands, became the terror of princes and peoples. Later as Cortez and Pizarro, they conquered and plundered the New World, fought at Pavia as captains of freelances, and as soldiers of fortune during the Thirty Years War rented their services to the different generals and rose to power, or were broken upon the wheel like Schinderhannes and Cartouche. Today they are called in Russia Nihilists, as yesterday they were known in the Ottoman Empire as Mehemet Ali. A representative government allows these men with the powerful Ego to act out their impulses, maintain their individuality, without disturbing or even threatening the State. Much less exertion is required to be elected to Parliament than to climb to Wallenstein's position, and it is even easier to become prime minister in a constitutional state than to overthrow an ancient throne. A member of Parliament can hold his head high where Hans would be obliged to stoop, and a prime minister may have to struggle but never to obey another's will. Hence Parliamentism in a country is the safety valve which prevents the powerful individuals of the nation from causing destructive explosions. If we study the psychology of the professional politicians in all those countries with a representative form of government, we will find that the compelling force which drives them into public life, is the necessity for a larger space in which the growth and activity of their Ego can continue without restraint. This is called ambition. I have nothing to say against this term if it is defined correctly. What is ambition? Is it what the German word for it, Ehrgeiz, honor greed, represents, a craving for external titles of honor? This motive may influence some grocer who has found a fortune in his coffee-sacks and is now trying to get into office. But it plays no role in the life-career of a Disraeli, a Kossuth, a La Salle or a Gambetta. Such men as these do not care for the respectful greetings of self-important or obtrusive nonentities on the street, nor to wear gay uniforms, nor to have reporters, biographers and artists on illustrated weeklies, at their heels continually, nor for the notes from pupils in the young ladies' seminaries, begging for their autographs. Merely for the sake of these petty gratifications of their vanity they would never have assumed the terrible burden of public life, which repeats in the midst of our culture and civilization all the conditions of prehistoric existence. In public, political life there is no rest nor peace possible, every one is either fighting, hiding in ambush, lying, listening, hunting for trails, or removing the trace of his own, sleeping with one eye open and his gun in his hand, looking upon every one he meets as an enemy, his hand against everybody and everybody's hand against him, slandered, traduced, badgered, provoked and wounded—in short, he must live like a red skin on the warpath in the trackless forest. The so-called ambition which compelled the statesman to enter upon his political career, to select this dangerous and thorny path, was nothing else than the necessity of allowing his personality to develop completely and freely, a sensation of indescribable delight which the ordinary class of men never experience and which is only gained from the consciousness of a will which has overcome each and every obstacle. The case is similar in regard to the passion for ruling. It is a matter of much less importance to the genuine, born party leader to rule over others, than to prevent any one from ruling over him. When he bends the wills of others and makes them yield to him, it is principally to appreciate and rejoice in the consciousness of the strength of his own will. There is but one choice open to the man living in the midst of our modern conditions of State and society, unless he lives like a hermit in the wilderness—he must either rule or be ruled. As strong natures can not endure the latter, they are obliged to decide upon the former; not because it gives them any special pleasure, but because it is today the only way in which the individual can retain his liberty and independence. Those who love authority are not counting the heads beneath them, to satisfy their vanity, but those above them. Cesar preferred to be the first in some village rather than the second in Rome. In the latter place he would have ruled over millions, subject to but one, while in the former only a few hundred men would have recognized in him their master.

Would not the passion for ruling, have been gratified a thousandfold more in Rome than in the village? Yes, if Cesar had only been anxious to rule. But he wished to be conscious only of his own Ego; in Rome it came in contact with another and stronger will, while in the village it could expand in all directions without meeting another. In Cesar's remark lies the whole theory of the ambition which compels the politician to enter the arena of public life. Men of small calibre, the rank and file of politicians, may be influenced by other motives; they think it a matter of the greatest importance to secure for themselves and their friends the spoils of office, to bore a small hole into the State barrel and help themselves to its contents through their own little straw. These petty politicians and carpet-baggers, as they are called in North America, these office seekers are only the paid hirelings of the leaders; they are not an indispensable part of Parliamentism, but help fill it out as wadding. To the leaders however, the material advantages of then-position are but secondary matters. The point of the greatest importance to them is the unchecked expansion of an Ego that has painful cramps if obliged to stay folded up.

No word reappears so often in politics as "I". I and always I alone. This shows that a representative constitution has proved to be the triumph, the apotheosis o egotism. According to abstract theory it is an organized fellowship, but in practice it is self-interest reduced to a science. The fiction is that the representative relinquishes his individuality and is transformed into a selfless collective being, through whom those who elected him think and speak, decide and act. The reality is that the electors renounce by the act of election, all their rights in favor of the representative, and he gains the entire authority which they lose. In his programme and in the speeches with which he wins the vote of the people, the candidate of course pretends to accept this fiction. Before election he talks of nothing but the interests of the public, he is the guardian and promoter of the common good, he forgets himself in his anxiety for the welfare of the community. But these are only formulas which even the most good-natured simpleton has ceased to accept literally. What are the interests and welfare of the general public to the candidate? Less than Hecuba to the player. He wishes to rise in the world and his constituents are the rounds of his ladder. He work for the community? Not much! He expects the community to work for him. Some one has described the public as voting cattle. This is a picturesque and unusually appropriate expression. Representative legislation produces conditions resembling those of patriarchal times. The representatives take the place of the patriarchs and their wealth consists similarly in herds and flocks. But nowadays, these herds are not composed of actual cattle with horns and hoofs, but of cattle, figuratively speaking, who on election days are driven up to the ballot-box to deposit their votes. Rabagas is supposed to be a caricature and a satire. But he seems to me more like a faithful portrait. Why should we be astonished and smile at the fact that Rabagas, the great revolutionist, should force upon the people, when he had once attained to the summit of power by the help of the people, the identical forms of governmental oppression which he had denounced as crimes in his incendiary speeches against his predecessors? To me this change seems natural and consistent. The politician has no other purpose and no other motive for his actions than the gratification of his egotism. To compass this he must have the support of the masses. And this support is only obtained by the usual promises and party cries which the politician rattles off as glibly as the beggar on. the church steps repeats his customary prayer. The candidate submits to this old-established custom mechanically, almost unconsciously. This wins for him the support of the voting public and he steps into power. His egotism is thus satisfied; the voting public vanish from his horizon completely and do not reappear until he is threatened with the loss of his authority. Then he will do what is necessary to retain it, as he did before what was necessary to obtain it. He will either bind upon his brow the wreath of promises and party cries or else threaten the grumblers, as the emergency may require. This sequence of logical premises and conclusions is called by the world representative legislation.

CHAPTER IV.

We must study the details of the profession of politician before we can appreciate how shamelessly the practice of Parliamentism belies its theory.
How does a man become a representative to Congress or Parliament? Only once in ten years or so does it happen that the voting public seeks some sagacious and honest fellow citizen and begs him to be its representative, and even in this case it is usually under the influence of certain circumstances which deprive it completely of its ideality. Some party has an interest in placing the authority in the hands of this chosen man, perhaps because his name will be an ornament to its standard, or else to oppose a strong candidate to the dangerous one nominated by the other party. In this case the candidate's name is advertised and his virtues celebrated, without any effort on his part, without any solicitation from him, and the office falls to the most suitable one among the citizens according to the abstract theory of representation. But the case is usually entirely different: some ambitious individual steps up before his fellow-citizens and tries to convince them that he, more than any one else, deserves their confidence. What motive impels him to this step? Because he feels an impulse within him to make himself useful to the community? Who can believe this? Men are rarely met with in our times, who have such a sense of fellowship with the people and with mankind at large, that it compels them to seek their happiness in working and sacrificing for the community. Even in such men their very

nature renders them more sensible to rude and vulgar impressions than other men, as they are more ideal and susceptible. And do such ideal, sensitive natures expose themselves voluntarily to the mental and physical annoyances of a political campaign? Never! They can suffer and die for humanity but they can not pay empty compliments to a horde of dull voters. They can do what they consider to be their duty, without regard to reward or appreciation, but they can not sing their own praises before a crowd m extravagant phraseology. They withdraw into their study or into a small circle of congenial minds and avoid the rude turmoil of the market place, as a usual thing, with a timidity which others often mistake for superciliousness, but which is in reality, only their fear of contaminating their sacred ideal. Reformers and martyr spirits sometimes appear before the multitude but only to instruct it, to point out its faults, to tear it away from its cherished customs, not to flatter it, confirm it in its errors and repeat in honeyed terms what it loves to listen to. Hence they are more often stoned than crowned with flowers. Wycliffe and Knox, Huss and Luther, Arnold de Brescia and Savonarola have each exerted a powerful influence upon large numbers of people and aroused passionate devotion as well as bitter hatred. But I do not believe that they or a Rousseau, a Goethe, a Kant, or a Carlyle, would ever have been appointed to represent the people in the legislature in any country or city district, by their own powers alone, without the help of any supporting committee. These men would not stoop so far as to pay court to their constituents to inveigle their votes, and thus conquer with his own weapons the opposition candidate, who would carry everything before him by merely following the ordinary routine. The method by which a political office is to be obtained often deters a man of true refinement from attempting it, but it is no obstacle to the egotists who are determined to attain to influence and distinction and are willing to do any thing to promote their ends.

A certain man decides to enter upon a political career. The mainspring of his decision is self-interest; as he requires popularity to attain to the position he covets, and as popularity is usually only won by those who promote or appear to promote, the public welfare, he begins to work for the interests of the public, or to pretend that he does so. He must possess certain qualities in order to ensure success, which do not make him more loveable. He must not be modest, for in that case he would not push himself forward, and this he must do if he wants to be noticed. He must be ready to dissemble and lie, for he is obliged to assume friendly interest in certain men, who are, if not repugnant to him, yet certainly indifferent, otherwise he would make enemies of them. He must make hundreds of promises that he knows beforehand he will not be able to fulfill. He must learn how to assume and play upon the lower aspirations and passions of the public, their prejudices and customary beliefs, for these are the most widely extended, and he must win over the majority to his side. These traits combine to form a physiognomy absolutely repulsive to a nobler man. Such a figure in a novel would never arouse the sympathetic affection of the reader. But in real life the same reader casts his vote for him every time.

A political as well as a military campaign has its science of warfare, its strategy and its manual of tactics. The candidate seldom comes into direct personal contact with the constituents. A committee stands between them, whose authority is created only by their own presuming audacity. Some individual comes to the conclusion that he would like to assert himself somewhat. He summons his fellow-citizens to a public meeting, entirely on his own responsibility. If he feels that he is not yet of sufficient importance to make it a success alone, he invites some friends to join with him, or he calls upon a few rich and empty-headed nonentities and tells them that it is their privilege and their duty to place themselves at the head of their fellow-citizens, assume the guidance of public opinion, etc. The wealthy idiots feel very much flattered by this invitation and lose no time in signing their names to the summons, which is then published in the newspapers or posted on the walls, and their signature gives it brilliancy in the eyes of all those who judge a man by his bank account, rank or social position. Thus the public meeting is arranged and a committee formed to take charge of it. Each committee of this kind is composed of two elements, the energetic and the unscrupulous schemers who are working for some personal advantage of a moral or material nature, and the consequential narrow-minded blockheads, solemnly in earnest, who are taken on board by the former for ballast. Others can become members of the committee if they choose, even if they are not invited to join. All that is necessary is to speak loudly and fervently in the meeting and thus attract the attention of the crowd. A man with a powerful voice and a rapid utterance, no matter what he says, will soon attain to a certain degree of authority in a mass meeting, and as these qualities make him desirable as a member of the committee, and formidable as an antagonist, he is consequently welcomed into the committee

The committee can organize itself around the man who wishes to become the candidate, or it can be formed uninfluenced by him. In the former case the candidate guides the whole procedure; he organizes his staff, he summons the public to meetings, appoints orators to speak in them, and fights his own battles. In the latter case the committee is a band of wandering adventurers "whose leadership can be won by any enterprising man, and whose services are rented out to any candidate that may require them to conduct the campaign. Many politicians have worked in this way for others, before they set up their own claims for candidacy; they made and unmade representatives; they gave or rather sold offices to those who were willing to pay for their services in hard cash or minor offices and advantages of different kinds; in certain rare cases merely for vanity, so as to be recognized as the most influential men in the voting district. In a mass meeting loud talking wins the day. The crowd only listens to those who speak sonorously, deal in fine promises and everyday matters, easily understood. On election day the most influential voters whom the candidate has taken especial care to win over to his side, deposit their votes according to the dictates of their vanity or of their interests; the majority however, vote for the candidate in whose behalf the committee has labored most zealously. They put into the box the name that has been buzzing about their ears for so many weeks. They do not know the man to whom it belongs, they know nothing of his character, his capability, his opinions; they vote for him because his name is the most familiar. If they were asked to lend him an old tea-kettle for a few hours they would search out his antecedents more carefully. But they are ready to confide to him the highest interests of the community, as well as their own, without knowing anything more about him than that he is recommended and endorsed by a committee of men who are often as perfect strangers as the candidate himself. And it does no good to rebel against this act of violence, for such it is. A private citizen who accepts seriously his constitutional rights and wishes to learn more about the man to whom these important trusts are to be confided, tries in vain to resist the tyranny of the committee, forcing upon his acceptance a candidate of whom he knows so little. His resistance is impotent and his conscientiousness is smothered and lost in the indolence of the crowd. What can he do? He can stay away from the polls on election day, or vote for the man of his individual preference. But neither of these proceedings will help him in the slightest. The man will be elected nevertheless, for whom the great mass of the thoughtless, the indifferent or the intimidated deposit their votes, and this mass proclaims always the name which has been kept most loudly, forcibly and constantly before the public. It is true that theoretically every citizen is at liberty to endorse the man of his individual choice, to convene meetings for him, and create a party to support him. But in real life it is much more difficult to win adherents by extolling the superior virtues of a candidate, than by promising advantages of all kinds. In consequence of this fact the citizen who conscientiously tries to practise his political rights with a view to the welfare of the community, will always find himself in the minority, while the majority are following the lead of the professional politicians who carry on their public life as a regular lucrative business career.

This is the physiology of the elections of members to representative bodies. The one elected is supposed to be the man in whom the majority have confidence, whereas he is in reality, only the choice of an insignificant minority. But the minority is organized into a compact whole, while the majority of voters are a mass of loose molecules which the former can mould to its will. The membership should be presented to the wisest and most capable citizen; it falls however, to the one who pushes himself forward most audaciously. Cultivation, experience, honor and intellectual superiority are unessential qualifications in a candidate. They do not detract, but they do not aid him in the slightest in his political struggle. But what he needs above all is self-appreciation, audacity, fluency of speech and vulgarity At the very best, it is possible for the candidate to lie an honest and shrewd man, but he can never be of a refined, sensitive and modest nature. This explains the great scarcity of characters in representative bodies, while talents are frequently met with.

The professional politician has now obtained the coveted position by his false promises, his tail-wagging before the public, by unabashed self-laudation and declamatory speeches full of common-places, aided by his comrades who are all fighting with the same weapons and whom he will aid in turn. How will he exercise the authority with which he has been invested? He is either an exceptional individuality or an average man of his class. If the former, he will found a party, if the latter, he will join one already established.

That quality which makes its possessor a leader of men, is the will. It is a natural endowment which has nothing in common with reason, imagination, foresight or magnanimity. A powerful will can be combined with a narrow mind, dishonorableness, selfishness, malice and general lowness of sentiments. It is an organic strength and can belong to some moral monster, as well as a fine figure and muscular development to some corrupt or mentally insignificant being. Whatever his other qualities may be, the man of the most powerful will always take the lead in any assembly, guides and controls it. He will destroy the weaker wills that oppose him; his relation to them will always be that of the iron to the earthen pots. A superior intelligence is able to bring a stronger will into subjection. But how? Not by conquering it in an open hand to hand fight but by apparently submitting to its control and at the same time whispering in its ears the desired ideas and opinions, so skillfully that it learns to consider them as its own. The most important ally of the will in Parliament, is eloquence. This is also a natural gift, entirely distinct from high intellectual culture or character. A man can be the greatest thinker, poet, general or legislator in the world, and yet not be able to make an effective speech, and the reverse is also true, he can have an especial talent for eloquence with an average, mediocre intellect. The history of representative legislation records few examples of great orators who ever did anything to enlarge the mental horizon of their race. The most famous extemporaneous speakers, whose share in important debates led to decisions affecting the history of the world, and crowned them with fame and power—their speeches when read produce such a paltry impression that the reader exclaims: "What can it have been that made this speech have such incomprehensible effect?" It is not the rational sentence that finds an attentive audience in the crowd, but the one forcibly delivered. The most brilliant and easily comprehended argument has little chance of moving a large number of hearers unless its delivery has been carefully prepared and rehearsed beforehand. While it happens very often that they are entirely carried away by the inspiration of some foolish orator and pass resolutions in a rash, almost unaccountable precipitation, which they can not even explain to themselves upon cool reflection.

When the party leader unites to his indomitable will the talent of eloquence, he plays the chief role upon the world's stage. But if he does not possess this gift he stays behind the scenes and as manager, dictates and controls the actions of all the players on the stage, invisible to the public, but the highest authority, the moving spirit of the whole parliamentary comedy. He has eloquent orators then to speak for him, as he has often high but timid and vacillating intellects to think for him.

The means by which the leader of men exercises his power, is the party. What is a political party? In theory it is an union of men who combine their individual energies to attain the realization of their common ideas in regard to the laws and the policy of the Government. In reality there is no great single party, that is, ruling or capable of ruling, by its size and strength, which is founded on the basis of a single platform.

It sometimes happens that small groups are formed consisting of ten or twenty persons at most, attracted by the similarity of their ideas in regard to the affairs of public life. Large parties however, are only called into existence by the influence of private ambition, private self-interest or the power of attraction of some predominant central personality. Men are divided by nature into two classes; one of them can not endure the control of others, hence, as I have noted in the preceding pages, it must become the ruler, according to the present arrangement of things in this world; the other is born to obey, for under the necessity of making decisions and carrying out the dictates of its will, it shrinks from the responsibility of the consequences of its actions, the indispensable adjuncts of liberty and self-government. The first class is naturally in a diminishing minority compared to the other. As soon as a man of the comfortable, obeying kind meets a man with a strong will and passion for ruling, he yields to him of his own free will and places the guidance of his affairs and the responsibility for the same in his hands not only with pleasure, but with a sensible lightening of his heart. Such obeyers are often capable of carrying out the tasks imposed upon them by another's will, with the greatest energy, sagacity, perseverance and even sacrifice of self. But they must receive the impulse from another's will. They may have every talent; they only lack the power of the initiative, that is, a will. These men enter at once into the service of the leader whenever they come in contact with him. All the material functions of the representative legislative assemblies are performed by the party leaders alone. They alone decide, make wars and triumph. The public sessions are scenes without any real significance. Debates are carried on so as not to allow the fiction of parliamentism to be dropped. But only in the rarest cases has a debate led to any really important parliamentary resolution. Debates and speeches give the speech-makers fame, power and position; but as a general rule they have not the slightest influence upon the result determined beforehand, consequently the parliamentary proceedings might be entirely suppressed without detriment and only the decisions arrived at by the parties in obedience to the will of the leaders, be put to the deciding test of a vote.

The causes which lead to the downfall of a party leader who has obtained control of the reins of government, are not the blunders which he makes in the ad ministration of the supreme authority; these only serve as pretexts for attacks upon him. They are either the appearance of a more powerful antagonistic will or the detection of mercenaries whose greed for the spoils of victory he has not been able or willing to satisfy, or a combination of these two causes. This is so truly the case that a ministerial crisis, which appears to transfer the power from the hands of one into those of the other party utterly and diametrically opposed to it, is yet powerless to effect any radical change in the interior policy of a Government. The relation of the individual to the State remains the same as of old, the private citizen need hardly notice when he reads his newspaper, that another party has climbed to the summit of power and another Cabinet has replaced the old. The designations Liberal and Conservative are simply masks for the real motives of all parliamentary contests, conflicts, campaigns and changes—ambition and egotism.

This is the colossal lie of our modern political life with its many different strata. In several countries the fiction of representative legislation is the screen behind which is concealed an absolute, "by the grace of God" monarchy. In those nations in which it is an actual reality, where the representative body really reigns and governs, it amounts to nothing but a dictatorship of certain persons, who in turn, obtain control of the supreme power. Theoretically representative legislation ensures the fulfillment of the will of the majority; in reality it only carries out the will of half a dozen party leaders, their advisers and standard-bearers. Theoretically the opinions of the representatives should be formed or influenced, by the arguments advanced in the parliamentary debates; in reality they are not influenced by them in the slightest, but depend entirely upon the party leader or upon private interests. Theoretically the representatives should have only the good of the commonwealth before their eyes; in reality their only thought is how to advance their private interests and those of their friends at the expense of the commonwealth. Theoretically the representatives are supposed to be the best and wisest of all the citizens; in reality they are the most ambitious, the most pushing and the coarsest. Theoretically the vote deposited in favor of a candidate means that he is known and trusted by the voter; in reality the voter knows nothing whatever about him except that a set of ranting speech-makers have been deafening him for weeks with the candidate's name and placarding it before his eyes. The forces which theoretically keep the parliamentary machine in motion, are experience, foresight and abnegation of self; in reality they are strength of will, egotism and fluency of speech. Culture, intelligence and noble sentiments are defeated by noisy eloquence and indomitable audacity, and the halls of legislature are ruled, not by true wisdom, but by individual, obstinate wills.

Not an atom of the right of representative legislation supposed to be gained by universal suffrage, falls to the individual average citizen. Now as much as ever before is my poor Hans obliged to pay taxes and to obey the authorities, bruising his elbows again and again, by coming in contact with the thousand absurd restrictions that hem him in on every side. All the share he has in the whole business of representative legislation, with all its fuss and ceremonies, is his fatigue on election days, from walking to the-polls, and his dissatisfaction that more entertaining and profitable reading matter is crowded out of the newspapers to make room for the uninteresting, interminable congressional debates.

THE ECONOMIC LIE

CHAPTER I.

Those circumstances of our civilization which affect the largest number of human beings, with the most painful and lasting results, are the .grievous errors prevailing in the economic world. There are plenty of people *?ho have never taken any interest in abstract question/?, to whom God is a matter of as much indifference as primal causes; the encyclical as uninteresting as the theory of evolution, whose faith or knowledge is alike superficial. Many people also are totally indifferent to the political problems of the day, and the number is much larger than is usually supposed, who do not care in the least whether they are governed in the name of a personal king or of an impersonal republic, so long as the State remains visible in the shape of public officials, tax-collectors and drill-sergeants. But on the other hand, there is not a single man of our civilization who is not daily confronted by the question of supply and demand. The circumstances of the economic world force themselves upon the dullest observation and the most secluded intelligence. Every human being possessed of consciousness, experiences certain wants and grumbles at the difficulty or rebels against the impossibility of satisfying them. With bitterness does he see the disproportion between his labor and the enjoyments he is able to purchase as the results of it, and compare his own share of the gifts of nature and productions of art to those enjoyed by others. He grows hungry every few hours, he is fatigued and weary at the close of each working day, every time that he sees a beautiful or brilliant article he longs to possess it, in obedience to that natural instinct of human nature to attract notice and admiration to its personality by ornamental or distinguishing appendages. Thus he is led by the circumstances of his physical conditions to reflect upon his relation to the general movements of political economy, the production and distribution of wealth. There is consequently no subject in which the masses are more vitally interested than this. During the Middle Ages millions were aroused to action by the name and cause of Religion. In the latter part of the last century and up to the middle of this, the nations of the world were aflame for their abstract needs of enlightenment and political liberty. The cry for bread for the masses fills this latter part of the Nineteenth Century. This cry is the sole import of that European policy which tries to turn the people from this engrossing idea by side issues of all kinds, by persecution of some social class, by wars, colonization schemes, expositions, dynastic comedies, parliamentary twaddle and civil service reforms, but it is constantly brought back to it by the pressure of public opinion which demands a consideration of the great, worldwide problem of the day, the question of how to support one's self. Crusades for the rescue of a Holy Sepulchre, for the conquest of a Golden Fleece, are no longer possible. The causes of modern revolutions are not constitutions on paper and democratic party cries, but the longings experienced by so many to toil less and live better.

At no period in the world's history were the contrasts between rich and poor so decided, so prominent, as at present. Those writers on political economy who commence their scientific works with the axiom that pauperism is as old as humanity itself, betray either a lack of reflection or truth. There is an absolute and a relative poverty. Absolute poverty is that condition in which a man is partially or totally unable to satisfy his actual wants, that is, those which are the result of the organic act of living. Hence it is that condition in which he finds it impossible to procure sufficient food, or where to procure it, he is obliged to curtail the rest and sleep which his system requires and without which he pines and dies prematurely. Relative poverty, on the other hand, signifies a condition of lack of means to satisfy the wants which man has artificially acquired, not the indispensable requisites for the preservation of life and health, but those of which the individual usually becomes conscious by the comparison of his manner of living with that of others. The working man feels poor when he is not able to smoke and drink his whisky, the shop-keeper's wife, when she can not dress in silk and fill her house with superfluous household goods, the professional man, when he can not accumulate capital sufficient to free him from the haunting anxiety in regard to the future of his children and the support of his declining years. This poverty is evidently not only relative—the shop-keeper's wife appearing rich in the eyes of the working man, the professional man considering as the height of luxury, what would seem shabby to those brought up in the luxury of an aristocratic home,—it is also subjective, as it only exists in the imagination of the individual in question and is by no means an objective, appreciable lack of the indispensable conditions of existence, entailing suffering upon the organism. In short it is not physiological poverty, and old Diogenes proved that this is the boundary line of the subjective sensation of happiness, viz. that a man can be well and comfortable as long as his physical wants can be easily and abundantly gratified.

From the point of view of a man of this civilization of the Nineteenth Century, who is a slave to all the customs and wants of civilized life, the great majority of mankind appear to have been always relatively poor in the past, growing poorer and poorer as they are more and more removed from the present. The clothing was coarser and less frequently renewed, the dwelling places were less comfortable, the food more primitive, the utensils less in number, there was less money in circulation and less abundance of unnecessary articles. But the picture of relative poverty is not affecting. Only an empty-headed fool could find anything magic in the fact that an Esquimau woman protects herself from the cold by a sack-shaped garment made out of seal-skin instead of a complicated affair of velvet as expensive as it is ungraceful. In fact, I doubt whether the sentimental wish expressed by that good king, Henry IV. that every peasant might have a chicken in his kettle every Sunday, would have ever touched or inspired genuine peasants as long as they could eat their fill of pork. But absolute physiological poverty as a permanent condition, never has appeared except as a consequence of the highly developed and unhealthy state of civilization. It is actually inconceivable in the natural condition of mankind and even at a lower stage of social development. The procuring of sufficient nourishment is the chief and most important act in life of all organic beings, from the polyp to the elephant, from the bacteria to the oak-tree. If it fails, it dies. It never voluntarily submits to the permanent lack of nourishment. This is a biological law, governing man as well as all other living creatures. A primitive man does not accomodate himself to circumstances of want but struggles to overcome them. If he is a hunter, and the game leaves his usual hunting grounds, he starts in search of others. If he is a farmer on unproductive soil, he packs up and emigrates when he learns of more fertile fields that he can get. If other men stand between him and his food, he takes his weapon and kills them, or is killed by them. Abundance is then the reward of strength and courage. So the tide of emigration sets from unfruitful districts into those blessed by the sun; the heroism of a Genseric, of an Attila, a Ghengis Khan and a William of Normandy, has its origin in the stomach, and on the bloodiest and most glorious battle-fields, which the poets sing and history loves to dwell upon, the question of the midday meal was decided by the iron dice. In short, primitive man will not endure genuine poverty, that is, hunger. He takes up his arms against the encroaching wretchedness at once and wrests for himself the superabundance of the enemy or dies beneath his hatchet, before he perishes of privation. Absolute poverty is also incompatible with a civilization which has not yet passed beyond the standpoint of physiocracy. As long as a people are only familiar with agriculture, cattle-raising and domestic industries, although they may be poor in money and articles of luxury, yet the necessaries of life are within the reach of every individual. Only when man loses his direct dependence upon food-producing Mother Earth, only when he forsakes the furrow in the field and passes beyond the reach of Nature who offers him bread and fruits, milk and honey, game and fish, only when he shuts himself up behind the city walls and gives, up his share of forest and stream, procuring his food and drink no longer from the grand store-house of the animal and vegetable kingdoms, but by an exchange of the products of his labor for the gifts of nature monopolized by others, only at this period does the possibility arise for a small minority of persons to accumulate great wealth and for a large majority to sink into absolute poverty, physiological distress. A nation which consists of free tillers of the soil, is never poor. It can only become so by the subjection of the farmer into a slave, working for another, who deprives him of the results of his labor on his land, or else applies his labor in some other way so that he can no longer till the land, or else by the growth and increasing number of cities, absorbing and diminishing the agricultural public. A highly developed civilization thus condemns a group of individuals increasing daily in numbers and importance, to absolute poverty. The cities grow at the expense of the farming population. It favors the great manufacturing industries at the expense of animal and vegetable production, and produces a numerous wages-receiving class, whose members can not call a single inch of ground their own and live under abnormal conditions of existence, condemned to slow starvation the day that their factory, work-room or dock yard is closed. This is the point to which all the countries of western Europe have arrived, considered to be the wealthiest and most highly civilized in the world.

Their population is divided into a small minority, living in the midst of an aggressive and extreme luxury, partly attacked by a very frenzy of extravagance, and a great mass, consisting of persons who can only support life by the hardest exertions, or who in spite of all their efforts, find it impossible to attain to a normal human existence. The minority is daily growing richer, the contrast between its life and that of the millions is daily growing more decided, its importance and influence in the community is hourly increasing. When we are speaking of the unprecedented, foolish extravagance of certain millionaires and billionaires of our days, some self-conceited, would-be historian is sure to interrupt us and quote with a smile of compassion for our ignorance, the words of some musty old writer describing the extravagant goings-on in Rome under the Empire, or even in the Middle Ages. He will maintain that the disproportion between the very rich and the very poor was in former ages, far greater than at present. But it is all only a trumped-up, learned fraud. There never was a fortune in the Middle Ages like the hundred millions of a Vanderbilt, a Baron Hirsch, Rothschild, Krupp etc., as we know them today. In ancient times such an amount might have been accumulated by some favorite of a tyrant, or a satrap or pro-consul, by plundering a country or a continent, but the wealth thus amassed had no permanence. It was like the treasures in the fairy-tale. Today in his possession, tomorrow, lost. Its owner dreamed a few hours, and was then awakened by the dagger of an assassin, the persecution of his sovereign or by the brutal confiscation of his wealth. There is not a single example of the descendance of such a fortune from father to son for even three generations, or the calm and undisturbed enjoyment of it by the possessor, in the Roman Empire or in any Oriental state. And in former times, the number of these millionaires and billionaires was incomparably smaller than in these days, when, in England alone, there are from eight hundred to a thousand millionaires, and in Europe altogether,—not counting in any other continent—there are at least a hundred thousand persons with fortunes of a million and over. On the other hand, never before were there so many property-less individuals as at present, men who according to my definition above, do not know in the morning what they can get to eat during the day, nor where they can sleep at night. The slave in ancient Rome, the serf in Russia, were completely without property, as in fact they formed part of the property of their master, but their actual physical wants were supplied, they had always food and shelter. During the Middle Ages the outcasts, gypsies, robbers, strolling players and tramps of all kinds were the only persons without the pale of property holding. They could call nothing on earth their own, no table was ever set for them, the ruling-authorities even deprived them theoretically, of the right to look upon the gifts of nature as spread for them. They fought their way out of the wretchedness in which the social systems of their day sought to imprison them, by begging, robbery and poaching, and even if the gallows and the wheel were more frequently the causes of their death than old age, they had notwithstanding, a full and merry life up to the very steps of the scaffold. The modern proletariat or lowest wages-receiving class, has no precedent in history. It is the child of our times.

The modern day-laborer is more wretched than the slave of ancient times, for he is fed by no master nor anyone else, and if his position is one of more liberty than the slave, it is principally the liberty of dying of hunger. He is by no means as well off as the outlaw of the Middle Ages, for he has none of the gay independence of that freelance. He seldom rebels against society, and .has neither means nor opportunities to take by violence or treachery what is denied him by the existing conditions of life. The rich is thus richer, the poor poorer, than ever before since the beginnings of history. The same thing is true of the extravagance of the rich. We are continually being bored by the anecdotes told by grubbers in history, as to the wonderful banquets spread by Lucullus. But it remains yet to be proved that ancient Rome ever saw a feast that cost $80.000, like the ball given by a New York Croesus, of which the newspapers have been giving us accounts recently. A private individual who set before his guests dishes made of nightingales' tongues, or presented a hundred thousand sestertia to some Grecian hetera, made such a stir and commotion in Rome that all the satirists and chroniclers of those and afterdays repeated his name again and again. Nowadays no one speaks of the thousands upon thousands who pay $40.000 for a set of china, $100.000 for a race-horse or let some adventuress spend a million for them in a year. The extravagant luxury of the ancient world and of the Middle Ages, aroused attention and astonishment by its rarity. Besides it had the modesty to limit its display to a comparatively small circle. The masses saw nothing of it. Nowadays the insolent parade of the wealthy is not confined to the ball-rooms and banquet halls of their set, but flaunts along the streets. The places where their aggressive luxury is most prominently displayed are the promenades of the large cities, the theatres and concert halls, the watering places and the races. Their carriages drive along the streets splashing mud on the bare-footed, hungry crowd, their diamonds never seem to sparkle with such brilliancy as when they are dazzling the eyes of the poor. Their extravagance loves to have journalism as a spectator and delights to send descriptions of its luxury by the columns of the papers into circles which otherwise would have no opportunity to observe the life-long carnival of the rich. By these means an opportunity of comparison is given the modern wages-receiver which was wan ting to the poor man of ancient times. The lavish squandering of wealth that he witnesses around him, gives him an exact measure by which to gauge his own wretchedness, in all its extent and depth, with mathematical precision. But as relative poverty is only an evil when it is recognized as such by comparison with others, the millionaires are exceedingly unwise to flaunt their luxury in the eyes of the poor, whose misery is sharpened by the contrast. The unconcealed spectacle of their existence of idleness and enjoyment, arouses necessarily the discontent and envy of the laboring classes and this moral poison corrodes their minds far more rapidly and deeply than their material deprivations.

But these material deprivations must not be underestimated. The great masses of the poor in civilized countries maintain their bare existence under conditions worse than those of any animal in the wilderness. The dwelling place of the day-laborer in a large city of the old world, is far more filthy and unhealthy than the den of a beast of prey in the forest. It is by far less perfectly protected against the cold than the latter. His food is barely sufficient to sustain life, and death from actual starvation is of daily occurrence in the capitals of the world. The writers on political economy have invented a phrase to quiet the uneasy conscience of the rich—the "iron law of wages." According to this law the wages paid in any locality are at least what is actually necessary to support life there. In other words, the laborer is certain of earning sufficient to satisfy his actual necessities, even if he has no surplus. This would be very fine if it were only sustained by facts. If it were true, the rich man could say to himself, morning and evening, that everything is arranged for the best in this best of all possible worlds, and no one would have a right to disturb his digestion and his nightly rest by groans and curses But the misfortune is, that this famous iron law of wages is only a Jesuitical play upon words. At the best, it does not apply to those who can not procure work at all. And during the time when he has really work to do, it is impossible for the laboring man in western Europe, to earn enough so that he can have anything left over for days when he is out of work. He is thus reduced to beggary during part of the year, or to a gradual physical decline from lack of sufficient nourishment. But the iron wage-law does not apply even to the amount of daily wages earned by those actually employed. What is the minimum of income that will support an individual? Evidently it is that which will keep his system in a good condition, and allow him to develope fully and attain to the natural limit of his life. As soon as he attempts more than his system is capable of enduring, or gets less food, warmth and sleep than his system requires to remain at the summit of its type, then he falls into physiological distress. Overwork is as equally the cause of organic decline as insufficient food, but the latter is synonymous with slow starvation.

If the iron wage-law were actually what it pretends to be, then the wages-receiver would earn sufficient to bring his organism to and maintain it in that condition of development to which it is possible for it to attain, by the natural laws of its being. But experience shows us that the day-laborer finds this impossible anywhere in Europe. The optimistic political economist points with triumph to his iron wage-law, when he sees that the wages-receiver does not drop dead of hunger at the close of his day's work, but fills his stomach with potatoes, smokes his pipe, drinks his whiskey and persuades himself that he is satisfied and comfortable. But then comes the science of statistics and shows us that the average length of life of the wages-receiving class is a third and in some cases a half, less than that of the well-to-do individuals of the same nation, living under the same conditions of climate and upon the same soil. What robs the wages-receiver of the years of life to which as son of a given race and inhabitant of a given country, he is entitled? Hunger, wretchedness, want of all kinds, these slowly undermine his health and weaken his constitution. The wages he receives are also, at best, merely sufficient to protect him from pressing hunger and cold, they do not avert the gradual wasting away of his whole being, from insufficient food, clothing and rest. The statistics of the records of disease and death among the laboring classes of Europe, brand the "iron law of wages" as an infamous lie.

The portrait of the economic organization of society would not be complete if I omitted to describe along with the recklessly extravagant millionaire and the laboring man, condemned inexorably to disease and an early death, another class of beings who play in our present conditions of social life, nearly as melancholy a role as the industrial slaves of the great city. These are the cultivated men without any regular income, who have to support themselves by intellectual labor. The supply exceeds the demand in this branch of labor, to a frightful degree. The so-called liberal professions are everywhere so over-crowded that those who seek in them a livelihood, trample upon each other until the struggle for existence assumes in them the gravest and most hideous phases. Those unfortunates whose efforts are directed to obtaining a public or private situation, a position to teach, or success in art, literature, the law, medicine, civil engineering, etc., are capable of appreciating their wretchedness in a greater degree, on account of their higher intellectual development. Their intimate intercourse with those more prosperous keeps the picture of wealth constantly before them, side by side with that of their own poverty, which is thus never forgotten. Social prejudices require them to gain their livelihood in a way which without being hygienically preferable, lays far greater burdens upon their shoulders than those borne by the day-laborer. The price paid for prosperity in their career is constant humiliations, suppression of then true character and denial of their own individuality, a yoke more galling to a nature of true nobility than material want. Owing to the fact that these persona are capable of suffering more intensely, they bear with even more impatience than the wages-receiving class, the burdens imposed upon them by the internal economy of society and property holding. Those among them whose efforts have not met with success, are looked down upon by the man of wealth, who calls them failures, and affects to despise them. But these "failures" are the intrepid vanguard of the army that is besieging the proud fortress of society and that sooner or later will raze it to the ground.

CHAPTER II

Let us analyze more closely the separate elements of the picture we have just been drawing. We have seen the rich man revelling in superabundance without labor, the factory-hand, day-laborer, condemned to physical decay and the intellectual laborer trampled to death in the deadly competition. Let us turn our light upon the minority, the wealth possessing class. What are the sources of the riches of the men who compose this minority? They have either made them for themselves, or increased what they received by inheritance, or else limit their efforts to retaining; what they have inherited. I will discuss this matter of inheritance at length farther on, only remarking here that man is the only living being who carries the natural care for his offspring—one of the manifestations of the instinct for the preservation of the race—to such an extreme, that he wishes to remove the necessity of providing for themselves not only from those of the next generation until their maturity, but from his most remote posterity, during their entire lives. The increase of inherited property usually takes place without the slightest interference on the part of the owner, and is certainly not the result of his labor. The large and ancient fortunes consist mostly of real estate. The value of the land and of the buildings rises every year and the income from them increases in proportion to the growth of civilization. The products of the manufacturing industries become cheaper, provisions dearer and the dwelling places in the constantly increasing cities more cramped and expensive. Some political economists deny that provisions are growing dearer. But they can only bring sophistical arguments to support their assertion. It is true that in days of more restricted commercial intercourse, famine and starvation were more frequent, and a failure of crops in certain places was succeeded by such an extortionate price for the cereals as would be today inconceivable. The rapidity and extent of the variations in the cost of provisions in the past, has ceased, but the average price of meat and farm produce is constantly rising, and this rise is only retarded not prevented, by the short-sighted policy of skinning the enormous tracts of virgin soil in America and Australia. The day is not far distant when this piratical cultivation of the soil in the new continents must come to an end; the plough will find no more unclaimed lands to conquer. Then the cost of provisions will rise beyond measure, while the continual improvements made in machinery, and the constantly increasing utilization of the forces of nature now and yet to be discovered, will cause the price of all manufactured goods to fall in proportion. This two-fold current in the economic world, the upward tendency of the prices of provisions and the downward tendency of the prices of manufactured products, continues to increase the wealth of the land-owner and the poverty of the factory employé. The latter is obliged to produce a constantly increasing number of manufactured goods to exchange for the agricultural products necessary to sustain life; the former receives in return for his farm produce a constantly increasing number of manufactured articles. The factory-employé finds it more and more difficult to satisfy his wants, the land-owner is able to enjoy more and more of the results of the former's labor. The number of proletaires grows daily larger, toiling for the land-owner, who is thus practically their lord and master. The wealth of the inheritor of land and houses is not increased by his own efforts, but by the faulty organization of the conditions of land-ownership according to the present economy of society. According to these conditions, the land, the natural working-tool of mankind, is placed in the hands of a few, and as a consequence the lowest classes, robbed of their share of the soil, are obliged to crowd into the great cities.

New fortunes are accumulated by trade, speculation or manufactures. We will pass by the extremely rare cases in which a man with the cooperation of chance, attains to great wealth by discovering some gold and diamond mine or petroleum springs and is able to retain and work them for his exclusive benefit. At the same time, thanks to the existing ideas of property ownership, these exceptional cases have a certain theoretical value as confutations of another so-called scientific axiom of the doctrines of political economy, viz. that capital is in all cases, accumulated labor. What labor does a diamond of the size of the Koh-i-Noor represent, which some adventurer may find on the ground in South Africa and sell for a million? The economist is ready with his answer: the gem is certainly the result of labor, that is, of the labor performed by the finder in stooping and picking it up. The established science accepts this explanation with a satisfied acquiescence and proclaims the theory to be saved. A sound human intellect however, refuses to accept this would-be science, which is invented by blockheads, for blockheads, with the purpose of ornamenting and excusing in empty, flowery terms, the injustice of the present systems of political economy.

Legitimate trade, that is. the equitable exchange of the raw materials and the finished products between the producer and the consumer by means of a third person, the trader, who makes a profit on the goods he handles, giving them to the last buyer at a larger or smaller increase in the selling price over the cost, in these days rarely leads to the accumulation of great wealth. There are too many people who are satisfied if they have the wherewithall to support life, or can lay by a moderate amount, and the competition for the custom of the consumer is too great, for a tradesman to amass an especially large fortune except in isolated instances. The general tendency of the wholesale and retail trade is to suppress all unnecessary middle-men, to place the consumer in as direct intercourse with the producer as is possible, and to reduce the profits of the middle-men, to an amount only sufficient to cover their necessary expenses of handling the goods, and supply them with the necessaries of life. The merchants' profits can of course become much greater, even extortionate, if he is able to limit or suppress free competition. If any one can obtain salable goods under difficult conditions or dangers, in Central Africa, or among the wild tribes of Asia, he can sell them at a very great profit, because the number of those who are ready to venture life and health for the sake of possible wealth, is comparatively small, and he has, for a while, a free field of operations. But the undisturbed possession of such a profitable trade does not last very long, as the dangers and difficulties decrease in proportion as the country becomes better known, and the opening of other countries, formerly inaccessible to foreign trade, brings them under the laws which govern general competition. In twenty or thirty years this source of great wealth would be sealed up. Central Africa, Asia and China will be reached as easily and safely as any European or American country; the merchants will be obliged to pay as dearly there and sell to consumers as cheaply as is possible without actual loss. The trade in Congo ivory and Chinese cotton will then realize profits no more abundant than those we are accustomed to at home.

Enormous profits can also be made by a single dealer, or close combination of dealers, if they are able to control some indispensable article, to monopolize its sale, so that the purchaser can only receive it from their hands. He must resign himself to the alternative of doing without it, or paying the price charged for it by the robber band. But this proceeding does not come within the limits of legitimate trade; it is an act of violence which the laws of certain countries (France, for instance), regard and punish as a crime. It brings us to the second source of enormous fortunes, speculation.

Speculation is one of the most intolerable and revolting manifestations of disease in the economic organism. Those profound sages who maintain that everything that exists, is superexcellent, have also attempted to defend speculation, to justify it, to assert its necessity even to enthusiasm. I will immediately prove to the panegyrists what the principle is, whose cause they are espousing. The speculator plays in the economic world the role of a parasite. He produces nothing, he does not even perform the questionable service of mediator, performed by the merchant. He confines himself to taking away from the real workers, by stealth or violence, the largest part of the proceeds of their labor. The speculator is a robber who robs the producers of the articles produced by forcing them to accept inadequate compensation for their toil, and the consumers, by forcing them to buy from him at an enormous advance. The weapon with which he falls upon producers and consumers like a highwayman, is double-barrelled, and is called elevation and depression of prices, or cornering the markets. He makes use of this murderous implement in the following manner. When his intention is to plunder the producer, he begins to sell certain goods that he does not possess, at a price lower than the current market rates, promising to deliver them to the purchasers a fortnight, a month or three months later than the date of sale. The purchaser of course, buys of the speculator because he asks lower prices. The producer now has only two courses open to him. If he is rich enough to carry his goods without selling until the day arrives when the speculator is obliged to deliver those he has guaranteed to the purchaser, then the speculator will not be able to get the goods at as low prices as he had hoped, and will be obliged to buy them at the producer's price, and lose money upon them, thus being robbed instead of robbing.

But if the producer can not do this, and this is by far the most frequent case, then he is forced to sell his goods immediately at such prices as the goods will bring in the market. He must underbid the speculator, who then becomes his purchaser, for the consumer has already ordered what he wants from the speculator. Thus when the time comes for him to deliver the goods, he is able to buy them of the producer at a lower price even than the one contracted for.

The producer may have become bankrupt by the operation, but the speculator has got his pound of flesh and is happy. If his aim is to plunder the consumer then he buys up all the available goods offered of a certain kind at the producer's price. He can do this without trouble as the transaction does not cost him a single penny; he pays for his purchase, not in cash, but in promises. He need not settle his account for weeks or months, as the case may be. Thus without real possession, frequently without going to the expense of a single dollar, the speculator becomes owner of the goods, and if the consumer wishes to buy any of them he must apply to the speculator arid pay the price he demands. The speculator receives into one hand the money given him by the consumer and after abstracting a portion as large as possible, which he puts into his own pocket, he hands over the remainder with the other hand to the producer. In this way the speculator, without labor, without benefiting the community, becomes wealthy and influential. Capital extends to him the highest favor, unlimited credit. When some poor fellow of a working man wants to start in business for himself, he meets with the utmost difficulty in borrowing the small sum he requires to purchase his tools and raw material, and to support himself until the sale of his first productions. But when some idler with sufficient audacity decides to live upon the labor of others and wants to carry on some speculative buying and selling on a large scale, both producers and consumers place themselves at his disposal, without waiting even to be entreated. They say that they run no risks; the credit demanded only exists in theory. The producer does not give up his goods; he only promises to deliver them on a certain day at a certain price, of course only upon the receipt of cash. The consumer on the other hand, does not pay down the purchase price, but only agrees to pay it on the day that the goods are delivered to him. This theoretical credit is sufficient however, for the speculator to create for himself, out of nothing, the most scandalous wealth.

Every working man, every one without exception, is tributary to the speculator. All our wants are foreseen, all the necessary articles of our consumption are bought up beforehand by speculators, on credit, and sold to us as dear as possible, for cash. We can not eat a bit of bread, nor lay down to rest beneath our roof, nor invest out savings in stocks, without paying to the speculators in bread-stuffs, in land and buildings and Stock

Exchanges, their assessments. The taxes which we pay to the State are oppressive, but by no means so oppressive as those exacted from us by speculation. Certain persons have ventured to defend the Stock and Grain Exchanges as necessary and useful institutions. It is a miracle that they were not suffocated by the enormity of their assertions. What, the Exchanges of the world useful and necessary? Have they ever kept within the limits of their legitimate business? Are they ever simply the meeting place of the bona fide purchaser and the bona fide seller, where honest demand and honest supply can come together and transact their business. The simile comparing the Commercial Exchange to a poison tree, is incomplete, because it only symbolizes one phase of the transactions carried on /there, their effect upon the moral nature of the people. The Exchange is a den of robbers in which the modern successors of the robber knights of the Middle Ages, make their abode and cut the throats of all who pass that way. Like the robber knights they form a kind of aristocracy, which gets a handsome livelihood out of the people. Like the robber knights they claim the right to exact contributions from the merchants and artisans. But, more fortunate than the robber knights, they run no risk of being hung high and dry, if a stronger than they comes upon them in their high-handed course of purse-slashing.

We sometimes console ourselves with the reflection that speculators in times of panic are sure to lose at on* stroke all that they have been accumulating in the years of unchecked robbery. But this is a pleasing delusion with which the pastor's lambs try to comfort themselves, who like to see punishment follow crime as the finis. Even if a panic does force a speculator to disgorge his ill-gotten gains, it can not alter the fact that for many years perhaps, he has been living in the lap of luxury, at the expense of the laboring members of the community. He may lose his property at such a time, but no power on earth can deprive him of the champagne which has been flowing in streams for him, nor of the truffles he has eaten, the piles of gold he has gambled away on the green cloth, nor of the hours he has spent in all kinds of pleasures only possible to the rich. Besides, a panic is only disastrous to single, isolated speculators, not to speculation in general. On the contrary panics are the great harvest of speculation, the opportunities .for the slaughter of the entire saving and producing classes in a nation or in a continent, en masse. Then the few great capitals, the enormous fortunes, open their jaws and swallow not only the whole property of the investment-seeking public, but also that of the small robber capitalists, whom they usually good-naturedly allow to play around them, looking on like the lion at the mouse's gambols. Great depreciations of values are usually brought about and utilized by the financial giants. They then buy up everything that has value and a future, to sell it again when the storm has passed away and the skies are blue, at an enormous profit to the very same people who have just sold it at such ridiculous prices. They buy it up again during the next panic, at the same low rates, and play the cruel game as often as a few years of peaceful industry have refilled the emptied money drawers of the producing classes. Financial crises are simply the piston strokes with which the capitalists pump the savings of the Industrial classes into their own reservoirs.

The advocates of speculating say that the speculator plays an important and necessary role in the great drama of political economy; that his gains are the results of superior sagacity, deeper insight, prompter decision and more adventurous daring. This argument pleases me; let us seize and examine it. Therefore, because the speculator has means of information at his disposal which are inaccessible to the general public, because he has less dread of losses than the prudent and honest man, and takes advantage of all possibilities in a more underhanded way, he has a right to take away from the laboring classes the results of their labor, and allow it to accumulate for himself, while he takes his ease. This right is consequently based upon the fact that he has better weapons—his sources of information, greater courage—as he hazards only the money of others, and superior strength of judgment and intelligence. Now let us see if the poorer classes have not even better weapons—rifles and dynamite bombs, greater courage—as they are willing to risk their lives, and superior strength—of bone and sinew. If this is the case, and it is, the advocates of speculation must concede to the laboring classes the right of taking away from the speculators the results of their so-called labor. If they do not concede this right to the one class as well as to the other, then the theory upon which the justification of speculation is based, is a lie.

The third source of great wealth is manufacturing on a large scale. In this case the owner or borrower of capital plunders his employés who sell him their daily labor. The difference between the actual value of this daily labor, as expressed in the price of the articles it produces and the wages paid for it, forms the profit of the manufacturer, allowing of course, for raw material and other running expenses. In most cases this difference is out of all proportion and usuriously exorbitant compared with the wages. It is often spoken of as the reward of the manufacturer's mental exertions. But the reply can be made to this assertion that the mental labor required to manage the technical and mercantile interests of a large factory, bears no comparison to that necessary in scientific investigations or literary productions and at the highest can only be ranked with that required in a public office or the executorship of an estate. And yet the results of the mental exertions of these latter are by no means so remunerative as the annual income of the great manufacture! The profits of manufacturers can not be looked upon as mere interest on the capital employed, because no manufacturer is content to sell his goods at a price which would bring him in a net income of four to six per cent, after all the expenses and the pay for his mental exertion had been deducted. This per cent is obtained by anyone on investments without risk, even by the man of leisure. The price at which the manufacturer sells his goods is regulated on the one hand by the amount of competition with other manufacturers with which he has to contend, and on the other hand, by the larger or smaller supply of labor. His first care is to pay his employés as little as possible, his next, to sell to the purchaser as dear as possible. When the supply of laborers allows him to hire labor at the lowest prices, and the absence of competition or other circumstances, make it possible for him to sell his manufactured articles at a very high price, he does not entertain the idea of limiting his income to six or ten per cent, but he bends all his energies to making a hundred or even more per cent on the capital employed. The advocates of this plundering of labor by Capital say that the division of this net income of the factory between the capitalist and the laborer would only keep the former poor, while raising the wages of the latter so slightly as to be immaterial, amounting to merely a few pennies a day, divided among so many. A noble, a modest argument forsooth! It is possible that the wages-receiver might receive only a few pennies more a day, if he were able to retain for himself all the fruits of his daily labor. But by what right is he obliged to present his employer with even the tiniest share of his daily earnings, when the employer has already the interest on his capital and a sufficient remuneration for his problematical mental labor? Let us imagine for a moment that every inhabitant of the German Empire were forced by law to pay a penny every year to some Smith or Meyer, not in return for any services performed, nor in gratitude for any benefit he might have rendered to the community, but as a simple present. The favored individual would thus be ensured a yearly income of about a hundred thousand dollars; but none of the contributors would feel the loss of their penny. One penny! that is such a small amount that it is not worth the trouble of speaking about it. And yet such a law would elicit from the entire nation a cry of indignation, and every citizen would revolt against its arbitrary injustice. But the economical law which obliges the poorest part of the nation, the factory employés, to present to this same Smith or Meyer, a contribution of not one cent, but of ten to fifteen dollars in the lowest cases, and often of from one to one hundred dollars, in the course of the year,—this law seems quite a matter of course to those who happen to be exempt from its jurisdiction. The injustice is about the same in both cases. But the world at large appreciates but slightly or not at all, the injustice perpetrated upon the proletaire, because it has continued for so many centuries, because mankind has become accustomed to it by habit, and also because it has not yet assumed that paradoxical form in which a truth must reveal itself before it can force an entrance into unreceptive minds.

We have thus seen that great wealth in almost all cases, is due to the appropriation of the results of others' labor, not one's own. By their own labor alone, men are only able to support life from day to day, occasionally to lay by sufficient for times of sickness and old age, rarely to attain to regular prosperity. Some physicians, lawyers, authors, painters and other artists, have been able to turn their personal efforts to such advantage as to obtain annual incomes of hundreds of thousands of dollars, and thus accumulate fortunes of millions, without resorting to speculation or illegitimate profits. But such persons are rare, numbering probably but two hundred or even one hundred, living at one time throughout the civilized world. And even their wealth, examined closer, has something of a parasitic character, with the sole exception of that amassed by the author. In his case, if he becomes a millionaire, it is owing to the fact that he has written a book of which one or two millions copies have been sold, showing that his wealth is the direct remuneration of his intellectual labor, paid him voluntarily and willingly by mankind in general. But when an artist sells a painting for a hundred thousand dollars, a surgeon performs an operation for which he receives $10,000, a lawyer receives the same sum as his retaining fee, or a prima donna is paid $5,000 for one evening's performance, these amounts do not represent the price paid by the mass of people as the legitimate and voluntarily proffered reward for individual exertion. They are the mathematical demonstration of the fact that a small number of millionaires are living in the civilized world, with no means of judging of the real value of any work, because their riches are not the result of their own labor; they satisfy every one of their whims without regard to its cost, and fight among themselves for the possession of certain things, a painting for instance, or the song of a certain prima donna, the service of this physician or lawyer and of none other—willing to pay any price to satisfy their caprice. Aside from the rare instances of success in the pursuit of the liberal professions above described, the rule is without exception that a great fortune necessarily owes its origin and growth to the plundering of one's fellow-men. When the real estate inherited by a certain man increases in value, it is not the result of his own exertions but of the fact that the number of working-men torn from the land and soil is constantly increasing, that all forms of industry are growing in extent, that the cities are becoming more and more populous, that the labor of civilized society is being confined more and more to manufacturing industries, thus causing the price of provisions to risk in the same proportion as the price of manufactured articles is falling—in short, because other men are working, not because the landed proprietor exerts himself. When the speculator amasses millions it is by the abuse of a superior strength, either of information, sagacity or of combination, with which he deprives the laboring and classes of their property, as the brigand relieves the wayfarer of his purse, first knocking him down with his club. When the manufacturer becomes a Crœsus, it is by systematic plundering of his workmen, who receive for their exertions in his behalf, nothing more than food and shelter, like so many domestic animals, and both the very scantiest possible. The entire results of their labors flow into the money bags of their master.

It is in this sense that we must construe Proudhon's exaggerated and therefore false assertion that property is theft. We can only make it seem true by placing ourselves upon the sophistical standpoint that everything that exists is created for itself, and from the fact of its existence, deduces the right to belong to itself. According to this idea we are stealing when we pick a blade of grass, when we inhale the air, or catch a fish. The swallow is stealing when it eats a fly, the worm when it eats its way into the heart of the tree; all nature is peopled by arch thieves, everything that has life is constantly stealing, taking materials that do not belong to it, eating, inhaling and making them part of its organism in any and every way. The only instance of absolute freedom from stealing on this mundane sphere, according to this view, would be a bar of platinum, which takes nothing from other objects, not even oxygen from the air to form rust on its surface. No, property is not theft when it arises from trade, that is, from the exchange of a certain measure or labor for a corresponding measure of goods. But an enormous capital, that is the accumulation of vast amounts of property in the hands of one man, such as no individual would be able to amass as the results of his own labor, even at its very highest valuation, such fortunes are due to the robbery of the laboring classes.

This band of robbers, for whom the whole community toils, is powerfully organized. It has, in the first place, the making and administration of the laws in its own hands, as it has had for centuries. At every new law promulgated, we might exclaim with Molière: "Vous êtes orfèvre, Monsieur Josse!" "You are a capitalist, Mr. Lawmaker, or at least, you hope to become such, and declare everything to be a crime that might hinder you in the pursuit, enjoyment and possession of your capital." Everything that a man can get hold of in any way except by open, hand to hand violence is and remains his own. And even when the genealogy of a property can be traced to literal robbery or theft (such as conquest, seizure of church property or political confiscation of others' goods) this crime becomes an unimpeachable title to possession, if the owner has been able to hold the property for a certain number of years. The state law that calls out the police, is not sufficient for the millionaire. He makes superstition his ally and gets from Religion an extra padlock for his money chest, by smuggling into the catechism a sentence which asserts that property is sacred, and envy and covetousness for our neighbor's property, a sin to be punished with the fires of hell. He distorts even the laws of morality and furthers his selfish aims by inculcating upon the vast majority of the people, toiling for him, that labor is virtue, and that man was only created to labor as much as possible. How comes it that the best and truest intellects have believed in the reality of this fiction for thousands of years? Labor a virtue? According to what law of nature? No living being in the whole organic world works for the pleasure of working, but only for the purpose of self and race preservation, and only so much as is necessary for this twofold purpose. People say that organs only remain sound and develope when exercised, and that they wither when they lie idle. The advocates of this system of capitalists' morality who have found this argument in physiology, do not mention the fact that organs are much more rapidly destroyed by over work than by no work. Rest, comfortable leisure, is infinitely more natural, pleasant and desirable for man as well as for all other animals, than work and exertion. The latter is only a painful necessity, required for the preservation of life. The inventor of the story of the Garden of Eden in the Bible, showed that he appreciated this fact with honest naivetè, by placing his first human beings in a paradise where they could live without any necessity for exertion, and labor, the sweat of man's brow, was the terrible punishment for their disobedience. Natural, zoological morality proclaims that rest is the highest reward of labor, and that only so much work is desirable and commendable as is indispensable to prolong life. But the robber band do not accept this idea of the case. Their interests demand that the masses should work more than is necessary for them to support life and should produce more than is required for their own consumption so that their masters can take possession of this overproduction for their own use. Consequently they have suppressed the morality of nature and invented another, which they set their philosophers to tabulating, their parsons to praising and their poets to singing. According to their system, idleness is the beginning of all crimes and labor a virtue, the most excellent of all virtues.

The robber band is however, constantly contradicting itself with the most short-sighted policy. The robbers carefully avoid even the pretense of submitting to their own code of morality, and thus betray the small amount of respect they have for it in reality. Idleness is only a crime in the poor man. In the rich man it is an attribute of a higher type of humanity, the token of his exalted rank. And labor, which his double-faced morality asserts to be a virtue for the poor man, is from his point of view, a disgrace and a sign of social inferiority. The millionaire pats the laboring man on the shoulder, but excludes him from his social intercourse. Society which has accepted and adopted the morality and views of the band of capitalists, glorifies labor in its most choice terms, but at the same time, assigns the laborer to the lowest rank. Society kisses the gloved hand and spits on the horny hand of the son of toil. It looks upon the millionaire as a demi-god, upon the day laborer as an outcast. Why? For two reasons. Firstly, because the prejudices and ideas imbibed in the Middle Ages have been perpetuated to the present time, and secondly because manual labor in our civilization is synonymous with lack of education.

During the Middle Ages idleness was the prerogative of the nobility, that is, of the higher race of conquerors, labor, the compulsory performance of tasks by the people, that is, by the lower race of conquered and subjugated beings. Consequently the man that labored betrayed the fact that he was a son of the race which had given proof on the field of battle that it had less virile manhood and strength, while the lord, the man of leisure, receiving his means of livelihood from his estate or by conquest, looked down upon the working-man with the contempt of a white man for a Bushman or Papuan, which is founded on the appreciation of his anthropological superiority. Today leisure and labor have ceased to be tokens of race. The millionaires are no longer the descendants of the conquering tribe, the proletaires are no longer the sons of the subjugated people. But in this as in so many other cases, the historical prejudice has survived the conditions under which it originated. The rich man still considers his employé, who works for him and supplies him with his luxury, merely as a kind of domestic animal, as the nobleman centuries ago, looked upon his vassal, neither of them recognizing in him a complete human being, their equal in any way.

Manual labor is also synonymous with a lack of education in our civilization. In fact the whole organization of society renders cultivation inaccessible to those without means. The son of a poor man can hardly go to the public school, much less to high school and college, being obliged to earn money as soon as any one can be found to employ his services. We can admire in this case another example of the conformity to the end in view of the present conditions of State and society. The expensive institutions of learning are supported by the State, that is, by the tax-payers, working-men as well as millionaires, but they only benefit those who at least possess sufficient income to live till their eighteenth or twenty third year without supporting themselves. The factory employé who can not let his own son enjoy the benefits of a higher education, because he is too poor to afford it, is yet constrained to have the son of the rich man study at his expense, when he pays the taxes which are applied to the maintenance of the intermediate and high schools. The English and Americans are still consistent up to a certain point. Their higher educational institutions, even if they are not accessible to rich and poor alike, are yet no burden upon the community, because they are either maintained by private enterprise or by endowments. But on the continent of Europe, in conformity to the prevailing policy of plundering the people for the purpose of benefiting a small minority, the institutions for higher education are supported from the Budget, that is, from the amount of taxes paid to the State by the nation, although their benefits are only enjoyed by a few, by no means even one per cent of the total population. And who are the chosen few for whom the State supports colleges and technical schools, requiring appropriations amounting to millions;* Are they the most capable young men of their generation? Does the State take pains to admit to their lecture rooms only those persons in whose minds the instruction imparted by the professors will surely bring forth fruit? Does it refuse to allow blockheads to usurp the place and opportunities for learning intended for receptive and creative intelligent faculties? No. The State offers these higher branches of learning not to all but to a few, and these few are not chosen for their special intellectual endowments and capacity for assimilating this higher culture, but for their financial conditions. The most dense-headed simpleton can go through college and absorb the mental food spread before him by the professors, without its ever proving of the slightest benefit to the community, if he has money enough to support himself and pay his tuition fees. The most talented young man on the contrary, is excluded from the halls of learning because he lacks these necessary means—a matter of real detriment to the community which may lose by it some Goethe, Kant or Bacon.

Thus the pernicious conditions of society and political economy in our civilization, form a circulus vitiosus from which there is no escape; the laboring man is looked down upon because he has no cultivation; he can not educate himself because education and cultivation cost money, which he has not got. The rich retain for themselves to the exclusion of the poor, not only all the material enjoyments of life, but the intellectual as well. The noblest blessings that civilization has to offer us, culture, poetry and art, are, as a fact, only free to the rich, and cultivation in its most comprehensive sense, is the most important and most exclusive of all their privileges. When some young man of the lower classes succeeds in mastering the higher branches of education by means of almost superhuman exertions, by deprivations and humiliations, begging if need be, and receives a diploma in the university, he never returns to the position of his father. Free from the prejudices and ideas of society, which consider a man who obtains his livelihood by manual labor as a being of the lowest social status, he could take up the trade of his father and show the world one example of a day-laborer standing upon the same scale of culture as the ink-flourishing public functionary and the recluse professor. But he does not do this, he strengthens these prejudices by enrolling himself as a member of the privileged class, by affecting to look upon manual labor as degrading, and by getting his support, like the other members of the upper classes, from the laboring people. There are many kinds of manual labor by which a skilled mechanic or artisan, can earn without extra effort, a good living while preserving his independence; on the other hand, nine tenths of the situations in the business houses, railroads, and in the civil service, only pay very limited salaries. And yet the college graduate prefers one of the latter positions by far, even with its accompanying office slavery, to the better income with liberty. As a government employé he belongs to the privileged class in society, to the exclusive brotherhood of cultured Philistinism, but as a working-man, he would stand outside of the castes with whom society affiliates, and be looked upon as a barbarian who did not breath the same mental atmosphere as the cultivated set. These circumstances would all be changed if the college graduate would take his place at the lathe and the man with the leather apron be reading Horace at his. nooning, and the blacksmith or shoemaker, with their diplomas in their pockets, after the day's work is finished with the anvil and last, sit around an esthetic five o'clock tea table and discourse as learnedly as some young lawyer or clerk in chancery. For honest labor is honorable and dignified, whether it is applied to making overcoats or planning the construction of railroads, and their mental culture being equal, the civil engineer has no more claims to respect and consideration than the tailor. But the college graduate does nothing to bring about such a condition of affairs. He prefers to starve in his shabby-genteel overcoat rather than to live in comparative plenty, wearing a leather apron. This is the cause of one of the most threatening phases of the social problem: the over-supply of men in the liberal professions.

The college graduate thinks himself of too much account to descend into and be lost in the lowest class of society, by voluntarily assuming the trade of a manual-laborer, and according to the ideas prevalent in society he is correct. He demands of the world that he be supported as a master, not support himself, like a slave. But the world has only a limited demand for the kind of work which the college-bred man considers suitable for him. Hence, in the older civilized countries, at least one half of the graduates are condemned to spend their lives in hoping and envying, obtaining none of life's blessings, fighting hard for the small amount of daily bread they require, and often going hungry, standing beside the overloaded, groaning table of the upper ten thousand, while suffering the pangs of semi-starvation. Certain friends of humanity, of that stamp who consider wars and pestilences as blessings for the human race, because they leave more room and better conditions of existence for those remaining alive, these people express their convictions that cultivation is an injury to mankind, that the increase in the number of intermediate and high schools, is an attempt to destroy the happiness of the masses, because m them more discontented professional failures future barricade fighters and dynamiters are being raised and let loose upon the community. As things are now these reasoners are in the right. As long as the college-bred young man considers himself disgraced by manual labor because the laborer is despised, as long as he sees in his diploma an instrument by which to compel society to rally to his support and as long as he considers himself entitled by his education to the parasitic life of the wealthy classes—as long as these conditions endure, his education will bring him far more unhappiness, in five cases out of ten, than he would ever experience if he were without it and leading the life of a handicraft man or even of a day-laborer.

This can only be remedied by giving back to education its natural role. It must be its own object. We must learn to consider that a cultivated mind is in itself, a sufficient reward for the efforts made to get the cultivation, that we have no right to expect any other reward for these efforts, and that its possession does not relieve us in any way from the duty of productive labor. A cultivated mind has a fuller and richer consciousness of its Ego it grasps better the phenomena of the world and of life, it can appreciate and enjoy the beauties of art and of literature, and its existence gives its possessor a far more liberal and intensive life in every respect than that led by the ignorant. We are ungrateful if, in addition to these priceless blessings for the inner life, we demand of education that it should also provide us with our daily bread: this should be the task of our hands. But if on one hand, the man of culture ought not to despise the immediate production of articles for the market, society on the other hand, should make education accessible to all those capable of receiving and profiting by it. Compulsory school attendance is only a weak beginning. How can poor men afford to send their children to school until they are ten or twelve years old, when they are unable to feed and clothe them during that time, and the little ones must labor for their own support. And is it justifiable, is it consistent, for the State to say: "You must learn to read and write; thus far shalt thou go and no farther?" Why does compulsory school attendance cease at the elementary grades? Why does it not extend to the higher branches? Ignorance is either an infirmity in the individual and consequently in the community, or else it is not. If it is no infirmity, why are the children compelled to attend the primary and elementary schools? If it is, why is it not cured completely by a complete and rounded education? Is not knowledge of the laws of nature as valuable as the multiplication table? The coming voters, in whose hands lie the destinies of their native land, do not they need any acquaintance with history, politics and national economy? Can they get the full benefit of the art of reading which they have mastered, if they are not instructed in nor even introduced to the masterpieces of prose and poetry in their national literature? The intermediate schools provide for this, at least. Why then is not attendance upon the intermediate schools made compulsory? The obstacle is a material one. The poor man who has already experienced great difficulty in supporting his child until he graduates from the primary school, would find it utterly impossible to carry the burden of his maintenance until he had reached an advanced age, until his eighteenth or twentieth year. He is compelled by sheer necessity to convert the laboring power of his child into money, at the earliest possible moment. In order to have the benefits of the intermediate schools shared by as many pupils as attend the primary schools, the labor of the scholars should be organized and utilized, as is the case in some educational institutions in the United States, where the pupils carry on a farm or work at some manual trade, in connection with their studies, with sufficient success and pecuniary returns, aided by outside benevolent contributions to a certain extent, to support themselves during their school life. A far better and more consistent plan would be for the community to supply not only instruction, but the entire material support of the scholars during their years of study. "That would be pure Communism!" exclaims some obstinate adherent of that organized egotism which we call the existing science of political economy.

I might flatter him by disclaiming the horrid word and saying: No, that would not be Communism, but the solidarity of the community. But I disdain to play hide-and-seek with thought, and thus I say frankly: yes, it would be a bit of Communism. But are we not living in A complete state of Communism? Is it not Communism for the State to provide compulsory education for the whole generation of children from their sixth to their twelfth year? Is not the mental food thus provided for them, one kind of food? Does it not cost money? Is it not the community which supplies this money? And the standing army? Is not this also founded upon pure Communism? Does not the community support in this way a whole generation of young men, between their twentieth and twenty-third year, and not with mental food alone, but with actual food and clothing, house and home? Why should it be more difficult or more unreasonable for the State to support a million children during their entire school life, as far as the university, than to support half million young men during their years of military service? The expense? It would be no greater than the expense of keeping up the army. And the maintenance and development of an army is of no greater importance to the safety and prosperity of the nation than the more complete education of the generation growing up around us. And besides: why can not the two aims be combined? Why can not the State feed and clothe the entire male generation until the seventeenth or eighteenth year, as it now feeds and clothes the regular army, and during this time, in connection with the primary and intermediate schooling given to them, let them be receiving their military instruction? The national labor would gain vastly by the substitution of the less costly arms of the scholar soldiers for those of the strong and trained young men of twenty to twenty three, of whose valuable labor the community is now deprived. The actual gain in this way to the nation would represent an amount of money sufficient to cover the entire extra expense of the scholar army over the present army, whose capability for labor is condemned to three years of unproductiveness, at the very blossoming time of its development.

Such a system to be complete, must be founded upon a certain other condition. Not every mind is capable of receiving and assimilating the higher and highest branches of learning. If the State is to take charge of the whole population of scholars throughout the country and thus make education possible to all, even to the son of the poorest man, then it must take care that its benefits are not wasted upon those who are unworthy or incapable of profiting by them. At the close of each school year a strict and exhaustive examination of the scholars should take place, and those only be allowed to enter the grade above, who were able to sustain the examination. In this way the talentless scholar would drop out of school after having acquired the elementary branches, which much of a mental load as he is capable of bearing; the mediocre intelligence would leave school after having acquired a part or the whole of the intermediate branch, while only the pupils possessing real talent would work their way into the highest educational institutes, the scientific, technical and art academies. By this system liberal education would become the property of the entire people, instead of being as it is now, a privilege only enjoyed by the wealthy classes. Manual labor would be no longer synonymous with lack of cultivation, and the educated young man would incur no disgrace if he earned his livelihood by the direct production of articles for the market. The overcrowding of the liberal professions by presuming and unauthorized mediocrities would be prevented. Genuine talent that had been obliged to display and prove its authenticity and its claim to the title in a dozen competitive examinations of constantly increasing severity, would find in its diploma, the absolute guarantee of an honorable livelihood; the problematic existences would disappear and shabby gentility cease to exist. This system would thus be found a complete cure for one of the most dangerous wounds in the body of society.

Our picture of the political economy of our civilization in the preceding pages, included the privileged class, the men of wealth and leisure, who live on the labor of others, the group of college-bred young men who consider that their possession of a diploma entitles them to live the life of a parasite on the working classes, the same as the millionaire's wealth entitles him, and the proletaires, the lowest class in society, torn from the soil intended by nature to support man, without property of any kind, toiling for a mere subsistence. What a tragic figure in the midst of our civilisation! What a pregnant criticism of the world's progress, this factory employé! The lines are often quoted in which La Bruyère describes the peasant vassal of his day: "a kind of gloomy, timid animal, emaciated, living in dens: eating grass on all fours, covered with rags, fleeing affrighted at the approach of other men, and yet bearing the semblance of a human being, and yet being a man." This description will also apply to the day-laborer of Europe.

Miserably fed, principally on potatoes and the refuse of the meat shops in the shape of sausages, poisoned with bad liquors, which give him the deceptive sensation of a satisfied appetite and renewed strength, badly dressed, in blouse and overalls which proclaim him from afar as the poor man, the degraded social being, condemned to physical uncleanliness by his lack of money, he hides his wretchedness in the darkest, filthiest corners of the great cities. He not only has no share in the finer provisions that the earth brings forth, but he is also partially or totally deprived of light and air which one would suppose were at the disposal of every living being in unlimited quantities. His insufficient nourishment and the excessive demands upon his laboring forces, exhaust his vital energies to such an extent that his children are predisposed to rachitis and he himself, succumbs to an early death, frequently preceded by some chronic disease. His unhealthy dwelling place fastens upon him and his offspring the curses of scrofula and consumption. He is a kind of forlorn post which every disease tries in turn to master. He is worse off than the slave of ancient times, oppressed the same, dependent in the same way upon master and overseer, he yet gets nothing in return for the loss of his freedom, not even the food and shelter given to a domestic animal. Another point in which his wretchedness is more acute than that of the ancient bond-slave, is the fact that he is conscious of it and also of his dignity and natural rights as a man. He is even worse off than the savage wandering through the primeval forests of America or camping on the grassy plains of Australia, for, like him, dependent solely upon himself, like him, living from hand to mouth, day by day, and suffering the pangs of hunger if he lays idle for a few hours, he is, unlike him, deprived of that keen delight which is produced by the complete expansion of all the physical and mental forces in the struggle to overcome natural obstacles, animals and men. He is moreover obliged to pay over a considerable share of his earnings, which are so far from being sufficient for his support, to the community, in exchange for chains and blows. Civilization, which promised him liberty and prosperity, has not only refused to keep its promise, but excludes him directly from its highest blessings. Modern sanitary science which has made the home of the rich so comfortable and healthy, has not paid any attention to his lurking place. He is far more uncomfortable in the fourth class coach when travelling by rail than when he used to trudge along on foot or ride behind some broken-down horse in his rude cart. He never hears or knows anything of the triumphs of scientific investigation. The production of the creative arts, the poetical master-works of his native tongue are sealed books to him, because he has never been trained to comprehend them. Even the labor-saving mechanical appliances which ought to prove such a blessing to him, have rather increased than diminished his slavery. It is certainly a great forward stride in the progress and happiness of mankind that the forces of nature can now be harnessed and employed in the performance of all brute labor. What distinguishes man above all other living beings is not his muscular system, but his brain. As a source of strength he is inferior to the mule and the ox, and if mechanical labor is all that is required of him, he is degraded to be a mere beast of burden. But machinery has not proved as yet the savior, the liberator and the ally of the workman as was first hoped, but on the contrary, has made him its slave. Now as much as ever before, does his value in the industrial arts depend directly upon his muscular strength, and he has thus become the weak, imperfect and abject competitor of machinery. Deprived of his share of the soil, he is not able to supply his wants by raising the products of nature; submission to the inevitable is his only recourse. He only becomes aware of his fellowship with mankind by the duties laid upon him, for which he receives no privileges in return. When he is not able to exchange his labor for money, or when disease or old age put an end to his work temporarily or permanently, the community looks after him, indeed. It gives him alms if he takes to begging, it lays him on the cot in the hospital if he has a fever, it puts him—sometimes—in a poor-house, if he is too old and feeble for anything else; but how impatiently, how grudgingly, does it fulfill these duties! It offers its unwelcome guest more humiliations than mouthfuls. While it is satisfying his hunger and covering his nakedness, it is declaring that it is a disgrace to accept these benefits from its hands, and affects the most profound contempt for the unfortunates who are suing for its bounty. The laboring classes find it impossible to lay by anything for days of no work or of sickness and old age. How can they have a surplus when even the necessaries of life are lacking? They can not think of demanding wages above what they need to satisfy their most pressing wants, because the number of these disinherited beings is too large and is constantly increasing, there are sure to be plenty who would accept their situations at any wages that would keep them from dying at once of starvation.

These circumstances are utterly beyond the control of the laboring man. He may toil with the utmost diligence, with the greatest exertion of his vital energies, he can never earn more than is sufficient to supply his most immediate wants—aside from the fact that the lowest wages now paid represent the expenditure of all the workman's energies. On the contrary: the more he works, the more intolerable does his position become. This sounds paradoxical, but it is nevertheless true. The more that the operative produces, the lower goes the selling price of his productions, while his wages remain the same if they do not become less. Thus he spoils his own market by straining every nerve, and depreciates the value of his own labor. This phenomenon would not occur if the production of the great manufacturing industries was regulated by the demand. Then over-production would never occur, the price of the articles would never be depressed by an over-supply, and the producing laboring man would be paid higher wages for an increased amount of work. But Capital perverts this natural operation of the forces of political economy. A man builds a factory and commences the manufacture of goods, not because he has become convinced that a demand hitherto unsatisfied exists for the goods he is to produce, but because he has capital, for which he is seeking a profitable investment, and also because he has some neighbor who has accumulated wealth with his factory. Thus individual whims or want of judgment, instead of the laws of political economy, decide the investment of capital. The market is thus flooded with an over-supply of certain manufactured goods because some man has been following a false trail in his mad chase after the Almighty Dollar. The mistake brings its own punishment, it is true. The manufacturer offers his goods at lower and lower prices, until they no longer pay the expenses of production, and then he is financially wrecked. All the other manufacturers of that same article go down with him, and that branch of production is involved in a national or world-wide financial crisis. But the real victim is the factory employé. As the price of the manufactured article sinks lower and lower, his wages are decreased in proportion until the manufacturer has exhausted his capital. And when the unequal battle between supply and demand ends in the victory of the former and production ceases, then he is left entirely without bread, for a longer or shorter time as the case may be. These are the roles played by the manufacturer and the operative in the great manufacturing industries. The latter makes it possible for the former to accumulate a great capital. This capital seeks profits and believes they can be found in the opening of additional factories. This leads to over-production and increased competition, with their train of depression of prices and reduction of wages, closing with the crisis which deprives the operative of the opportunity of earning anything. Thus the industrial slave makes his master rich, while his own daily bread is reduced in quantity day by day and finally taken away from him entirely. Can there be a more beautiful illustration of the way in which the existing conditions of the economic world conform to truth, justice and propriety!

CHAPTER III.

The first question which arises in our minds as we look upon this picture of the financial and social conditions of life, is: must they necessarily remain as they are? Are we confronting the operations of the able laws of nature, or the consequences of man's folly and imbecility? Why does a small minority revel in the enjoyment of every good, in whose production it takes no part? Why is a certain class of human beings, consisting of millions, precondemned to hunger and wretchedness? This is the most important point of the problem that is to be solved. The question is: do the poor starve because the earth does not produce food in sufficient quantities for them to have their share, or because they can not obtain possession of what is produced in plenty? We can exclude the latter alternative from our discussion. If provisions were produced in ample abundance with a sufficiency for all, then the share which would fall to the poor man and which he can not afford to buy, would be left over, Experience proves that nothing of the kind takes place. As each year comes around, the entire harvest of bread-stuffs and other food products, is used up by the time the new harvest is gathered in. The annual supply of provisions is exhausted when the new supply pours into the markets, and yet not every individual of the whole human race has been able to eat his fill every day in the year; no bread-stuffs are thrown away from over-supply and meat never rots for lack of purchasers. To be sure the rich waste more goods than they actually require to satisfy the regular requirements of the body, but amongst these goods the most material, provisions, are in the smallest proportion to the rest. The millionaire squanders the results of man's labor to gratify his whims, his love of luxury or his vanity. He throws aside clothing which is far from being no longer serviceable, He builds houses of unnecessary size and fills them with superfluous furniture. He takes men away from useful production and maintains them in criminal idleness as lackeys and companions, or in semi-occupation as coachmen, body servants, etc. But in regard to provisions, he consumes at the utmost hardly more than four times what he actually requires to satisfy his organic wants, even making allowance for the most wasteful housekeeping. Let us assume that there are a million of such extravagant beings in the civilized world; with their families we can estimate the number at five millions. These five millions would consume provisions sufficient for twenty millions, so that in addition to their own natural share they use up that of fifteen million other human beings. This would only explain the fact that fifteen millions are entirely deprived of their share of food, or that thirty millions merely receive one half of what they are naturally entitled to. But the number of those human beings in Europe alone, who suffer from hunger and want, can be estimated with certainty at twice that number, that is, sixty millions. Consequently we must accept the other alternative and decide that the earth does not produce sufficient food for all, and hence that a part of the human race is condemned without mercy to absolute, physiological want.

Is this the result of natural causes? Does the earth produce no more because it is incapable of producing more? No. It does not give food, because food is not asked of it. When the science of economy, created and upheld by Capital, was confronted by the problem of the disproportion between the hungry multitudes and the amount of food products destined to satisfy their hunger, it did not torment its thinking faculties very long, but soon came across an honest fellow named Malthus who proclaimed without prejudice or partiality: "The time has come when the earth is no longer able to support her children. Therefore we must diminish their number." And he preached prudence in marrying and temperance after marriage—but only for the poor, A trifle more and he would have advocated the castration of every individual born without a regular income, and the reorganization of humanity upon the pattern of the societies of ants and bees which have but a few individuals possessing the power of propagating their species, while the majority is composed of sexless individuals who have only the right to labor for those more completely developed. Such a condition of affairs could not fail to complete the happiness of the millionaires. It never entered the heads of the pious Malthus and his disciples, to state their principle in a reversed form: "The provisions produced by the earth are not sufficient to support her children. Therefore we must increase the amount of provisions," and yet it seems as if this would be the most natural remedy for the economic distress. There surely can not be any man in existence, in possession of his reasoning faculties, who would dare to assert that it is impossible to increase the amount of agricultural products. If there does exist such a fool, he can easily be silenced by a few figures. Europe supports 310 millions of inhabitants upon an area of 9.710.340 square kilometers; that is, it supports them aided by the contributions of provisions it receives from India, southern Africa, Algeria, North America and Australia. Enormous quantities of grain and meat are imported from these countries into Europe, which sends them nothing in return, except perhaps, wines. And yet with all this stream of food flowing into the country a considerable portion of the population suffers from actual want. Europe as a whole, thus confesses its incapability of supporting 32 human beings on one square kilometer. But Belgium supports 5.536.000 inhabitants on an area of 29.455 kilometers, consequently in this country one kilometer is amply sufficient to support 200 human beings, a number six times as large as that which we have found to be the average for Europe as a whole. If the soil throughout the whole of Europe were cultivated like that of Belgium, it could support a population of 1950 millions, much more completely and abundantly than the 316 millions it now supports so poorly. Or if the number of the population remained the same, each man would have six times as much food as he could consume. But we are reminded that Belgium imports provisions also, showing that its agricultural products are not sufficient to feed the nation. Very well, let us assume that Belgium buys one quarter of the provisions it requires in foreign lands. Even proceeding upon this assumption we find that it supports 150 inhabitants on each square kilometer, which figure applied to Europe gives us a population of 1458 millions which it could support, more than all mankind now numbers. Let us take another example. China, without its dependencies, has an area of

4.024.890 square kilometers, upon which are dwelling 405 millions of human beings. 1 The square kilometer supports 100 people and supports them completely, for China, far from importing provisions, exports large quantities of rice, preserves, tea, etc. According to the unanimous testimony of all travellers in China, hunger and want are only experienced there in years when the crops fail to come to maturity. And this famine is only the result of the undeveloped means of transportation, not of a deficit in the agricultural products of the whole Empire. Thus we see that if the soil of Europe were tilled and managed like that of China, it could support 1000 millions of human beings instead of its 316 millions who are so poorly fed that they are emigrating annually by hundreds of thousands to other parts of the world.

Why is not more exacted of the soil when experience shows that it responds so readily to all demands made upon it? Why does not mankind make the effort to raise agricultural products sufficient for every human being to have enough and to spare? Why? Owing to one single reason: the accumulation of capital has led to a one-sided and unnatural development of our civilization. Civilization is crowding towards manufactures and trade all the time, turning its back upon the production of food. Physiocracy which teaches us that the true wealth of a country lies solely in its agricultural products, has been held up to ridicule during the last hundred years, by the official science of political economy, which has condescended so far as to be the court jester of the present arrangement of the economic world, founded upon egotism and Capital.

The son of the soil forsakes his plough, the freedom of the country and nature and the pure, abundant sunshine and air, to force his way into that fatal prison, the factory, and take up his abode in some pestilential tenement house in the big city, in obedience to a kind of suicidal instinct. The same instinct seems to impel the human race as a whole, to abandon the food-producing soil and cast themselves into the slough of manufacturing industry where they suffocate and starve The whole genius of mankind, all its powers of invention, contrivance and investigation, all its enquiry and experiments, are applied exclusively to manufactures. We see the results: the machines grow more and more wonderful, the systems of labor more and more perfect, the production of goods more and more prolific. But hardly one inventive genius in a hundred busies himself with the production of food. If only one half as much study and ingenuity were applied to this production as to the industrial arts, physiological want would not only cease to exist on earth, but would become absolutely inconceivable. But this branch of human industry, the most important of all, is the very one that is neglected to such a degree that we wring our hands in despair. In the domain of manufactures we are highly civilized beings, but in regard to the cultivation of the soil, we are still in a barbarism as dark as midnight. We congratulate ourselves upon our marvelous ingenuity in employing and rendering valuable by means of our manufactures, the refuse and waste formerly considered absolutely worthless. But at the same time, we are allowing at least one half of the refuse from food-products, the contents of the city sewers, to escape us, without being utilized, and be emptied into the rivers, to pollute them. The sea, their final destination, does not return in its fishes and pearls a thousandth part of the value of what we pour into it. This waste of millions of tons of the most valuable waste products is positively atrocious and yet it is comical when we see the anxiety and care with which the tiniest drop of sulphuric acid is saved and utilized in the chemical laboratories, and the tearing haste with which an inventor secures a patent when he has succeeded in perfecting a process by which the refuse from some manufacture can be turned to a profitable account. We boast of having harnessed the powers of nature and yet we allow millions of acres of land to remain barren, although we know theoretically that there is not a single district that must of necessity remain a desert. We know that every kind of soil, even if it consists of iron shoe nails or crushed stones, can be made productive by heat and water, whose application is not beyond human power except—perhaps—at the poles. We point with pride to our coal and copper mines which are tunneled deep into the earth and under the ocean, and yet we are not ashamed of the bare mountain sides above them, from which man, the same being who has burrowed into their depths, is unable to produce anything. We can control the lightning from the skies and yet are not able to procure more than an atom of the inexhaustible treasures of food that are concealed in the oceans which deprive us of three fourths of the entire globe. How can we explain the fact that in a period which gives birth to such mechanical marvels as our labor-saving appliances and the more delicate tools and instruments capable of such astonishingly minute and accurate work, we allow swamps, rivers without fish, uncultivated tracts and waste land, to exist in the midst of Europe? How can it be that the generation after Gauss is so weak in its mathematical faculties, that it does not reckon upon its fingers how much more expensive it is to supply the albumenous food needed by the body, by meat from cattle, which require so much productive land to be left waste for their pasturage, instead of by fish, with which the sea is teeming, while it can be used in no other way, or by poultry, which do not require large meadows to roam over, and can be abundantly fed from the refuse of the kitchen?

However I will not proceed any further into details. The fact seems to me sufficiently demonstrated that the cultivation of the soil is the step-child of our civilization. It hardly takes one forward stride where manufactures take a hundred. The only progress realized in the production of food for mankind during several centuries, is the introduction of the potato into

Europe, which makes it possible for the operative, the proletaire, to imagine that his hunger is satisfied, when at the same time his body is slowly starving to death for want of proper nutriment, while it enables the capitalist to screw down the wages of his employés to the lowest possible point. Fruit and vegetable gardens, mushroom beds, show us what a wealth of provisions can be produced on the tiniest scrap of ground. Experience teaches us that man's labor, as a general thing, can nowhere be employed more lucratively than in agriculture. If a man should work over his field with the shovel and spade instead of the summary plough he would find that a plot of ground of incredibly small size would be sufficient to support him., But mankind is suffering for want of food, provisions are growing more and more expensive, and the wages-receiver must work an increased number of hours each day to get enough to eat. Nature shows man that he can not live apart from her, without the soil, that he requires the field as the fish requires water. Man recognizes that he sinks lower and lower when he forsakes the soil, that the farmer is the only one who remains healthy and strong, while the city yaps the very marrow in the bones of its inhabitants, rendering them liable to disease and unfruitful, so that each family absolutely rots out in two or three generations. The city would become in a hundred years an enormous cemetery, without a single living being within its walls, if it were not for the fact that there is a constant influx of people from the country to fill up the ranks left vacant by death. In spite of their knowledge and appreciation of these facts men continue to abandon the fruitful fields and flock to the cities, to tear themselves away from life and throw themselves into the arms of death.

Now the professor of political economy steps up again and says with an air of bland confidence and intrepidity that the measure of development to which the manufacturing industries of a country have attained, is at the same time, the measure of its civilization, and that an advanced stage of manufactures is a blessing to the nation as it makes the goods produced so cheap as to be within the reach of the poorest. This is one of the most widely spread and most frequently repeated lies with which Capital seeks to deceive mankind. A plague upon such cheapness! It is a benefit to no one, except perhaps to the manufacturer and merchant. We have seen how this cheapness of the manufactured articles is brought about: by the competition between capitals, carried on at the expense of the operatives, and by the conscienceless, criminal exhaustion of the powers of human labor. The factory employé must be chained to his machine ten, twelve, perhaps fourteen hours a day, so that cotton cloth may be sold at this cheap rate. He finds no opportunity to enjoy even the mere privilege of living. He spends his life inside the dreary factory walls, making continually a succession of identical, automatic movements, as the machine requires it. He is the sole living being in the universe who spends the greater part of his life-time in work contrary to nature, merely to keep himself alive. Of course the goods decline in price as the result of such labor. At the same time they deteriorate in quality. The entire development of our manufactures tends constantly towards the substitution of lower grade raw material for higher grade, and to the employment of the smallest possible amount of it in the finished article. Why? Because the raw material, if of an organic nature, is derived from the animal or vegetable kingdoms, and can only be procured for its actual value in labor, hence it is expensive. The earth does not allow herself to be cheated; she gives cotton and flax, wood and wool, but only in proportion as she receives the equivalent in labor and nourishment. The cow and the sheep can not be screwed down to nothing; they will only produce their hides and wool, horns and hoofs, if they are properly supplied with food. Man alone is more stupid than the earth, more easily imposed on than the cow and the sheep. He gives up his nerve and muscular strength without demanding its full value in exchange. Hence the manufacturer has every reason to be saving of the expensive raw material, and lavish of the cheap human labor. He adulterates and diminishes the quantity of the former but gives the finished products a handsome appearance by laborious or complicated processes of labor, that is to say, by an unstinted use of human labor. In the finished piece of calico offered by the English manufacturer in the market, there is the smallest possible amount of cotton fibre and the largest possible amount of human labor. The calico is cheap because the manufacturer is not obliged to pay his human slaves for their toil as much as the earth requires for her cotton fibre. But it is far from necessary that these goods should be so cheap. Their low price leads to an extravagant use of them. Even the poor people in our present civilization, renew their clothing and household goods oftener than is strictly necessary, and throw aside articles that could still yield good service, that in reality to continue to yield service, as is shown by the great trade in secondhand clothing etc., between Europe and the colonies. At the close of the year the European has spent the same amount for clothing as he would have spent if the goods had been far higher in price, for in the latter case, he would certainly have worn them longer. Thus we see the practical results of this vaunted lowness of prices, the pride of the economic world. It does not bring any actual relief or saving to the consumer, because the tyrannical custom of lavish use of the goods keeps pace with it. It is a curse to the labor that produces the goods because it diminishes the amount of its earnings more and more, while compelling it to constantly increasing exertions. Every individual that does not belong to the minority of wealthy idlers, is a producer of some one article and a consumer of others. Hence the result of the whole vaunted development of the manufacturing industries in our civilization, is nothing more than a mad chase growing wilder and fiercer every day, in which each participant is at the same time hunter and hunted, driving the soul out of the body and ending in a sudden collapse with lolling tongue and breath entirely spent.

Longer, harder toil for the producer, frenzied, criminal extravagance in the consumer—these are the direct results of the development of manufacturing industries, which tends constantly towards increased production and lower prices. Let us assume that all finished products were four times as dear as they are now, while provisions remained the same— this is easily conceivable if the development of the agricultural industries should overtake or pass beyond that of the manufacturing industries. Where would be the harm? 1 see none, but on the contrary, enormous benefits to mankind. Each individual would renew his clothing once instead of four times a year, and his household goods once in twenty years, instead of once in five. The factory employé would receive four times the wages at present paid him; that is, if he is now obliged to toil twelve hours to earn sufficient to support life, he would obtain the same result with three hours' labor. The expenses of the individual consumer would amount to the same sum total as before, at the close of the year. But one enormous result would be gained; the laboring-man would cease to be a galley-slave and become a man. That highest of all luxuries, of which he is now completely deprived: leisure, would conic within his reach. This means that he could have his share of the higher pleasures of civilized life, that he could visit museums and theatres, read, converse, meditate, that he would cease to be a machine and could assume the rank of a man among other men. We must call to the laboring classes: You are caught in a horrible whirlpool. Escape or you are lost! The more you toil the cheaper become your productions, the consumption of them grows more lavish, you must work still longer and harder tomorrow to get the means to support your sheer existence. Stop work for awhile! Loaf part of your time! Decrease your work by a half, by a quarter! Your earnings will remain the same if every one only consumes what he actually requires, and only labors as much as he is obliged to.

The professors of political economy are not of this opinion. They have a horror of leisure for mankind and believe that all good and happiness lie in the most extreme exertions of man's laboring faculties. Their doctrine can be condensed into two commandments: Thou shalt consume as much as possible, no matter whether the consumption is justified by actual necessity or not; thou shalt produce as much as possible no matter whether the productions are needed or not. These wise men make no distinction between the fire-works destined to flare up for a minute or two, to astonish some idle blockheads, and the machine that turns out useful bedsteads and wardrobes, year after year. The fire-works cost $10.000; they represent, in addition to the materials, the labor of fifty men for one year, who were during that time in perpetual danger. The machine costs $2.000. But the professor of political economy continues his dissertation with gentle impartiality: The fire-works are worth five times as much as the machine; the workmen are equally usefully employed in producing them; the production of the fireworks added to the wealth of the country as much as if five bed-making machines had been produced; and, if it were possible to keep a million workmen employed in the manufacture of such fire-works, producing thus a billion dollars worth of them annually, and disposing of them, then the country could be congratulated upon the blossoming of such an interesting industry and the workmen upon their diligence and ability.

According to established theories, this train of thought is without a flaw. According to actual practice it is a scholastic sophistry of the worst kind. Certainly it is true that if a man can get as much money for a rocket as for a fowl, then the rocket is worth as much as the fowl, and he who makes a rocket adds as much to the wealth of the nation as he who raises a fowl. And yet it is a lie. No, it is not the same to humanity whether rockets or fowls are produced. No, the Alpine guide is not as valuable to the human race as the fireman of the steam thrashing machine, although it may pay him higher wages than the latter. I know that my distinctions are leading me to attack all articles of luxury. 1 do not hesitate then to declare that no human being has the right to demand the gratification of his whims, as long as the actual necessities of others are unsatisfied, to employ workmen in the production of fire-works, for example, as long as others are famishing, because this workman is withdrawn from the cultivation of the soil, or to condemn the factory operatives to fourteen hours a day of slavish toil, so that the price of velvet may be low enough for him to clothe himself in the material the most pleasing to his esthetic taste.

The great end and aim of humanity in the field of political economy, is not the production of commodities for which a price can be obtained, but to satisfy with its labor the actual organic wants of the body. There are but two kinds of organic wants: food and propagation. The former has for its purpose the preservation of the individual, the latter the preservation of the race. We might apparently trace these two wants to one single source and omit the necessity for the preservation of the race as not being actually necessary. But only apparently. The impulse for race preservation is as much stronger than the impulse for individual self-preservation, as the vital energies and strength of the race are more powerful than those of the individual. It has never yet happened that a considerable body of human beings, an entire tribe, were prevented for any considerable length of time from obeying their natural impulse to perpetuate the race. If such a case should ever happen, if there should ever arrive a general national sex-famine, the most horrible scenes of days of famine that the world has ever seen would fade into insignificance compared with the passions and acts of violence that would then be seen. The two great organic wants of mankind must hence be satisfied; every thing beyond these is of secondary importance. It is possible for an individual whose appetite is fully satisfied, who is protected from the cold, with a shelter against the wind and rain over his head and a companion of the opposite sex by his side, to be not only contented but absolutely happy and without further desires. A hungry individual can not be happy nor even contented, even if he were dressed in gold brocade and listening to a magnificent orchestral concert in the Vatican Museum. This is so self-evident that it is absurd to state it. It is the prosaic moral of the fable of the cock who found a pearl and complained because it was not a grain of corn. And yet this truism is beyond the mental grasp of the official political economy. It has never occurred to any of the professors of this sublime science to test their doctrines by the homely wisdom of Lafontaine's book of fables. Applied to the development of our civilization in regard the matters of political or national economy, the fable of the cock and the pearl means simply this: "Less Manchester cotton goods and Sheffield knives, and more bread and meat!" What theory has neglected up to the present time practice will soon set about in earnest: viz. to demonstrate the preposterousness of the definitions and principles of the present science of political economy invented and maintained by arid for Capital, and accepted without enquiry by the world. Already, the world over, man is laboring beyond all reason and producing beyond all demand. Almost every civilized country is trying to export manufactured articles and import provisions. The markets for the former are beginning to fail. We can say without fear of exaggeration, that the great manufacturing industries of the principal countries in Europe have found all the markets they ever will find. These conditions can only grow worse, never better. The countries which are not yet developed as regards manufactures are gradually becoming so. Processes of labor will be still more improved, machines still further increased and perfected, and then? Then each country will be able to supply its own demand for manufactured articles and have an abundance left over that it will try to dispose of to its neighbor, but in vain, for the latter will have no use for them. The very last naked negro on the upper Congo will have his fifty yards of cotton cloth and his gun, the very last Papuan his boots and his paper collars. The European will have then reached the point of buying a new suit of clothes every week, and having a machine to turn over the leaves of his magazine. This will be the Golden Age of the political economists who are so captivated by unrestricted production, unbounded consumption and an unlimited development of manufactures. And in this Golden Age, when the entire country will be set as thick with factory chimneys as it is now with trees, the people will live on chemical substitutes for food instead of bread and meat they will toil eighteen hours out of the twenty four and die without knowing that they have ever lived. Perhaps it will not be necessary to wait until this Golden

Age arrives, for the fact to dawn upon certain enlightened minds or circles, that this excessive, one-sided industrialism is a wholesale suicide of the human race, and that everything which the science of political economy alleges in its favor is a lie and a fraud. We have already become convinced of the fact that a country which exports bread-stuffs, if it exhausts the soil and does not return to it in some way or other, the matter of which it is deprived by the growing grain, is gradually growing poorer, although untold millions may be pouring into it from other countries. We will become convinced of another fact sooner or later, that the exportation of labor, of muscle and nerve, in the shape of manufactured articles, will make a people grow poorer and poorer, no matter how much gold it receives in exchange for them. The European factory operative is even now, the slave of the negro on the Congo. He stills his hunger with potatoes and vile whisky, he spends his life in the machine-rooms and dies of tuberculosis, so that some barbarian may lead a more comfortable existence than has hitherto been the case. This feverish labor which is not applied to the production of food but to industrial over-production will finally produce a nation of hungry money-bags. The world may then behold the spectacle of a country where a piano of the very latest make stands in every cottage, the people rustling in brand-new clothing, but with rachitis in their bones, no blood in their veins and consumption in their lungs.

CHAPTER IV.

The sentiment in regard to the unendurable conditions of affairs in the economic world is universal. The wretched operative whose daily hunger keeps the subject always in his mind, knows that he produces wealth by the labor of his hands, and he is demanding his share of the riches he thus creates. But he commits the mistake of founding his demand upon all sorts of reasons that do not stand the test of criticism. There is only one single true and natural argument which he can call to his aid, and that is unanswerable: the argument that he has the power to take possession of the goods which he produces, that the rich are in the minority and unable to prevent this appropriation, consequently that he has the right to keep what he makes and to help himself to what he needs. The whole of the present structure of society is built upon this argument as its sole foundation. This argument makes the weaker individuals and peoples slaves of the stronger; it makes millionaires out of shrewd and unscrupulous men and sets up Capital as the absolute master of the whole world. The minority, the loafers and plunderers, make constantly use of this argument to silence the demands of the laboring and plundered classes. But the wages-receiver, whose mind in spite of all its Radicalism, is still entangled in the meshes of the ideas of right and morality inculcated by Capital, he hesitates to employ this unanswerable argument, based upon the laws and instincts of nature. He prefers to seek the justifiableness of his claims in all kinds of out of the way excuses and ideas, among which Communism is the most widely accepted and believed. Thus, in the most foolish manner, he enters upon territory in which he is sure to be defeated.

Capital has no difficulty at all in proving the absurdity of this theory. In fact Communism, as all socialistic schools comprehend and preach it, is the outgrowth of a preposterous chimera, evolved from the inflamed imagination of certain dreamers, deaf and blind to the realities of the world and human nature. Actual community in property or the negation of individual rights in property, has never existed since the world began. That condition of property holding which a superficial observer might consider to be Communism, and of which several examples have occurred in historic times, some even existing in a few isolated places at the present day, is founded upon the basis of individual ownership of property, separate from the mass of property existing in the world at large. When such a perfect cohesion and sense of fellowship exists among a small number of individuals owing to their common descent or to other causes, that a family, a village or a whole tribe, considers itself as one single being of a higher order of creation, then it is conceivable that this collective individual should possess an indivisible collective amount of property, which the single individual could not control and use for his own advantage and to the prejudice of others. This kind of collective property holding, which exists in several places in Europe at the present time, such as the Russian Mir and the united households of the Croatians and Slavonians, has nothing in common with Communism, that is, fundamental and universal community in property throughout the world, as can easily be demonstrated. Just let an outsider, an individual not accepted as a member of the circle of joint owners of the common property, let him attempt to get possession of the smallest fragment of it! The entire tribe, village, Mir, etc, will rise up in arms at once to repel the intruder. The joint possessors of the common capital are imbued so strongly with the sense of proprietorship in it, that they rebel against any appropriation of any part of it by outsiders, with as much liveliness of indignation as an individual proprietor would experience if an attack was made upon his purse. And even this collective proprietorship, which is by no means actual Communism, but only a more primitive form of personal ownership of property, can only exist as long as every member of the community experiences directly and profoundly his cohesion and fellowship to and with the rest. Its perpetuation depends also upon the similarity of the labor performed by the members, so that the efforts made by each can be compared easily and directly with those of the rest, and no doubts arise as to their relative value or importance. As soon as a division of labor takes place and different kinds of production are carried on in the collective community, the necessity will arise to compare the relative values of certain kinds of labor, each useful in its way, but differing completely in every other respect. It will be impossible to estimate justly and satisfactorily to each member, the utility and pecuniary value of his labor, as it differs in kind from that of those around him, consequently the collective proprietorship in the results of the efforts of all must necessarily come to an end, and the ownership of property individualize itself in a very short time. Thus we see that the solution of the economic problem is not to be looked for in Communism. It is a natural condition possible only in very low forms of collective associations, and could not exist in a form of animal life so highly developed as in our human society. Individual possession is the natural condition not only of men, but of most animals. The source of the impulse for individual proprietorship is the necessity for the gratification of individual wants. Every animal must supply itself with nourishment and many require also an artificially prepared shelter or natural hiding-place. The food and the nest or den which it has found or made for itself, is considered by the animal as its property. It feels that these things belong to it, and to no other being, and will not submit without resistance to being deprived of them by any other individual. A life that makes foresight and provision for the future a necessity, leads to the extension of this sentiment of proprietorship and to the development of the impulse for acquiring increased individual possessions. A beast of prey, which lives upon fresh meat, fixes the limits of his proprietorship in the total amount of fresh meat existing, at the quantity which he requires for one single meal. But an animal which lives upon a vegetable diet, if his home is in a region where there is a winter with a cessation of vegetation, helps himself from the common store-house of nature to far more than is necessary to supply his immediate wants. He accumulates more food than he can possibly require during the coming months, thus decreasing without any organic necessity, the amount of food at the disposal of other animals, he becomes a capitalist and an unscrupulous egotist. In this way squirrels, field mice, marmots, etc., heap up quantities of nuts and fruits of all kinds in their holes to provide for the coming winter, which is not all consumed at the return of spring, when they can find food again in the fields and forests. They not only realize the possibility of their personal proprietorship but they accumulate wealth, they become rich, in the sense of owning more than they require for their actual wants. Man belongs in the category of animals to whom provision for the future is necessary. The acquisition of individual property, to increase it beyond what is actually required for the moment, to defend it against the encroachments of others, these are natural vital actions and instincts in him to which he is impelled by the fundamental impulse of self-preservation, and which are impossible to eradicate. Even under the most violent compulsion of laws framed in opposition to them, they would assert themselves again and again with their elementary strength.

But if individual proprietorship is a natural instinct, and hence utterly refuses to be suppressed, there is one application of the right of personal possession against which reason absolutely revolts, and for whose existence no natural causes can be produced—this is inheritance. It is true that the impulse for the preservation of the species impels all living beings to care for their offspring and to provide the most favorable conditions of existence possible for them. But this care never extends beyond the moment when the young creatures are sufficiently developed to care for themselves without outside assistance, as the parents did before them. There is only sufficient stored up food in the seed of the plant or in the white of the egg, to supply the embryo with nourishment during its earliest stage of life—the time of absolute helplessness. The mammiferous animals give milk to their young only as long as they are unable to graze or hunt food for themselves, and the parent birds cease to bring worms to their little ones as soon as they have successfully accomplished their first independent flight.

Man alone wishes to provide his descendants with their stored up food, their albumen, their milk and their worms, to the third and fourth, to untold generations. Man alone is anxious to keep his children and great grand-children, into the most distant future, in the embryonic condition in which the young of all animals are provided for by the beings to whom they owe their existence; he will not abandon them to their own resources. When a man accumulates a fortune, he wishes to bequeath it to his family in such a way that its members will be, if possible, relieved for ever from the necessity of earning their own livelihood. This is contrary to all of nature's laws. It is a violent disturbance of the regular arrangement of the world, according to which every living being is compelled to win for himself his place at the great table of nature, or else perish. This disturbance of nature's regulations is the cause of all the evils of the economic world. And while it condemns enormous masses of individuals to wretchedness and want, it at the same time, takes its revenge upon its originators. It is in vain that the rich withdraw from the commonwealth their accumulated possessions with unconsciously criminal egotism, in order to ensure a life of luxury and leisure to their children and their children's children forever, they never accomplish their design. Experience teaches us that no wealth lasts through several generations without some business efforts. Inherited fortunes never remain long in a family, and even Rothschild's millions may not protect his descendants of the sixth or eighth generation from poverty, unless they possess those qualities which would have enabled them to win a high place for themselves in the world without any inherited millions. These fact? show the operation of an implacable law, which is constantly striving to bring about an equilibrium in the economic life of society, so grievously disturbed by the unnatural conditions of inherited property. An individual who has never been confronted with the necessity of calling his most primitive organic instinct, the acquiring of food, into play, soon loses the ability to retain his possessions and to defend them against the greed of those without possessions, who encroach upon him on every side. Only when all the descendants of a family are absolutely mediocre natures, and live far from all public and private agitation, in complete obscurity, the world forgetting and by the world forgot, leading a regular vegetable existence, can they hope to retain undiminished the possessions that form their heritage. But as soon at this family produces an individual gifted with more imagination, who surpasses in any direction the standard of mediocrity prevalent in the family, with passions or ambition, eager to shine or at least to appreciate life's possibilities, the family inheritance is doomed to decrease or ruin, because this off-shoot of the wealthy family is absolutely incapable of replacing even one penny of the sums he spends in the gratification of his whims. It is with wealth as it is with an organism. The latter must have vital activity to maintain life; as soon as the vital processes cease in its cells it falls a prey to corruption, and is consumed by the microscopic beings with whom nature is teeming, seeking whom they may devour. In the same way we can say that life becomes extinct in a fortune in which the vital processes of exchange and circulation are not carried on, so that it is preyed upon and soon devoured by the greedy companions of corruption, the parasites, swindlers, cheats and speculators. The body of a fortune can be artificially protected against decay and putrefaction as well as a human body; the latter by antiseptics, the former by a special law—which ensures the perpetuation of the property intact, that is, the law of entail. This law of entail is an invention which affords us an interesting proof of the fact that the rich egotists have always had a dim suspicion of the unnaturalness of the right of inheritance. The man of wealth feels that he is committing a crime against humanity and that nature will take her revenge upon his descendants for his contempt of her laws, consequently he erects a last barrier against her assault. He forsees that his children will not have arms strong enough to hold fast to their heritage, so he ties it to their bodies with ropes and cords that no one can unfasten. But even the law of entail, this carbolic acid bath for dead fortunes, loses its efficacy after a while and ceases to protect the inherited wealth against corruption and decay and the family against economic shipwreck.

The right of inheritance must be abolished. This is the only natural and hence the only possible cure for the ulcers in the body of society caused by the present conditions of political economy. Such a proposition seems extremely radical at the first glance, appearing to be practically the confiscation of all individual property. But examined loser, we find that it is only the consistent development 01 certain phenomena now existing, which cause no one uneasiness. The right of primogeniture is maintained in those countries which cling most tenaciously to the feudal organization of society. This right consists in the systematic disinheritance of all the children, all the descendants, with the exception of one, the first-born; so that it is identical with my proposition, with this one exception. Hence we see that the most conservative peer of England carries my proposition into action, although it may seem so revolutionary to some of my readers. If we see nothing wrong and certainly nothing impossible, in the exclusion of all the children and descendants of an English nobleman, except the first-born, from their share in the enjoyment of the fortune he leaves behind him at his death, why should we consider it wrong or impossible to treat all the children of the man of wealth in the same way? It is true that the peer who disinherits his younger children gives them other possessions, education and training, which enable them to take their places in society. But if all accumulations of property passed into the possession of the community upon the death of the accumulator, the State would be able to give all the youth of the land an education and training adapted to their capacity, and all the disinherited would have at least the same advantages as are enjoyed today by the disinherited younger son of the peer. But the peer provides for his younger children to whom he bequeaths none of his wealth, by employing his family and political connections to obtain situations for them in the service of the State, community or among his friends, which have more or less the character of a benefice or perpetual office. What is this more than an organized solidarity, which offers the individual even greater securities for a comfortable existence than an independent fortune? It is true this solidarity is narrow and selfish; it is confined to one caste and has for its sole purpose the plundering of thy majority for the benefit of a few parasites. Let us imagine the limits of this solidarity widened to include the whole community and its purpose, not to support parasites, but to perform necessary and useful work; let us imagine a state which provides instruction and if the parents are incapable of bearing the expense—food, clothing and shelter for all the children within its limits until they are old enough to enter upon their business career, and when this time arrives, supplies them with tools and materials for independent labor. In such a community of fellowship would not each individual be well provided for, and would the absorption of the father's wealth at his decease, into the public treasury be an act of injustice against the children?

I can not deny for a moment that the practical realization of this scheme would at first meet with many and difficult obstacles. The parents would try to escape from the necessity of bequeathing their property to the State by presenting it to their children and others while they were still alive. This would result in the practical inheritance of a part of their patrimony by the children, and it could only be prevented by the State with difficulty. But this source of fraud is of very small importance to the system as a whole. The adoption of it would exert such an influence upon the views and opinions of humanity that they would soon be radically changed from what they are at present. The parents would learn to appreciate the fact that in the new, reorganized community, lack of fortune did not mean poverty and wretchedness for the child, consequently the impulse to ensure a regular income to it through life would become much weaker. The State would find little or no trouble in getting control of the notes, bonds, stocks, etc., which form the greater part of the floating capital of the world; all household goods, works of art and single objects of value might be exempted from confiscation and retained by the children as mementoes of their parents; there would be no possibility for evading the law in the matter of real estate. But the most important, indeed, the only essential point of the whole system is this: the land with all the houses, buildings, factories, trading establishments, etc., that on it are, must become the unalienable property of the community and come into its direct possession at the close of each generation. Any one desirous of owning land or factories, will receive a title to them for his life-time from the State, for which he must pay an annual rental, which will be a certain percentage of the total amount of capital represented.

This idea is no unprecedented revolutionary innovation, as some would suppose, but merely the further development of certain conditions existing at the present day in many countries, especially in England and Italy. In these countries there are many landed proprietors who do not cultivate their land with their own hands, but rent it to tenant farmers. There is nothing to prevent society from placing the manufacturer and the tillers of the soil upon the same footing as the English tenant farmer, with one great proprietor as the master of them all: the State. This arrangement of the economic world would make it possible for the single individual to accumulate personal property by his sagacity and industry as at present, although not to such an enormous extent as the fortunes of the pirates and parasites of our modern civilization. The talented, the industrious man would find in a more luxurious manner of living the reward for his greater ability or efforts, the man of mediocre capabilities and the indolent man, would be obliged to live more frugally, while the individuals who shirked or refused to work would be the only ones condemned to want. The accumulation of enormous quantities of land in the possession of one single tenant could not occur, as he would experience such difficulty in finding laborers to till his land, owing to the fact that as any one willing to work could rent land from the State, no one would have any inducement to drudge for another when he could be his own master and enjoy the blessings and fruits of independence. The development of the system leads necessarily to a condition in which each individual would require only so much land as he alone, or with the help of his family, could successfully cultivate. The unnatural development of manufacturing industries at the expense of the agricultural, would thus be prevented. For as the individual would have it in his power to become an independent farmer as easily as a, factory operative, he would not enter upon the latter career unless it offered him a pleasanter and more profitable existence than farming, and the multitudes now seeking work in such numbers in the factories, underbidding each other, and satisfied with the very smallest possible amount of life's goods and enjoyments, such a class would be inconceivable in a society reorganized according to this system. Real difficulties in carrying it out would not arise until the country became too densely populated and the soil exhausted. When these conditions arrive and it is found impossible to supply all the demands for productive land and factories, then a part of the young people must decide upon emigration. However, an extremely intensive cultivation of the soil, such as I mentioned above, will postpone this necessity to a far distant future.

There is no doubt but what this system is a kind of Communism. But let him who shudders and turns pale at this word, remember that we are living now in the midst of a complete Communism, only it is a passive instead of an active Communism. We have no community in possessions, but we have a community in debts. No one is shocked at the fact that every citizen merely on account of his being a citizen of the State, is a debtor to an amount varying in different countries; in France for example, it is nearly $120 per capita. Why should any one be shocked at the idea of the citizen owning, instead of owing, in consequence of a complete revolution, a corresponding amount of property, if the State should possess common property as well as common debts? In such a case the State would not be always taking taxes from its citizens, but distributing benefits among them, as it now does to a small number of them, comprising the privileged class. Besides, the State already possesses property of all kinds in buildings, lands, forests, ships etc. The existence of this property, which is certainly not individual possessions but belongs collectively and indivisibly to all the citizens together, is certainly communism but it is not recognized as such by the people, because the forms of government and the public institutions inherited from the Middle Ages, favor the idea that this common property is an individual property belonging to the king or ruler of the state whoever he may be. The public debts, public property and taxation are not the only forms in which Communism exists in our civilization. Certain kinds of credits are nothing but the rankest Communism. When one man lends another money from his pocket or offers him a draft secured by a mortgage upon his private fortune, which is accepted by a third person like so much cash, then it is practically an exchange of individual property. But when a bank offers unsecured notes in circulation—and in many banks the amount of unsecured notes is a third or more of the entire number of notes in circulation—and gives a man in exchange for his signature on a note, a number of these unsecured notes with which he can go forth and buy anything he wishes, then the transaction is an act of the most complete Communism. The bank does not give its saved-up labor, that is gold, but a certificate for certain labor to be performed in the future. The fact that the community will give up goods, receiving these unsecured notes in exchange, is a proof of the respect in which mankind holds this principle of human solidarity, and a recognition of the concomitant fact that the individual member of the community has a right to a share in the goods existing in it, even when he can not offer in exchange for this share any personally produced equivalent.

The absorption of all goods into the public property after the death of the accumulator, would lead to an almost inexhaustible public fund, without interfering with individual possession. Each member of the community would have then his individual and general property as he has his baptismal and family name. The public property with which he is born, is like his family name; the private fortune which he accumulates during the course of his life and of which he is the sole, unmolested proprietor and usufructuary, is his baptismal name, and both taken together represent his economic personality as the names represent his personality as a citizen. While he is toiling for himself he is working for the community, which will some day fall heir to all the surplus remaining after his expenditures have ceased. The public fortune will be a vast reservoir, receiving the surplus of the rich and dealing out blessings to the poor, regaining its normal level once in every generation and thus equalizing the inequalities in the distribution of property, which inheritance on the contrary, fixes indelibly and increases in each generation.

To such a new arrangement of the politico-economical organization of society the world must come at last, because reason and the ideas of mankind in regard to man and the universe based upon natural science, demand it. One single fundamental principle must govern society, and this principle must be either individualism, that is, egotism or the solidarity, the cohesive fellowship of mankind, that is, altruism. At the present day neither fellowship nor egotism are ruling alone, but a combination of both, which is as unreasonable as it is inconsistent. Possession is organized upon a personal basis and egotism reaches in the laws governing inheritance the utmost limits to which it can attain, by no^ only seizing by stealth and violence everything that it can lay hands on, but by clinging to the plunder forever and ever and excluding the rest of mankind from ever sharing in its benefits. The man of property however, will not allow the man without property to call that principle to his aid to which the former owes his wealth. Fortunes are accumulated in the name of individualism; but they are defended in the name of human solidarity. The rich man enjoys his disproportionate share of life's blessings of which he has made himself master by unblushing egotism; but when the poor man helps himself to them with some of the rich man's egotism and selfishness, he is arrested. In the form of usury and speculation the unscrupulous furtherance of self-interest is allowable, but it is strictly forbidden when it takes the form of robbery and theft. The same principle applied in the former case is a merit, in the other a crime. Human reason revolts at such ideas. If egotism is to be preached let it be consistent and assert its right in all cases. If it is right for the rich man to luxuriate in a life of leisure because he has been able to get possession of landed estates or to take advantage of the labor of others, then it must also be conceded to be right for the poor man to strike him dead and take possession of his property as the spoils of victory, if he has the courage and strength to undertake and carry through such an undertaking. This is logical. It is true that such logic would soon bring society to destruction and our civilization to the dogs, and men would become like beasts of prey wandering alone through the land and tearing each other to pieces. But any one who is not pleased with this abstract aim of our social development, egotism, has no other alternative before him but to accept the other sole principle, fellowship. The motto will no longer be: Every one for himself, but: One for all and all for each. Society will then assume the responsibility of supporting and educating the youth of the country until they can earn their own livelihood, of supporting those too old and feeble to support themselves, of coming to the aid of infirmity, without allowing hunger and distress to exist except as the punishment of voluntary idleness. But these responsibilities can only be accepted and fulfilled upon one condition: the abolition of the right of inheritance.

Great catastrophes are looming up on the field of political economy and it will not be possible to ignore them much longer. As long as the masses were religious, they could be consoled for their wretchedness on earth by promises of unlimited bliss in the future. But today they are becoming more enlightened and the number of those patient sufferers is daily growing less who find in the Host a satisfactory substitute for their dinner and accept the priests' order on the place waiting for them in paradise with as much pleasure as if it were some good terrestrial farm of which they could take immediate possession. The poor count their numbers and those of the rich and realize that they are constantly growing more numerous and stronger than the latter. They examine the sources of wealth and they find that speculating, plundering and inheriting have no more rational justification for existing than robbery and theft, and yet the latter are prosecuted by the laws. The increasing disinheritance of the masses by their deprivation of land and by the increasing accumulations of property in the hands of a few, will make the economic wrongs more and more intolerable. The moment that the millions acquire in addition to their hunger, a knowledge of the remote causes to which it is due, they will remove and overthrow all obstacles that stand between them and the right of satisfying their appetite. Hunger is one of the few elementary forces which neither threats nor persuasion can permanently control. Hence it is the power which will probably raze the present structure of society level with the ground, in spite of its foundations of superstition and selfishness—a task beyond the power of philosophy alone.

THE MATRIMONIAL LIE

CHAPTER I.

Man has two powerful instincts which govern his whole life and give the first impulse to all his actions: the instinct of self-preservation and the instinct of race-preservation. The former reveals itself in its simplest form as hunger, the latter as love. The forces which produce the phenomena of nourishment and propagation are still obscure to us, but we can watch their operation clearly. We do not know why one individual completes his circle of development in a certain number of years instead of another; why the large and powerful horse can only grow to be 35 years old, while the smaller and weaker animal, man, on the contrary, lives to be 70; why the raven lives 200 years, while the goose, so much larger, only lives 20 years. But what we do know is that every living being is destined to a certain length of life from the moment of its birth, like a clock wound to run a certain number of hours—this time can be shortened by the operation of casual, external forces, but under no circumstances can it be lengthened. In the same way we assume that the species is destined to last a certain term of years; like an individual it arises at a certain fixed moment, is born, develops, comes to maturity and dies. The cycle of life of a species is too extended for men to be able to determine by direct observation the moment of its beginning and end. But paleontology gives us sufficient data to enable us without hesitation, to announce as a fact the parallelism of the laws governing the life and development of the individual and of the species. As long as an individual has not exhausted the vital energies with which it was born, it strives with all the exertion of which it is capable, to support itself and protect itself against its enemies. When the vital energies are exhausted it experiences no longer any need for food nor any impulse to protect itself, and dies. In the same way the vital energies of the species are revealed by the impulse for propagation. As long as the vital energies of the species are at their prime every fully developed individual strives with all its might to provide itself with a mate. As the vital energies of the species begin to ebb, the individuals of which it is composed, grow more and more indifferent to the subject of propagating and finally cease entirely to regard it as indispensable. We possess an unfailing means of determining the exact degree of vital energy in a given species, race or nation, in the proportion between the egotism and altruism of the individuals comprised in it. The larger the number of beings who place their own interests higher than all the duties of solidarity and all the ideals of the development of the species, the nearer is the species to the end of its vital career. While on the other hand, the more individuals there are in a nation who have an instinct within them impelling them to deeds of heroism, self-abnegation and sacrifice for the community, the more potent are the vital energies of the race. The decay of a people as well as of a family, begins with the preponderance of selfishness. The prevalence of egotism is the unerring sign that the vitality of the species is exhausted, which will soon be followed by the exhaustion of the vitality of the individual, unless he is able to secure a reprieve by favorable crossings or changes. When a race or a nation attains to this point in its life-career, its individuals lose their ability to experience normal and natural love. The family instinct dies out. The men do not wish to marry because they find it inconvenient to assume the burden of responsibility for another human life and to provide for another being beside themselves. The women avoid the pains and inconveniences of motherhood and even when married, strive by the most unhallowed means to remain childless. The instinct of propagating, which has lost its aim of reproducing the species, dies out in some persons and in others, degenerates into the strangest and most abnormal complications. The act of generation, that most sublime function of the organism, which can not take place until it has reached its full maturity and with which are connected the most powerful sensations of which the nervous system is capable, is degraded into a mere wanton sensuality no longer having for its object the preservation and reproduction of the species, but merely a gratification of the senses, without the slightest aim or value for the community. Where love still appears, as a relic or case of atavism, it is not the union of two incomplete, half individualities into one whole and complete individuality of a higher type, it is not the transformation of a sterile single life into a fruitful dual life, that can be perpetuated in its offspring far into futurity, it is not the unconscious blending and extinction of egotism in altruism, it is not the discharging of the stagnant waters of an isolated, individual existence into the rushing, impetuous stream of the existence of the race—it is nothing but a strange longing incomprehensible even to itself, partly revery, partly hysteria, partly self-deception, reminiscences, self-application of what has been heard and read, combined with a sickly, sentimental, morbid imagination, and partly sheer lunacy, emotional or melancholy insanity. Unnatural vices spread and increase, but while indecency is holding its orgies in secret, an especially sensitive prudishness is displayed in public. The proverb which says that in the hangman's house no one speaks of the rope, is exemplified by a people whose conscience is guilty in regard to the sexes, and is fully conscious of its sins of omission and commission in this respect; it avoids any reference to the sexual life with the scrupulous anxiety of a criminal caught in the act. This is a description of the relation between the sexes in a decaying race whose vitality has become exhausted by the natural decline which is a consequence of age or by unfavorable conditions of existence, or else by the operation of injudicious and injurious laws.

If my assertion is conceded to be true that the form of the relations existing between the sexes in a given people is a measure of its vital energies, and if we apply this measure to the civilized peoples of Europe, we are obliged to draw the most alarming conclusions from what we see. The falseness of the economic, social and political conditions of our civilization has also poisoned the intercourse between the sexes all the natural instincts which should ensure the perpetuation and perfection of the race, are distorted and diverted into wrong channels, and the future generations of that part of humanity which is intellectually most highly developed, are sacrificed without hesitation to the prevailing selfishness and hypocrisy. Mankind at all times, has appreciated the fact, instinctively at first, then with its reasoning faculties, that there was nothing more important to it than its own perpetuation. All sentiments and actions which had any bearing whatever upon this most prominent interest of the species, have from the very first occupied the most extensive domain in its world of thought. Love is almost the exclusive theme of the light literature of all ages and of all peoples, and it is certainly the only one that has the power to fascinate permanently the mass of readers or hearers. The result of love, the union of the youth and the maiden into a fruitful pair, has always been surrounded by more ceremonies and festivities, preparations and formalities than any other act of man's life; in primitive times by customs and etiquette, and later, by written laws confirming these formalities. Even the formal presentation of manly weapons to the youths was a ceremony of but secondary rank, although in barbaric tribes, living in a condition of incessant attack and defence, this act was considered of the greatest importance. By these formalities, which make a marriage a matter of so much ceremony, the community has always kept control of the relations between the sexes, and the solemnity with which it treats the union of a loving couple, ought to arouse in them the consciousness that their embraces are no mere private affairs, like a dinner, a hunting expedition or an evening spent in singing and dancing, but matters of great public importance and significance, affecting the welfare of the whole community and aiding to determine its future. In order to prevent as much as possible the degradation of love into a mere pastime and to proclaim most emphatically its sublime purpose, the preservation of the race, society from its very beginnings, has only recognized as honorable and distinguished by its respect those relations between man and woman whose earnestness has stood the test of a public ceremony. It disapproves of those which have refused to submit to this formality and punishes them with avoidance or material penalties. In our civilization as well as in its state of primitive development, the impulse for procreation must summon society to be a witness to its gratification and place itself under its protection, or else it sinks into a contemptible and criminal vice. Today as much as ever before, marriage is the only kind of union between man and woman countenanced by the community. But what have the lies of our civilization made out .of marriage? It has become a mutual agreement in which there is no more room for love than in the partnership contract of two capitalists entering upon some new business enterprise together. The pretext for marriage is still as ever, the preservation of the species, its theoretical presupposition is still the mutual attraction of two individuals of opposite sexes, but in reality, a marriage is contracted not in the interests of the future generation, but solely with regard to the personal interests of the contracting parties. The consecration of morality and anthropological justification are utterly lacking in the modern marriage, especially among the so-called better classes. Marriage ought to be the victory of altruism, but it is the victory of egotism. The contracting parties do not wish nor expect to live in and for each other in the new relationship, but to carry on a more comfortable and irresponsible single existence. They get married to have their combined fortunes make life more agreeable, to provide themselves with a pleasanter home, to secure and maintain social prestige, to satisfy their vanity and to enter upon the privileges and enjoyments which society refuses to the single woman and concedes to the married one. In contracting a marriage everything is thought of: the drawing-room and the kitchen, the promenade and the watering place, the dancing-hall and the dining-room, one thing only is forgotten, the most essential of all: the sleeping-room, that sacred place, from whence the future of the family, of the race and of humanity, should dawn upon the world. Decay and ruin must be the destiny of those peoples in whose marriages the selfishness of the contracting parties celebrates its victory, while the child is an unwished-for, in the most favorable case, an indifferent accident, a resulting consequence not easily to be avoided, but always of secondary importance.

The objection may be made that among peoples living still in natural, primitive conditions of life, the majority of marriages are contracted after the same fashion as in the midst of our civilization. Among them also, affection plays no role in the establishment of a new household. In some tribes the man marries a maiden whom he sees for the first time after the wedding ceremonies are over. In others the would-be bridegroom carries off the first woman of some neighboring tribe that he meets and is able to capture. When the bride is chosen, the choice has nothing to do with love. She is selected to be the mistress of a home, because it is known in the tribe that she can work faithfully, take good care of the domestic animals, spin and weave well. In this case also the perpetuation of the tribe is left to blind chance or to egotism, and yet such peoples are full of youthful vitality and their development far from suffering from this condition of things, is progressing rapidly and satisfactorily. We can reply to this objection that marriages founded not on love but on selfishness and social station do not have the same bad results among uncivilized peoples as among the civilized, owing to anthropological causes. There is but little mental or physical difference between the individuals comprising a primitive people. The tribal type is shown in every man and in every woman alike, and an individual type does not exist at all or at most only as a germ. All the individuals seem to have been cast in the same mould and resemble each other to a perplexing degree; for breeding purposes they all have about the same value. Natural selection is not a necessarily preceding condition of matrimony; the result will be the same, whatever the motives, that led to it, may have been. Great similarity between individuals not only does away with the necessity of love, but also with its possibility. The impulse of procreation arouses in the individual a general wish for the companionship of an individual of the other sex, but it does not individualize, in a word it does not rise to its highest form, the concrete love for a certain individual and for none other. One entire sex has a general attraction for the other entire sex, it is quite immaterial to the man as well as to the woman, which man or which woman becomes their companion. When by chance some individual does arise who differs from the uniformity of the tribe and is distinguished above all the other members by surpassing mental or physical qualities, the difference is appreciated with an intensity of which we can form no conception, as we are so accustomed to see striking individual differences in the people around us. The great zoological law of sexual selection then begins to operate with the power of an elementary force of nature, and the desire for the possession of this superior individual becomes a fearful, furious passion leading to the most extreme actions. The case is quite otherwise in a civilized people, whose individuals all differ so widely. Among the uncultivated, that is, the less developed lower classes, the impulse for propagation is revealed much more frequently as a general attraction towards the other sex than as an individualizing, discriminating affection for one, and contrary to the universal sentimental romancing of non-observing poets, violent love for one chosen being is exceedingly rare among them. But among the upper classes, whose members are highly developed, of innumerable variety and the individual types sharply defined, the sexual impulse becomes exclusive and discriminating; if it were not so the offspring would not be full of vitality and energy. Hence, marriage, the only relationship between man and woman countenanced by society in which offspring are produced, should be the result of love. For love is the great regulator of the life of the race, the impelling force which promotes the perfecting of the species and tries to prevent its physical decay. Love is the instinctive recognition of the fact by one being, that it must be united with a certain other being of the opposite sex, so that its good qualities may be increased, its bad neutralized and its offspring prove at least no deterioration of its type, and if possible an improvement upon it. The propagating impulse alone is blind, and it needs the reliable guide, love, to enable it to reach its natural goal, which is at the same time the perpetuation and improvement of its kind. If this guide is lacking, if the union of man and woman is determined by chance or external interests, which have nothing to do with its physiological purpose, and not by mutual attraction, then the offspring of such an ill-assorted couple will be almost always bad or mediocre. The children inherit the faults of the parents which appear in an increased form in them, while their good qualities are modified or lacking entirely. The generation, the race thus produced is inharmonious, distracted within itself and decaying, doomed to become speedily extinct. Only one voice, the voice of love, tells the individual that his union with a certain other individual is desirable in the interests of the preservation and perfection of his kind, while his union with a certain other would be disastrous. Goethe employed a single word to express the essence of love, which comprehends it so wonderfully and defines it so exhaustively that volumes of definition could add nothing to it; this word is: "Wahlwandtschaft," which has been translated: "elective affinity." It is a term borrowed from the science of chemistry, and shows with marvelous penetration, the connection between the great elementary processes of nature and the process of love in man, which has been rendered so mysterious and unintelligible by the hysterical ravings of poets unable to discern and comprehend its true significance. Affinity in chemistry means that attraction between the particles of two bodies which causes them to unite and blend, thus forming a new compound completely different in almost all its properties, in color, density, effect upon other matter, composition, etc., from the two ingredients of which it is formed. Two bodies between whom this affinity does not exist, can remain for ever in the most intimate contact without blending together, without forming a new compound or producing any vital process—their combination will never be more than a passive juxtaposition. But if there is an affinity between the particles of the two bodies, they need only be brought into contact to produce an instantaneous phenomenon of action, spontaneous, beautiful and fruitful. The human organism is the scene of exactly similar operations. Two individuals exert this mutual attraction upon each other, or they do not. If they stand in affinity to each other, they love each other, they rush to each other with impetuosity and become the source of new formations. If there is not this affinity between them they remain cold and passive, and their propinquity will never lead to an episode of the universal vital processes of nature. These are elementary properties inherent in matter, which we do not attempt to explain. Why does oxygen unite with potassium? Why will not nitrogen unite with platinum? Who can tell us? And why does a man love this one woman and not this other? Why does a woman want this man and spurn all other men? Evidently because this attraction and indifference are founded on the innermost chemical properties of the beings in question and proceed from the same sources as the organic processes of life itself. Marriage is thus a vessel in which two separate bodies, two chemical individualities, are enclosed together. If there is an affinity between them the vessel is full of life; if there is none, the vessel contains death. But who enquires about the affinity in a modern marriage? There are only two kinds of relations between man and woman: those which were produced by a natural mutual attraction, and have always reproduction as their aim and purpose, consciously or unconsciously, and those in which this aim is not the principal one, which are merely the gratification of selfishness in some one of its many phases. The first kind is justifiable and moral, the latter come within the limits of prostitution, no matter how moral they may appear to outsiders. The outcast being who plies her trade in the great cities at night, accosting the first passer-by whose features ever she can not discern, prostitutes herself; the low wretch who dances attendance upon some old woman, and is paid in cash for his attentions, prostitutes himself — there is only one view possible of such actions. But I ask wherein lies the difference between the man who is supported by the woman who loves him, and the man who is wooing an heiress or the daughter of some influential man for whom he does not experience the slightest love, in order to obtain wealth or position by the alliance? And wherein lies the difference between the wretched creature who sells herself to some stranger for a trifling amount, and the blushing bride who is united before the altar to some unloved individual, who offers her in return for her companionship, social rank and dresses, ornaments and servants, or even merely her daily bread? The motives are the same in both cases, the actions the same; their names, according to truth and justice, should be the same. A mother may be respected by every one as entitled to the highest esteem, she may consider herself a model of extreme morality, and yet when she introduces some wealthy suitor to her daughter and tries to overcome her natural indifference to him by judicious persuasion and advice, somewhat after this fashion: that it would be very foolish to throw away such a chance for a comfortable provision for the future, that it would be in the highest degree imprudent to wait for a second opportunity which might never arrive, that a maiden ought to think of practical things and get all the silly rubbish of romantic love stories out of her head—"with a little hoard of maxims preaching down a daughter's heart,"—this model mother is an infamous go-between, no more and no less than the old hag who whispers corrupt counsel into the ear of some poor working girl in the park and is punished by the laws when found out. The elegant young bachelor, such a welcome guest in the drawing rooms of society, hunting for a fine match in the mazes of the German, until he finds some wealthy heiress to whom he can pay his court with melting glances and tenderly modulated tones, who puts off his creditors until the day after the wedding and portions off his mistress from his bride's dowry—is not his degradation as deep as that of any low wretch whom he would not touch without gloves? A woman who sells herself to buy bread for her aged mother or her child, stands upon a higher moral plane than the blushing maiden who marries a money bag, in order to gratify her frivolous appetite for balls and travel. Of two men, he is the less deceived, the more logical and rational, who pays his companion of an hour in cash each time, than he who gets a companion for life by the marriage contract, whose society was purchased as much as in the former case. Every alliance between man and woman in which either one is influenced by the substantial or selfish advantages to be gained by it, is prostitution, no matter whether it has been sanctioned by the justice of the peace or the parson, or not.

But this is the character of almost all marriages; the rare, exceptional cases in which a man and a woman are united in a legitimate way without any other reason or desire than to belong to each other in love, are condemned by reasonable persons and young people are cautioned not to imitate them. Poor girls and those only moderately provided for, are carefully warned by their parents to stifle the dangerous natural impulses of their hearts, and to gauge the sweetness of their smile by the figure of the bachelor's income. When this artificial coquetry is not sufficient alone to catch a husband whose reliability in regard to his income can be depended upon, the mother and aunts rally to the rescue and back up the innocent child's efforts with crafty manœuvres. The case is different where rich girls are concerned. They are not the hunters, but the game. A certain class of men are trained and drilled for the chase of a dowry, and go regularly to work according to certain fixed rules. They wear trousers and vests of immaculate cut, cravats of a carefully selected color and shape, and carry an eye glass screwed into one eye. Hours are spent in arranging their hair and moustache, a delicate perfume surrounds them; they dance superbly, are thoroughly at home in all society games, rhapsodize on sporting matters and are thoroughly versed in theatrical gossip. At a later stage of the game they distribute bouquets and bonbons, and love-letters in prose and verse are evolved. By these means the golden pheasant is soon brought down, and the simple creature who imagined that she had been playing a role in a lyric drama, discovers too late, that she has only been employed as a factor in an arithmetical calculation. When both parties to the marriage possess about the same amount of fortune and position in life, these are counted, compared and measured beforehand. In such a case no trouble is taken to disguise or conceal in the slightest, the true motives of the marriage and the real comprehension of its significance. Two fortunes, two positions, two influences, are united. The man wants a wife to get his dinner for him or sew on his buttons, or else to wear a silk dress with elegance and preside at the head of his table; the woman wants a husband who will work for her, or else make it possible for her to go to balls and receptions and receive society in her own home. This open acknowledgment of the motives is not allowed in marriages between unequal fortunes and positions. Then one or other of the contracting parties must lie. The poor girl pretends affection for the money-bag, the wooer makes a false display of love for the gold fish he has caught. Nature and truth can celebrate at least one melancholy victory: that the corrupt egotism which has diverted marriage from its natural goal, recognizes and accepts its real moral and physiological significance, by assuming in its wooing the mask of love.

What is the fate of the men and women who have become united in matrimony after this fashion? The "degenerates," the morally decayed offspring of parents who were married in obedience to the command of material interests, conceived and born without love, brought up without tenderness, they become finally entirely incapable of love and can grow old without ever having perceived, even for one moment, the impoverishment of their inner life. The husband cultivates his palate and stomach, he becomes a connoisseur in wines and cigars, his liberality wins him a favorable recognition in the demi-monde, his name is spoken with respect in the clubs, he dies rich in civil and social honors and if sincere, would have this inscription carved upon his tombstone! "The only love of my life was—I, myself!" The wife invents crazy fashions, strives to surpass all her equals in insane extravagance, dreams day and night of dress, jewels, furniture and carriages, intrigues, lies, slanders other women, destroys the heart-happiness of others, impelled by a fiendish envy, and is able, if the means at her command correspond with her inclinations, to leave a broad swath of desolation and misery behind her, like an army of locusts or a pestilence. Both man and wife vegetate in a mephitic intellectual sphere, without light or inspiration. Their lives are without a single ideal. Their natures, deprived of every organ of flight, without elasticity and aspiration, crawl flat in the mire. They are germs of corruption spreading disease wherever they go, destroying society and dying in the putrefaction they have produced. "Degenerates" are found principally among the upper classes. They are at once the results and the causes of the egotistical organization of society. In society marriages are not entered into on account of love, but to obtain rank and wealth. Wealth and rank are thus maintained, but their owners decay. This is in obedience to the self-regulating and restricting tendencies of every living organism, hence of humanity at large. The suppression of love, the enlargement of egotism which are the prevailing tendencies of the upper strata of society, would lead to the speedy decay of the race if they became universal. The impulse for self-preservation in mankind thus leads to the inevitable decay of families founded on loveless and selfish unions. The universally conceded rapid decay of aristocratic houses has hardly any other cause than this. In addition to the marriages of this kind contracted by "degenerates", there are also those entered into by sound, normal beings, capable of love, who yet have married without love from a lack of understanding, from heedlessness or from a cowardly dread of the dangers of the struggle for existence in the midst of a society organized and governed by sheer egotism. It is remarkable that such marriages, contracted in direct opposition to nature and reason, are called marriages of reason. The sin they have thus committed against that fundamental law, sexual selection, is avenged upon them sooner or later, and the later, the more severely. The impulse to love can not be eradicated from their hearts and is continually seeking an outlet through the unyielding walls of legal and social conventionalism, with incessant and most painful exertions. It may happen that such an individual never meets one with whom it has an affinity, throughout its entire life career; in this case the marriage remains undisturbed and the relations between man and wife united from prudential motives, formally correct. But their existence is unfinished and unsatisfactory, they always have the tormenting sensation of a sorrowful unrest and expectation, they are always hoping for something yet to come, that will awaken them from the stupor of their empty lives. The whole being is felt to be fragmentary and they long for the missing portion, but never find it even in the most brilliant gratifications of their vanity or self-interest, because love alone could supply it.

The lives of such persons as well as of the "degenerates" miss the consecration of the ideal; but, more subjectively unhappy than the latter, they have a continual consciousness of what is lacking. They are not blind, but seeing men deprived of the light. This is the case if destiny does not bring them in contact with some being with whom they have an affinity. But if they meet with such an one the catastrophe is inevitable. The conflict between the conjugal duties and the elementary striving for union with the individual for whom they feel an affinity, is constant and wearing, the substance, the love, rebels against the form, the married state, in which it is confined. Either the substance is crushed or the form is destroyed. A third solution is also possible, and as it is the most ignoble, it is the most frequently employed: the sides of the form which are visible to all eyes remain undisturbed, but in the rear a narrow crack is made through which the substance can find its way out. To express it more practically: the loving party in the loveless marriage either dissolves the marriage by force, or struggles with and subdues his love by the sacrifice of his life's happiness, or else deceives his spouse and breaks his conjugal vows in secret. Common natures seize at once upon this last means of escape, but natures of true nobility have to struggle through and bear with the tragedy of rebellion against the prejudices of society and the fatal contest between passion and duty, with all their bitter intensity. If society were founded upon the laws governing the species, such loveless marriages would be impossible and such catastrophes inconceivable. If it were organized upon the basis of organic laws and solidarity, it would in such a struggle take sides with the lovers and cry to them: "You love, therefore be united." But society, officially, is the enemy of the species and is only ruled by egotism; it therefore takes sides with the conjugal duties and says to the contestants: "Renounce each other." But as, in spite of its unnatural conditions, it has retained the knowledge that this is impossible, that it is as easy to renounce life itself as love, and that such a revolting command would not be obeyed any more than an order to commit suicide, it adds in a whisper and with a sly wink: "or at least do not give any cause for scandal." Thus love gets its rights at last, but only from those who are willing to accept the hypocrisy of society, so that, instead of elevating and ennobling the character, it becomes under such conditions a cause of its deterioration, as it requires constant lying, perjury and dissimulation. A curious classification of individualities is produced by its operation in wedded life; the best and finest characters, exactly those which have the most value for the race as breeding material, are the very ones who scorn to accept any immoral and vulgar compromises, and as they will not break the solemn vows they pledged at the altar and have perhaps neither the decision nor means to openly and legally dissolve the marriage contract, the love that has entered into their lives too late is the cause of their ruin, and thus is of no benefit to the race; the every-day natures, on the other hand, whose perpetuation is of slight importance to the race, avoid the pains of martyrdom and satisfy their hearts at the expense of their ethical conscience.

The conventional marriage, nine times out of ten, as contracted among the civilized peoples of Europe, is hence, a deeply immoral relation, fraught with the most fatal results for the future of society. It compels those who enter into it, to find themselves involved sooner or later, in a conflict between forsworn vows and indestructible love, and gives them only two alternatives, vulgarity or ruin. Instead of its being a source for our kind to renew its youth, it is the means of its slow suicide.

CHAPTER II.

The fact that matrimony, originally intended to be the single permanent form of love between man and woman, has completely lost its scope and purport, that it is usually entered into without regard to the affinity between the parties, that young men and maidens are formally trained to consider love as something distinct from marriage, owing to the examples they see around them in every-day life, and still more to the light literature of all languages, that in fact they learn to look upon them as antagonistic in most cases, and when their hands are united in public, make the reservation in the secret depths of their souls, consciously or only indistinctly apprehended, that the inclinations of their hearts are not to be influenced by this formality—the economic organization of our civilization is to blame for these facts. This organization has selfishness as its foundation; it recognizes only the single being and not the species, its attention is confined strictly to the individual and it neglects in every respect the race; it allows a piratical system of economy to exist which sacrifices the future to the present, and among all its numerous watchmen and guards, attorneys and bailiffs, there is not a single being whose duty it is to look after the interests of posterity. What matters it to a society organized in this way, that the reproduction of the species occurs under the most unfavorable conditions? The living generation has only itself to think of. If it can complete its existence in the utmost possible comfort, it has fulfilled its duty to itself completely, and it is not aware of any other duty. The succeeding generation in its turn may look after itself alone, and if it is mentally and physically impoverished by the fault of the parents, so much the worse for k. Are the children born in a marriage without love, pitiable creatures? What does it matter, if only the wedded couple obtained the substantial advantages they sought by the marriage? Are the children of love without marriage usually sacrificed to the mothers' dread of social ostracism, and thus become martyrs to the ruling prejudices of society? What harm is there in this fact if their parents found the happiness they sought in the forbidden relations? Humanity is disappearing from the horizon of man, the sentiment of solidarity, of fellow-ship with his kind, which is one of the primitive instincts of the higher forms of animal life, is dying out, the suffering of his neighbor no longer disturbs man's pleasure, arid even the thought that mankind might cease to exist with the present generation, would not cause society to change a mode of living in which the individual can be temporarily comfortable. Hence the impulse towards procreation has become a means of selfish advancement, and as it is the most powerful of all the impulses of man's being, he can speculate upon it with impunity. Thus we see that men and women try to make the sacred act, on which depend the preservation and development of the human race, a source of personal, pecuniary profit. Why should we blame the man or woman of our civilization because he or she looks upon marriage as a charitable institution, a "Sheltering Arms," and when a proposal is made looks around to see if any one bids higher. They see that the world takes the amount of the fortune as the measure of the worth of the individual; they see the rich faring sumptuously and Lazarus lying in the dust at the gate, today as well as in the Biblical times; they know the crush and the weariness of the struggle for existence and the difficulty of winning a victory in it; they know that they can only count upon their individual selves and strength, and if they fall that they need expect no acceptable help from the community. What wonder then that they look upon every act of their life, marriage included, solely and exclusively from the standpoint of their personal, palpable advantage in the struggle for existence? Why should they allow love to influence them in the selection of a husband or wife? Because humanity would be better off by it? What do they care for humanity? What has humanity done for them? Does it satisfy their appetite when they are hungry? Does it give them work when they can find no work to do? Does it feed their children when they are clamoring for bread? And if they die will it support their widows, their orphans? No. And as it does not fulfill any of these duties towards them, they have only their individual selves to consider, and look upon love as an agreeable pastime and upon marriage as a means of increasing their share of the goods of this world.

The result of these ideas is a speedy degeneration of the civilized part of humanity, bat their direct, immediate victim is woman. Man does not suffer so very much by such a condition of affairs. If he does not have the ability or the courage to assume the responsibility of founding a family in the midst of a society which is hostile and piratical, instead of being kind and encouraging as would be more natural, he remains unmarried but without renouncing the full gratification of all his instincts. Bachelorhood is far from being synonymous with celibacy. The bachelor has the tacit permission of society to procure the pleasures of woman's companionship when and where he can, it calls his selfish enjoyments successes, and surrounds them with a kind of romantic halo, so that the amiable vice of a Don Juan arouses a sentiment that is composed of envy, sympathy and secret admiration. If he marries without love, to procure certain substantial advantages, he is allowed by custom to seek right and left the pleasures which he does not find in the society of his wife, or if this is not exactly allowed, it is yet not considered a crime which should exclude him from intercourse with respectable people. Quite the reverse is the case where woman is concerned. The woman of our civilization is taught to consider matrimony as her only life career and marriage her only destiny. Only by marriage does she attain to the gratification of all her physiological wants^ great and small. She must marry in order to exercise her natural rights as a complete and mature individual, in order to receive the consecration of motherhood or simply in order to be protected from poverty and distress. This last consideration does riot influence heiresses, but in spite of the fact that most of them realize the immorality of a marriage without love and that many of them carry their desire to marry from mutual affection to such an extent that it is almost a mania, leading them to consider all their suitors as fortune-hunters, yet they, most of all, are the victims of this fatal perversion of truth, which has substituted sheer egotism for love in the contraction of a marriage. There are too many men sufficiently degraded to consider a life-interest in a wife's fortune as a possession to be desired above all others. They will make every effort to win the wealthy heiress, not because they love her but because they want her property. They humor all her whims; if she yearns for love, they feign it with the more intensity the less reality there is in their protestations. The probabilities are that the heiress, young and inexperienced, bestows her hand upon the most unworthy suitor of all those with whom she is surrounded, because he is usually the most skillful and unswerving dissembler. She discovers too late that she also, in spite of her material independence, has married a man who has no affinity for her but only for her fortune, and that she must either renounce the thought of love, or must seek for it outside of her home, exposing herself to dangers of all kinds and the contempt of all moral censors. But heiresses are only a small minority in the world, all other women are compelled by the present organization of society to look upon marriage as the only possible refuge from disgrace and poverty, and even from starvation. What is the lot of the unmarried woman? Her familiar appellation, old maid, contains a scornful sting. The solidarity of the family does not extend usually into the maturer years of the children. When the parents die, the brothers and sisters separate, each one wishes to tread alone the path of life, and the constant companionship of the rest becomes a burden. The girl who is too sensitive to wish to be a hindrance to either brother or sister, especially if they are married, finds that she is alone in the world, far more solitary than the Bedouin in the desert. Shall she found a home of her own? It would be an inhospitable and dreary place, for no masculine friend could sit down by her fire-side without arousing the gossip of the neighborhood, feminine friendships are rare and beyond a certain point unnatural, and least of all would she introduce a sister in misfortune into her home to add to its melancholy and bitterness. Some wise being is ready with the advice: she need not concern herself about the gossip of other women, but let her assemble the congenial friends around her, whom she may meet. But with what right does this strong and independent character advise a gentle, timid girl to renounce for her life long, the satisfaction she obtains from the respect and appreciation of her equals, a satisfaction which appeals with effect even to the very strongest among us. The reputation is a very substantial possession and the opinion of one's social equals plays the most important part in the inner and outer life of the individual. And shall the solitary maiden throw away her title to this possession? She would then pass her life among strangers, more dependent than if wedded, more exposed to calumny than the married woman, the preservation of her reputation her incessant and tormenting care, for society requires it untarnished, although it does not offer her the natural prize for it, the husband. The bachelor can go into restaurants and saloons, pass his leisure hours in his clubs, which are becoming more and more a substitute for family life, he can travel alone, go to walk alone, and has a hundred ways of deluding himself into oblivion of the coldness and barrenness of his home, unblessed by the love of wife and child. All these solaces are denied to the single woman if she wishes to keep her reputation clear; she is condemned to a perpetual solitude in her sorrow over her wasted life. If she owns property she can only increase it with difficulty, it is much more liable to be diminished or lost entirely, for she is far less competent than man to conduct business affairs, that is, to protect her possessions against the sharks swarming around them, owing to her training and the customs of society. But if she has no property the picture grows indistinguishable from the hopeless darkness that settles down upon it. Only a few and unremunerative means of earning a livelihood are accessible to woman. The uneducated girl of the lower classes goes out to service and thus supports herself, but never learns the meaning of independence and liberty, while her character is crippled by constant humiliations. Slow starvation is the result of woman's independent efforts, and working by the day, she receives on an average one half as much as a man, although her natural wants are about the same. The educated girl of the upper classes becomes a teacher; in most cases she enters upon the slave's life of a governess; in some countries a limited number of subordinate official positions or clerkships are open to her, but none of them allow a cultivated and intelligent woman to practice her talents and inclinations, to satisfy her inner life, which alone makes poverty bearable; and those who can get these positions are the fortunate ones. The rest are poverty-stricken, wretched, a burden to themselves and others, oppressed by the consciousness of their aimless and useless life, unable to obtain for themselves any pleasures in their youth, their bread from day to day, or a provision for their old age. And with all this, the girl who vegetates in such a terrible solitude must have superhuman principles. We require this sad, morbid, starving, shivering girl to be a heroine! Prostitution stands near, waiting for her, enticing her. She can not take a step in her solitary and joyless life, without being beset by temptation in a thousand guises. Man who avoids assuming the responsibility of providing for her for life, does not hesitate to demand her love as a present, which requires no return from him.

His sensual selfishness pursues her without intermission and is the more dangerous, as her most powerful instincts are his secret allies. She must not only voluntarily continue her life of solitude and wretchedness, not only struggle to escape-from her strong and determined antagonist, man, who is spurred on by his passions, but she must subdue her own inclinations and put down the rebellion of her normal, natural instincts against the lies and hypocrisy of society . To emerge unharmed from such a struggle requires a heroism of which hardly one man in a thousand would be capable. And the reward of this heroism? There is none. The old maid who has lived the life of a saint amid these manifold temptations, finds no recompense, no assurance in her heart of hearts that she has been obeying a law of nature by her bitter, arduous life of deprivations; on the contrary, the older she grows, the louder her heart questions: "why did I struggle? Has my victory benefited anyone? Is society with its hard, selfish maxims, worthy of the sacrifice I offered upon its altar, my life's happiness? Would it not have been a thousand times better for me if I had yielded?"

When the average girl shudders at the thought of such a fate and marries the first man who enters upon her horizon on matrimonial thoughts intent, without too much scrutiny of affections and affinities—is she not right? There are a hundred chances to one that the lot of the married woman is more peaceful and pleasant than that of the old maid. But the lie acted by the bride when she marries without love, does not go unavenged. She is neither a faithful wife nor a conscientious housekeeper. In her unsatisfied longing for love she listens continually to the voice of her heart, accepts its lightest and most indistinct whisper as the hoped-for announcement of passion, and throws herself into the arms of the first man who has been able to fill her empty mind for a moment. She soon recognizes her mistake and continues her search for the right one, sometimes closing her career by falling over the precipice into social ignominy. In a more favorable case she may be merely coquettish, without going so far as to break her marriage vows materially or platonically. Her appreciation of the incompleteness of her life and the necessity of finding the missing part, the man destined by nature to supplement her and round her existence into completeness, these impulses may reveal themselves as semi-unconscious coquetry, which impels her to dress elegantly and attend the balls and evening entertainments where she meets strange men, to test her powers of attraction upon them and to experience theirs in return She is entirely wrapped up in herself, cares solely for her own interests and demands that life should only offer her personal pleasures. Her egotism makes it impossible for her husband to come within her sphere of vision, much less for her to have any consideration for him or to enter into his life. The household is indifferent to her except in so far as it exists for her. She spends money without regard for the exertions of her husband. She only married him so that she could live free from care, in comfort or luxury, and yet it is so hideously human to punish him because he was so ill advised as to take her to wife without first being convinced of her love. In this way a wretched chain of events is formed, of which every link is a calamity and vexation. The egotistical organization of society makes the struggle for existence unnaturally and unnecessarily difficult for the individual, consequently man does not seek love but substantial benefits in matrimony, and he pursues the heiress. The poor girl, for fear she may become an old maid, gives chase to the first eligible man she meets, who is able to support her; soon after the marriage she is discovered to be a costly article of luxury, of no possible value to the possessor but only a source of unlimited outlay. Many men able to support a wife and make her happy, are frightened by the spectacle of such wedded life and are deterred by it from getting married themselves. This condemns a corresponding number of girls to spinsterhood, their prospect of procuring a husband decreases, while their determination to capture one increases in proportion and their longing to make sure of him, leads them to suppress still more the promptings of their hearts. The consequences of marriages contracted under such circumstances have a tendency to deter an increasing number of matrimonial candidates from f. lowing their example. Man and woman become enemies, trying to steal a march upon and plunder each other. No one is satisfied, no one is happy, and the catholic confessor and the proprietors of the great dry goods establishments are the only ones who have reason to be pleased at this condition of things, as it brings them crowds of customers.

CHAPTER III.

But if the economic organization of the world is the principal cause of the falseness of the institution of matrimony, it is however, not the only one. A large share of the blame for the opposition between substance and form, between love and marriage, and for the frequent tragical conflicts between natural sentiments and conventional constraints, is due to the prevailing conception of morality, which is a consequence of Christianity. This morality considers the act of generation an odious crime, it covers its face before it as before an abomination, which at the same time does not preclude a stolen glance, and it lays upon everything which has the slightest connection with the sexual life, or even calls it to remembrance, the ban of a timorous silence. This is monstrous, it is unprecedented. This system of morality could not last an hour if it were not that in private all human beings, all without exception, set it aside as tranquilly as if it did not exist. It has not the smallest natural foundation and therefore not the faintest shadow of justification. Why should an organic function, the most important of all by far, because its purpose is the perpetuation of the species, why should it be less decent than others whose purpose is only the preservation of the individual? Why should eating and sleeping be legitimate actions which are openly practiced, spoken of and acknowledged, while generation is a sin and a disgrace which can not be sufficiently concealed and denied? Is not puberty the crowning point of the development of the individual, and its own reproduction its highest triumph and most glorious manifestation? All living beings, plants as well as animals, consider procreation the most sublime act of their vital energies, and summon nature with pride to be a witness of it, the flowers with their display of brilliant colors and their fragrance, the birds, "warbling sweet the nuptial lay," the fire-fly with its brilliant ray of light, the mammiferous animals by the roars and growls of then wooings and the fury of their rival—combats man alone is ashamed of his most powerful instinct and conceals it like a crime.

To be sure man has not been of this opinion in all ages; Tartuffe has not been always his guide in ethical matters. I do not refer to man in a state of nature but in. a condition of high civilization. A civilization, abundant, intellectually and morally profound, whose ideality far surpassed that of our modern civilization—the civilization of India and Greece—considered the relations between the sexes from a natural and unprejudiced point of view; it held the human form divine in equal estimation, without seeing anything more indecent in one organ than in another, it had no bashfulness in regard to the nude, consequently could behold it with a pure eye, without any corrupt secret thoughts. It saw in the union of two individuals of opposite sexes, the sacred design of reproduction alone, which consecrated this act as necessary and sublime, thus preventing the possibility of unworthy suggestions and trains of thought in a normal and ripened intellect. The Indian as well as the Greek civilization had not obscured and perverted this elementary impulse in man like our own civilization, and therefore was still penetrated with the natural admiration and gratitude for the process which is the source of all life throughout the universe, the process of reproduction. It paid honors to the organs which are involved in this vital action, it placed representations of them as symbols of fruitfulness in the temples public places and dwellings, invented special deities to personify propagation and paid them a worship which did not degenerate into gross and purposeless sensuality until the later periods of the moral decay. Surrounded by symbols which excited their curiosity, the young could not be brought up in that unnatural ignorance which is one of the chief aims of modern training; as the reason was permitted to comprehend the phenomena of the sexual life from the moment it began to take an interest in them, the imagination was not set morbidly to work, thus finding its way into wrong and dangerous paths; that which lay open to the eyes of all did not have the charm of secret and forbidden fruit, so that the unprejudiced, enlightened youth of this ancient civilization was more morally pure and less infected by premature desires than the young of our own flay, who in spite of the anxious pains taken to preserve it, can not be raised in that ignorance considered so salutary, but obtain their knowledge secretly from the most polluted sources, poisoning the mind and deranging the nervous system.

The radical change which has taken place in our conceptions of morality, is the consequence of the influence gained by the ideas of Christianity over the mind of civilized mankind. The fundamental doctrines of Christianity as they are proclaimed in the earliest writings, contradict each other in the most astonishing manner; they are based upon two opposing assertions which would have debarred each other absolutely, if Christianity had been founded by a logical thinker, with a clear understanding. On one side it preaches: Love thy neighbor as thyself, love even thine enemies; on the other, it declares that the end of the world is at hand, that the lusts of the flesh are the most deadly sins, abstinence the most pleasing to God of all virtues, and absolute chastity the most desirable condition. When Christianity preached the love of one's neighbor it raised the natural instinct of man's fellowship with his kind into a religious commandment and promoted the perpetuation and prosperity of the human race; but when, at the same time, it condemned sexual love, it destroyed its own work, it sentenced mankind to annihilation and placed itself in opposition to nature with an hostility which seems born of the devil, to use one of its own expressions. The doctrine of love for one's neighbor conquered humanity, because it appealed to its most powerful instinct, the impulse for the preservation of the race. The doctrine of celibacy on the contrary, would have prevented the spread of the new religion completely, if it had not been for the fact that it appeared at a time when society had become thoroughly corrupt, when licentious egotism alone was ruling supreme and the relations between the sexes, diverted from their purpose of reproducing the species, had become degraded into a source of selfish enjoyment alone, polluted by all manner of crimes, so that it seemed an abomination to the conscience of the good. When this state of things became altered, when Christianity was no longer the reaction from the moral corruption of ancient Rome, it ceased to consider it necessary to protest against the excess of immorality by an excess of purity, and the dismal, inhuman doctrine of celibacy was forced into the background. The church ceased to exact it from all but a few of its children, the priests and the nuns, and even made the concession to nature of elevating marriage into a sacrament. The vows of celibacy taken by the monks and nuns did not prevent however, the greatest excesses within the walls of the cloisters, and during the Middle Ages, when Christianity exercised its highest authority upon mankind, immorality was almost as bad as during the time of the decline of Rome. Ever since the beginning of Religion, the doctrine of celibacy has never been literally followed except by those individuals who were suffering from religious mania, a disease which is almost always co-existent with disturbances or irregularities of the sexual system, and which like them is a manifestation of a morbid state, proceeding from the same pathological modifications in the condition of the brain. But Christianity never completely abandoned this doctrine, the church canonized certain married couples as saints, because they had never touched each other, while together during a long married life sexual intercourse remained theoretically a sin in its eyes, even if it was allowed in practice, and in the course of centuries its constant pressure upon civilized mankind has forced it to its present standpoint, that is, to the conviction that sexual love is a disgrace, continence a moral duty and the gratification of the chief impulse of every living being, a sin deserving the severest penalties. Man has the same instincts in Christianism as in paganism; he desires and obtains woman's favor the same; but he has not the pure and ennobling sentiment that he is engaged in a laudable action, but is haunted by the idea that he is treading forbidden paths; it seems to him as if he were committing a crime that must be concealed, he feels degraded by the compulsion to deception and hypocrisy, and condemned to a perpetual lie against himself, the beloved object and mankind in general, by the necessity for leaving unavowed the natural aim of his affections the possession of the beloved being. Christianity will not concede that love is legitimate; there is therefore no room for love in the institutions permeated by it. Marriage is one of these institutions, its character is influenced by Christian morality. From the theological point of view, it has nothing in common with the love between man and woman. A marriage is not entered into to allow them to belong to each other, but to fulfill a sacrament. They would please God still more if they did not marry at all. The priest who is uniting a couple in matrimony before the altar, asks the woman whether she is ready to follow the man as her husband, and obey him as her lord and master. Whether she loves him, this question is not asked by the priest, for he does not recognize the validity of such a sentiment. According to his ideas the union which he has just sealed with his ceremonies, has its sole foundation in the solemn vows and covenants made before the altar, and not at all in any human, organic impulse which brings two beings together and unites them as one individual soul.

All the relations between society and the sexes are shaped by this Christian doctrinal opinion of the sinfulness of all carnal, that is, of all natural and normal love. Matrimony is sacred; its command of fidelity must not be transgressed, even when it starves the hearts of the wedded couple. The wife may have married without love, she may learn to know a man later who arouses her passionate love—society will not concede the possibility of such an occurrence. What, the wife loves another? That can not be! Such a thing as love is not recognized! The wife is married; that is all she can claim. She has her husband to whom she is bound by her vows of conjugal duty; outside of this duty the world has nothing for her. If she violates it, she becomes an adulteress and falls into the hands of the police, beneath the contempt of all right-minded persons. Society concedes to the husband the right to kill his faithless wife, and it commissions the judge to sentence her to imprisonment as a warning and an example, if the husband has been too forbearing. A girl has fallen in love with a man, she obeys nature's commands without waiting for the permission of the priest or the scribbling of the justice. Alas for the guilty wretch! She is banished henceforth from respectable, decent society. Even the innocent child, the result of her error, bears a stain from which it can not cleanse itself its whole life long. Theft is also forbidden by the community; but the judge has sometimes compassion upon the thief if he stole bread when he was starving, and lets him go unpunished. This is a concession by society of the fact that one's hunger at times may be stronger than one's respect of the law. But it makes no concessions to the wife who has loved notwithstanding her marriage vows, or to the girl who has loved without any marriage vows. It accepts no excuse for any violation of the laws with which it has regulated the intercourse of the sexes. It will not perceive that love as well as hunger is a sufficient cause to break the bonds of the written law. Are we not obliged to believe that this law, this system of morality, is the invention of scorified and calcinated old men or of eunuchs? Is it possible that society has been governed by these views of morality for centuries, a society in which the old men and eunuchs are in the minority, while it always contains many young men of twenty four and maidens of twenty? Governed—ah, there it is— society is not governed by these ideas! It has contrived a way to reconcile the inhuman laws and heartless customs with human nature, by pretending great respect and decorum before their faces, but cutting all sorts of capers behind their backs. Its non-recognition of love is a fraud. It takes off its hat in the presence of the judge who sentences the adulteress to prison, or of the severe mistress who sends away her servant who has been betrayed; but it claps applause to the poet who sings of love without even mentioning marriage, until its very palms ache. Every one in public assents unctuously to the proposition that it is a sin to obey the promptings of the heart, but in secret he listens to and obeys them with enthusiasm, and does not consider himself wicked in doing so. The theory of Christian morality only exists because no one applies it in practice. The bonds of an enormous conspiracy unite all civilized humanity, making every human being a member of this immense secret society—on the street they bow reverently to all the theological doctrines they may meet, but at home, with closed doors, they sacrifice to nature and wreak their vengeance upon any one who divulges the secrets of their Eleusinian mysteries; they express their abhorrence of the universal hypocrisy, and even have the audacity to acknowledge in public places the gods they have installed as presiding deities and worship in private.

In order to form an unprejudiced judgment of the institution of matrimony, we must first accomplish the difficult task of shaking off the prejudices in which we have grown up, and emancipate ourselves completely from the habit of the Christian conception of morality which has become so intertwined with all our thought. In opposition to the theological view, we must look upon man as a natural being and consider him in connection with the rest of nature; if we wish to test the justness of any human institution we must enquire whether it corresponds with man's constitution, his natural, fundamental impulses and the highest interests of the race. If we apply this standard to the institution of matrimony, it is very doubtful whether it will stand the test, and it seems extremely difficult to prove that it is a natural condition of man, and not a human institution. We have seen that the economic organization of society leads to the contracting of marriages from material interests and that the morality of Christianity refuses to recognize the validity of love. But now the last and most painful question of all obtrudes itself upon us: is matrimony a lie simply because it is usually entered into for mercenary motives and not for the possession of a certain individual, and is it a constraint merely because the morality of Christianity will not concede the fact of the existence of such a thing as love, in conjunction with the fetters imposed by the priest? Is not matrimony rather, as it exists today in our civilization, an altogether unnatural form of the relations between the two sexes, and in its present phase of development, that is, as a perpetual alliance for the whole life, would it not be a lie even if marriages were never contracted on any other grounds than those of love, and all its natural rights were conceded to passion?

We are so far removed from a condition of nature in regard to the relations between the sexes, that it is extremely difficult now to distinguish with certainty between what is physiological and necessary in this matter, and what has been so distorted, perverted and artificially added to, during centuries of inherited transmission, that it has come at last to have the appearance of nature. But a careful, critical analysis of the inmost promptings of the human heart, added to the deductions drawn from observations of the life of the higher animals, leads an adherent of the present institution to very discouraging conclusions. Marriage, as it has developed historically with our civilization, is based principally and solely upon the recognition of monogamy. But it appears that monogamy is not a natural condition of mankind, hence there is a fundamental contradiction between the individual impulse and the social institution, the cause of constantly renewed conflicts between sentiment and customs, in many cases bringing the substance into perpetual opposition to the form and making the state of matrimony a lie. Scarcely any reform is practicable that would bring the outward visible sign, the monogamic matrimonial relations of a wedded pair, into perfect harmony under all circumstances, with their inward attraction and affection for each other!

The institution of matrimony is founded altogether upon the supposition or knowledge of the fact that the interests of the perpetuating and perfecting of the race require a certain supervision by the community of the impulse of procreation, as I have attempted to prove above. But the fact that this institution has assumed the form of an union between two parties to last as long as they both shall live, this fact is no outcome of the interests of the species, it is not a vital condition of the kind, consequently is not produced by the impulse for its preservation, but it is a direct result of the economic organization of society and therefore probably as transitory as this organization. The conviction that matrimony must assume the form of monogamy, a conviction perhaps only semi-conscious, but still distinct enough to be formulated in laws and customs, was produced probably by this train of reasoning 1 , in a society which has no fellowship in the production, distribution and consumption of wealth, that is, in a society without any economic solidarity, in which every one toils and cares for himself alone and sees with unconcern his neighbor perish by his side, the children would starve if the parents did not bring them up. The mother can not carry alone the burden of the children's support, because in this egotistical society man will misuse his superior strength to crowd and push woman, as she is the weaker, out of all the light and more remunerative positions for earning a livelihood, that is, all for which she is fitted, to such an extent that she can hardly support herself by her own toil, to say nothing of supporting her children. The father must be compelled therefore, to aid the mother in carrying this burden. But this compulsion can only be exercised practically in one way: by forging a chain that will bind the man indissolubly to the woman whom he wishes to make a mother. This chain is the marriage for life. And to make it more easy to be determined which father is responsible for which child, to obviate any possible danger of imposing the duty of a child's support upon the wrong father, no man is allowed to have children except by one woman, and no woman save by one man. This is the single marriage or monogamy. And now the relations are simple and summary. You wish to possess a certain woman? All right: you must swear to maintain her and the children proceeding from the union, throughout your entire life. Do you become tired of the woman after a while? So much the worse for you. You have her now and you must keep her. You find that you made a mistake in your selection, that you deceived yourself when you believed that you were in love. You should have examined your own sentiments more closely, have considered the matter more ripely. It is too late now to have this excuse accepted. You are in love with another? That is no concern of ours. You must still carry the burden of your wife and children and we, society, will not allow you to shift it upon our shoulders.

The instinct of self-preservation of the race never ceases to act, as long as it possesses any vital energies. The only way the% in which the race can ensure the life of the women and children in an economic organization founded solely upon egotism and individualism, that is, ensure its own perpetuation, is by a life-long single marriage. Our economic institutions are necessarily followed by our institution of matrimony. In reality marriage has come to be a means of gratifying the selfishness of the parents, as it is not contracted from love, nor according to the laws of natural selection, nor in the interests of the offspring; while theoretically it is an institution dictated by the interest of the preservation of the race,—although it is true, a falsely comprehended interest—created not for the benefit of the parents, but of the children. Theoretically the adult generation is sacrificed to the undeveloped or unborn, the stomachs of the little ones are provided for at the expense of the hearts of their parents—inexorably in those countries lying still under the direct influence of the Christian theological views of the world, rather more indulgently in those in which the enlightenment of more natural and human conceptions has been diffused. Catholicism which, as we have seen, consider^ love to be unauthorized and a sin, will not allow a dissolution of the marriage under any circumstances; it will not con cede that two persons may have been mistaken in each other, or if they have been mistaken, that their life's happiness requires a separation. The peoples who are emancipated from Catholicism, make the concession to love. that it exists, that it has rights, that it can even make its appearance outside of wedlock; but they make the concession reluctantly and only partially; they allow the separation to take place only under difficulties, they pursue the divorced pair with invidious prejudices, and carry their heartlessness so far, that they forbid a marriage with the person for love of whom the divorce has been obtained, who has been loved before the legal separation of the wedded pair took place—a prohibition whose stupidity and barbarity are really frightful.

This is immaculately consistent from the standpoint of the self-seeking economic organization of society, but from that of physiology and psychology, on the contrary, we see in it a cause for the gravest reflection. The marriage Is contracted for life. Let us suppose the most favorable case: the wedded pair love each other truly. Will this love last as long as life? Can it last so long? Are the husband and wife justified in swearing fidelity unto death? Are they not committing a foolhardy or inconsiderate act when they pledge themselves for the immutability of their transient sentiments? The poets, who seem to have been entrusted with the task of almost hopelessly confusing and mystifying this matter, do not hesitate an instant with the reply to my question. They are firmly convinced that true love lasts for aye. if love ends, it is not love, they say. Hm, that is very easily said, but how about the truth of it? Every one who has observed life with his eyes open, can give the poets a hundred examples of love that commenced very passionately and yet cooled off very rapidly and very thoroughly. If the poets say that love is not love which fades away in time, we must ask them how we are to distinguish between real love and the spurious article, as the latter at the moment of its conception and also, during its brief blossoming-time is so deceptively like the former, arousing the same sentiments, impelling to the same actions, with the same accompaniment of excitement and agitation, ecstacy and despair, tenderness and jealousy as the former? Certainly there have been cases in which love only ceased with life. A cool and impartial analyst would perhaps find, even in these cases that the perpetuity of love could be ascribed to favorable circumstances, to the power of habit, the accidental absence of any disturbances or temptations, in short, to influences entirely independent of the two individuals, fully as much at least, as to the quality of their sentiment. We can not deny either the existence of such cases. In them lifelong single matrimony is a true, natural and authorized condition. In them form and substance are one, and the outward, visible bond never ceases to be the expression of the inward, spiritual union. But if such cases do exist without any doubt, they are, even according to the poets' own confessions, exceedingly rare. In what way ought those persons to consider matrimony who believed that they loved sincerely at a certain moment but find after months or years of reflection, or else awake suddenly to the consciousness upon meeting a certain individual, that their love was a mistake? Ought they to hasten and unite themselves for life? They soon cease to love each other, and then the yoke of matrimony is as unbearable a burden as if it had been assumed without love in the first place. Or ought they to wait before marrying until they become convinced that their love will last till death? This would be somewhat difficult; for as the true nature of the sentiment can only be recognized afterwards, the lovers would have to wait until their hour of death before they could say with a clear conscience: "Our love was in truth the genuine love, it lasted as long as life, we can now with good courage be—buried together, with no fear that we will ever grow weary of each other." If such a severe examination and such overwhelming conviction were required as indispensable conditions to matrimony, humanity would see no more betrothed lovers.

It is well that Romeo and Juliet died young. If the tragedy had not been concluded with the fifth act, I am not sure but what we would not have heard of quarrels between the charming young couple. I am sadly afraid that he would have taken a mistress after a few months and that she would have consoled herself with some Veronese nobleman for her desertion. It would be too horrible: a divorce case as epilogue to the balcony scene. I go still further and maintain that, as I understand the characters of Romeo and Juliet, it would have been certain to be the case, for they were both very young, very passionate, very unreasonable and very excitable, and a love which springs into existence at a ball, caused by the first sight of a beautiful physical form, does not usually last through many nights, in whose morning hours it believes it hears "the nightingale and not the lark." But did not Romeo and Juliet therefore, love each other? I should like to see any one who would venture to assert this! And ought they not to have married? That would have been a deadly sin not only from the standpoint of the perfecting of the race, but also from that of romance. If their marriage would have turned out badly, this fact is no proof against their love, but it is a proof against the anthropological justification of marriage.

The truth is, that among ten thousand pairs of lovers, there is barely one in which the man and woman love each other throughout their entire lives, to the exclusion of all others, not a single couple who would invent the perpetual, single marriage to answer to their own requirement, if it did not already exist. But there are sure to be nine thousand, nine hundred, who at some period of their lives experienced a strong desire to unite themselves with a certain individual, were happy if able to gratify this desire, suffered bitterly if it remained unfulfilled, and notwithstanding feeling, the sincerity of the original, after a longer or shorter period, developed until they came to have entirely different, often diametrically opposite sentiments for the object of their former passionate affection. Have these couples the right to get married? Undoubtedly. Their union must be promoted in the interests of the race. But will a lifelong single marriage be compatible permanently with their happiness! No honest observer of real life can reply affirmatively to this question. The fact is, that man is not a monogamous animal and all institutions which are founded upon the acceptation of monogamy, are more or less unnatural, more or less of a constraint to him. Inherited ideas which have become very deeply rooted in the human mind in the course of centuries of transmission, prove nothing against this biological fact. Let us listen very closely to the stillest, smallest voices in the hearts of lovers! Does the beloved being really fill the heart so completely that there is no room left for a wish or even for a perception outside of it, which has some other being for its object? I deny it. If we are honest we must allow that man and woman, even in the highest paroxysms of a new-born love, keep an obscure corner in their soul which is not illumined by the beams of the concrete passion, where lurk the germs of diverging sympathies and desires. We keep these germs concealed, owing perhaps to a sense of honor instilled into us by our training, we do not allow them to develope at once, but we are continually conscious of their existence and we feel that they would soon grow to be large and strong if we did not prevent their development. It may sound very shocking, yet I must say it: we can even love several individuals at the same time, with nearly equal tenderness, and we need not lie when we assure each one of our passion. No matter how deeply we may be in love with a certain individual, we do not cease to be susceptible to the influence of the entire sex. The most chaste and loving woman is still a part of the general feminine half of humanity, as the most honorable, loving man is still a part of the masculine half; he as well as she, experiences the mutual attraction of the opposite sex, and under somewhat favorable circumstances this general attraction may become the starting-point of a new, special attachment to a certain individual, as first love likewise, is usually nothing more than the collection and transferring of the pre-existing general attraction to the other sex, to a certain incarnation of it, ordinarily the first with whom one has an opportunity to become well acquainted. By this I mean chaste women and honorable men, as I repeat expressly. I am not referring to women who have a disposition to wantonness, nor to men born with a superficial, sensual temperament} whose number is far larger than the conventional moralists like to admit. Unconditional fidelity is not an attribute of human nature. It is no physiological companion phenomenon of love. That we exact it, is an outcome of our egotism. The individual wishes to reign entirely alone in the heart of the beloved, to fill it completely, to see only his own reflection in its mirror, because this effect upon another is his highest sphere of activity, his most powerful out-living, as selfishness or vanity can conceive of no more perfect gratification than the observation of such a phenomenon. As man feels himself a complete individual most profoundly and thoroughly, when he has conquered some antagonist in a free single combat, strength pitted against strength, man against man, he thus appreciates his own individuality most intensively and at the same time delightfully, when he knows himself to be the complete possessor of another individual. To exact loyalty is thus nothing else than the wish to extend the limits of one's own personality into another and to rejoice in their compass; jealousy is the intensely painful recognition of the limitations to this extension. We can therefore be jealous, without being ourselves in love, as we can wish to surpass a competitor in the race, without hating him personally; in both cases the point is to become conscious of ourselves as superior individuals, thus gratifying our vanity; it is a question of superiority, of strength, of physical training; and thus we exact fidelity without feeling ourselves laid under obligations of reciprocity. The most convincing proof that fidelity is not exacted by the natural aim of love, the interest of reproduction, but is a condition artificially implanted in humanity, an outcome of self-love, vanity and selfishness is this very lack of reciprocity. If it were a matter of organic necessity, the fidelity of the husband would be an obligation as inviolable as the fidelity of the wife; but as it is only a matter of succeeded egotism, the egotism of the strong in conquering the egotism of the weak in the course of the development of customs and morality, and as the husband is the stronger, he has been able to adapt and form laws, customs, opinions and sentiment to his own advantage and to the prejudice of the wife. He demands unconditional fidelity from his wife but does not concede to her the right to demand the same from him. When she forgets herself, she has committed a deadly sin, whose lightest penalty is public contempt; when he does the same, he has only been guilty of a charming little lapse from duty for which the law has no penalty, at which society smiles discreetly and good-naturedly, and which the wife pardons with tears and caresses if she took it seriously in the first place. And the unfairness of this dual standard is increased by the circumstance that in reality, it is not the same whether the husband or the wife is guilty of infidelity; for if the wife sins, she is passive in the matter— led astray by a man, that is, a power independent of her will; she succumbs to a force, which is stronger than her powers of resistance; but when the husband sins, he is not passive; he sins because he wishes to sin; there are very few Josephs outside of the Bible, and a Mrs. Potiphar is a rarity; the man takes the initiative in sin, he goes in quest of it, and commits it with concentrated purpose and premeditation, with energy and in spite of the resistance offered to him. India is the scene of the utmost extension of this power of the sheer egotism of the husband. In that country he considers his possession of his wife as so absolute, he carries his exaction of fidelity to such an horrible extreme, as to compel the widow, and even the betrothed, to take her place beside her dead husband or fiancé upon the funeral pyre; while the husband whose wife has just died is not obliged to hurt a hair of his head, but can return from the funeral to enter a new nuptial chamber if he wishes, without offending propriety. The selfishness of the husband has not assumed quite such a destructive phase in Europe. Only a few sentimental, hysterical romancers have risen to the height of exacting a fidelity which would continue to exist after the death of the loved one, and portray moonstruck lovers who condemn themselves to eternal mourning and continence, because they can not marry the beloved being on account of death or other obstacles. These visionaries are at least fair enough to lay the decree of this obligation upon both sexes alike, and their Toggenburgs are as often men as women. Their common sense readers however, do not believe in these romantic beings and consider any one in real life who tries to imitate them, a morbid, degenerate creature who tries to make a poetical virtue out of the necessity of the pathological condition of their body or mind. The morals of Christendom concede the facts, both in practice and theory, that love can cease to exist, that one can love repeatedly and that fidelity need not survive love, for they allow the remarriage of widows and widowers to take place and accept the new relations as perfectly moral and above the criticism of society. If at any time and in any place, the wife had been more powerful than the husband, there is no doubt but that all our conceptions of fidelity would have assumed another shape. Then the indiscretion of the wife would have been a fascinating weakness, which would partake somewhat of the character of a joke, while the inconstancy of the husband would have a tragic significance. Society in such a case would exact of man the same chastity outside of the marriage relation and especially before the marriage, as it now exacts of woman. Don Juan would then be Donna Juanna and in the theatre we would shed tears over the death of that poor, innocent Othello, strangled by the furious, jealous Desdemona.

I am well aware of the enormous difficulties in the way of solving peremptorily the problem of the fidelity and natural permanence of love, with our present customs and morals. If we examine the life of the higher animals, we can not fail to observe that the passion of the male for the female only lasts during the courtship or at the most, during the time which we might call the honeymoon, and that reciprocal fidelity, which only exists at all in a few isolated species, does not survive the birth of the young. No matter how violently our pride as human beings may recoil, we are yet constrained to seek for truth in these analogies from the animal kingdom, which is governed by the same vital laws as the human race, which differs from it biologically, in no particular, if we wish to know what attributes are natural and necessary, and what are artificial and arbitrary. This method of comparison would lead us to the conclusion that love exhausts itself in the effort to reach its aim and in the accomplishment of its purpose, as hunger ceases to exist when the desire for food is gratified, and that even for woman, one act in the drama of love comes to a complete close with the birth of the child, so that she can enter upon a new act with an entirely different cast of roles. If this is, as it appears to be, the true and natural condition of this human sentiment, then the permanent single marriage has no organic justification, it must become after the honeymoon in most cases, or after the birth of the child, an empty form and a lie, and lead to conflicts between inclination and duty even when it was originally contracted from love. Of course a multitude of arguments array themselves at once against this conclusion whose logical sequence could only be the abolition of the institution of matrimony and a return to the uncontrolled mating of the animal world. The chief of these arguments is this: It may be true that man is polygamous according to his natural instincts, that he experiences an impulse within him to enter into intimate relations simultaneously or in succession, with more than one individual of the opposite sex; but he has also other instincts and it is the task of civilization to educate the will of man so that he can subdue and suppress his instincts when he learns to know that they are wrong. Unfortunately this argument is not convincing; for it must first be proved that the polygamous instinct would be injurious to the preservation and development of mankind, as this would be the sole foundation for calling it wrong; in addition it gives us cause for reflection as we realize that our civilization, which has succeeded in subduing other instincts, has never yet succeeded in suppressing 1 the polygamous instinct, in spite of the fact that the church threatens it with the torments of hell, the law condemns it and our conventional morality declares that it is indecent; man lives in a state of polygamy in the civilized countries in spite of the monogamy enforced by the laws; out of a hundred thousand men there would barely be one who could swear upon his death-bed that he had never known but one single woman during his whole life; and if the principles of monogamy are more strictly observed by women, it is not because they have never had any inclination to disregard them, but because our conventional morality keeps a sharper lookout upon woman's conduct and punishes her lapses more severely than man's—an instinct however, which is so relentlessly attacked by the laws and morality, and which makes such a successful resistance to them, must have much deeper and more solid foundations than those others over which civilization has obtained control. Another argument has more weight: Human love although principally nothing more than the impulse for the possession of a certain individual with the purpose of reproduction, is yet something more; it is an enjoyment of the intellectual qualities of the beloved being; it is also friendship. This element of love survives its physiological element. Certain it is, that the sentiment felt for the loved one is not the same after possession, as it was before. But it is a profound and powerful sentiment still, sufficient to form the foundation for the desire and even for the necessity of a life-long union whose justification is no longer the natural aim of marriage, reproduction, but the want experienced by an intellectually more highly developed individual for companionship with one of similar culture. Even in the most constant hearts, even when the original passion was the most violent conceivable, love undergoes this transformation after the honeymoon or after the birth of the first child; it is still far from considering the yoke of matrimony a burden, but yet it is by no means a perfectly safe protection against the outbreak of a new passion. But there are other circumstances which aid the will in its struggle with t polygamous instinct. When the union of two persons, who gave evidence of their natures being harmoniously attuned Leach other to a certain degree, by loving for a brief period, has lasted a while it becomes a habit, which sustains fidelity most wonderfully. They perhaps, after time, cease to experience the slightest love or even friendship for each other, but their companionship is still kept up, and kept up as a matter of course. As in the process of petrefaction, all the original particles of the root of a tree for instance, gradually disappear and are replaced by particles of quite different, earthy matter, which yet take the exact place of the crowded out, organic molecules and leave the general outline unchanged, until there is absolutely nothing left of the original matter, without the outward appearance of the root having suffered the least alteration, in this process of transformation of the sentiments tiny, imperceptible atoms of habit replace the atoms of love as they vanish, so that when the love has entirely passed out of existence, the outward form of the union remains undisturbed—even if this form is cold, stiff and dead, it is all the more permanent and capable of resistance. If the union is blessed with children the tenderness of the parents is diverted to them and a new love springs up in their hearts which twines around both parents and unites them once more, as a vine joins two neighboring trees together with its luxuriant growth and covers them with foliage and blossoms, although they may be already dead and rotten at the core. Moreover, as the years pass the impulse to love grows weaker, from natural causes, and even if the germs of new attractions do not die out or vanish, it becomes easier every year for the will and judgment to prevent their development. There remains finally after the dawn of love has passed away, a sweet and deep memory of it through the remaining hours of the day of life, which produces a sensation of gratitude to the one loved once so dearly, and impels the two hearts to cling to each other still. On account of all these reasons it may be practicable to mate human beings monogamically for life, even if their disposition of mind or body seems to indicate that they were primally destined to a number of contemporaneous or succeeding relations. There will however, always be numerous cases in which nothing can prevent the outbreak of a new passion, not the friendship which accompanies love, nor the gratitude which it leaves behind it, nor habit, nor riper years, nor the bonds of the parental share and interest in the existence of the children; in these cases the obligation of fidelity should be removed and the marriage cease in form as well as in spirit. Society concedes the possibility of such cases and has introduced the institution of divorce in the most progressive countries. But nature has not yet attained her rights by its aid. The hypocritical prejudices which cling still so closely to the theory of strict monogamy, pursue the divorced parties and cast a shadow of disgrace upon them, which stigmatizes them as no longer perfectly respectable people. This causes timid and weak natures to prefer the lie to the truth, to choose infidelity to the marriage contract rather than an honorable dissolution of it, and to avoid the social destiny of divorces by continuing to seek shelter in the defiled and guilty wedlock. Society must learn to consider a divorced couple as exceptionally courageous and truth-loving natures who would not condescend to a compromise with their conscience but broke the form with decision as soon as the substance had ceased to exist and their natural feelings rebelled against it. Not until this view of the matter becomes generally accepted will the human heart get its rights, marriage become once more a true and sacred institution, wantonness and fickleness be deprived of their pretext of love, and conjugal infidelity become a disgusting crime which only the most vulgar and depraved natures will commit.

The problem that we have last been investigating is whether an union with a single person and for life, is adapted to the nature of man, even if it was entered into originally only from love. But how far are we removed from a condition in which society would be in need of such an investigation! Before we can proceed to the solution of the extremely anthropological problem as to whether an human being can love but once, and whether his mating instinct ought only to be exercised upon one single individual of the opposite sex, it must first of all be settled that love should be the antecedent of marriage and that the official bond must result from a mutual attraction of both parties, existing at least at the moment in which it is imposed. But the present economic organization of society is in direct opposition to such a state of affairs. As long as man is not sure of always finding work to do and by it securing an acceptable competency, he will seek to promote his material interests by marriage or, if he can not accomplish this, he will avoid it and prefer the gross gratifications which prostitution offers him or else temporary liaisons which impose little or no responsibility upon him. And as long as woman is constrained to look upon matrimony as the only career and means of support open to her, she will rush into it without asking about love, and as a consequence be either fearfully unhappy or else become a moral wreck. The miserable lot to which these conditions condemn woman in particular, is not improved nor changed by the quacks who recommend the emancipation of woman as a cure for this severest of the diseases of society. I will not enter upon a searching criticism of this theory of woman's emancipation, only remarking in a few words that the struggle for existence would assume phases even more ghastly than at present, if both sexes stood upon the same plane of equality. If woman should become the serious rival of man in many branches of industry, she would as the weaker, be crushed without consideration. Gallantry is an invention of prosperity and leisure. Want and hunger destroy this sentiment upon which woman calculates when she imagines a world in which she could wrestle with man for her daily bread. The most difficult and the most indispensable kinds of work man alone must undertake; he will rate them higher than those performed by woman and as at present, woman's labor will always receive a smaller remuneration than his. Why? Because he has the strength to make his views into laws and to accomplish his will; for no other reason. Woman is accorded a high and dignified position in our civilization because she is acquiescent, because she is content to be the complement of man and to acknowledge his material supremacy. In fact, if she attempts to question it, she is soon compelled to recognize its actuality. The fully emancipated woman, entirely independent of man and in many cases his enemy when their conflicting interests clash, must soon be crowded into the corner. It is in such a case a genuine wrestling match, and there can be no question as to which would succumb first. This emancipation would bring man and woman necessarily into the relation of a higher and lower race—for man is better equipped for the struggle for existence and competency than woman—with the result that the latter would be brought into a far worse condition of dependence and slavery than that condition from which this emancipation is to-release her. The aim of the emancipation preachers is to make it possible for woman to live without man and to renounce matrimony. This method of curing the evil is about as efficacious as that of some philanthropist who might give lectures during a time of famine on the subject of how man could be weaned most effectually from the habit of eating. The question would be then, how to supply the hungry with food, not how to teach them to do without it. And the little band of self-constituted agents of the victims of our civilization ought not to persuade and make it possible for woman to renounce marriage, but should try to secure her her natural share in the love-life of humanity. As I asserted in the preceding chapter that it is the duty of society to care for its children, to educate them completely, and as often as is necessary, to support them until they become capable of supporting themselves, I now assert that it is the duty of society to protect woman, its most valuable breeding material, against physical want. The community owes protection and support to woman. Man's role in the life of the species is that of the bread winner, the preserver and defender of the living generation; woman's role is that of the preserver and defender of the future generations, the improver of the race by natural selection, as she excites strife between the men, of which she is the prize and in which the ablest competitors secure the most valuable spoils. As a child the girl should receive the advantages of the public education of the young, and later, if it is necessary, she should be entitled to complete support, either in her parents' house or in a separate home of her own. Society should look upon it as a disgrace if any woman, young or old, beautiful or ugly, should feel the pangs of want in any civilized community. In a society reorganized upon these principles, in which woman would have no anxiety in regard to her daily bread, knowing that she is protected from want in any case, whether married or single, in which the children would be supported and educated by the community, in which man could not expect to buy as many women with his money as he wants, because hunger would no longer be his go-between, in such a society woman would soon from genuine affection, alone the spectacle of old maids who have found no husbands, would be as rare as that of old bachelors, who enjoy in their free, licentious life all the pleasures with none of the moral burdens or limitations of matrimony, and prostitution would only be practiced by a small number of degenerate beings who can only breathe in corruption and infamy and whose unbridled impulses are without the slightest value for the preservation of the species. When material considerations enter no longer into the contracting of a marriage, when woman is free to choose and is not compelled to sell herself, when man is obliged to compete for woman's favor with his personality and not with his social position and property, then the institution of matrimony will become a truth instead of the lie it is now, the sacred and sublime spirit of nature will bless every embrace, every child will be born surrounded by the love of its parents as with a halo, and will receive, as its first birthday present, the strength and vitality with which every couple that has been formed by the attraction of affinity endows its offspring.

Printed in Great Britain
by Amazon

80631172R00119